THE CHEMEKETA HANDBOOK

Your Guide to College Writing

Daniel Couch

The Chemeketa Handbook: Your Guide to College Writing

ISBN: 978-1-943536-48-1
Edition 1.2 Fall 2018

Chemeketa Press

Chemeketa Press is a nonprofit publishing endeavor at Chemeketa Community College. Working together with faculty, staff, and students, we develop and publish affordable and effective alternatives to commercial textbooks. To learn more, visit www.chemeketapress.org.

Publisher: David Hallett
Director: Steve Richardson
Managing Editor: Brian Mosher
Instructional Editor: Stephanie Lenox
Design Editor: Ronald Cox IV
Editorial Support: Stephanie Lenox, Steve Slemenda, Travis Willmore
Cover Design: Ronald Cox IV
Interior Design: Micaleigh Daniels, Emily Evans, Candace Johnson,
    Keyiah McClain, Amanda Pruett

Additional contributions to the design and publication of this textbook come from the students and faculty in the Chemeketa Visual Communications program.

Chemeketa Faculty

The development of this text has benefited from the contributions of many Chemeketa faculty in addition to the editor, including:

Sara Dennison, Bethany Gabbert, Alissa Hattman, Traci Hodgson, Roy K. Humble, Adam Karnes, Shannon Kelley, Stephanie Lenox, Karl Meiner, Brian Mosher, Mary Ellen Scofield, Steve Slemenda, Sam Snoek-Brown, Michael Ward, John Whitney, Travis Willmore, and the Chemeketa Community College librarians, who are amazing.

A portion of the proceeds from the sale of this handbook will help support the important work of the Chemeketa Writing Center. The rest of the proceeds will be used to develop new textbooks.

Printed in the United States of America.

Table of Contents

A Note to Students v

A Note to Faculty... xi

Part 1: Writing Basics

Chapter 1
Paragraphs   3

Chapter 2
Sentences   23

Chapter 3
Punctuation and Mechanics   85

Chapter 4
Word Choice   123

Part 2: Research Basics

Chapter 5
Research Basics   151

Chapter 6
MLA Style   179

Chapter 7
APA Style   217

Chapter 8
Chicago Style   255

Index/Glossary 291

Expanded Table of Contents..................................... 303

Notes for Multilingual Writers Index 313

A Note to Students

The Chemeketa Handbook shows you how to write in college. The first half of the book presents rules for paragraphs, sentences, punctuation, mechanics, and word choice. The second half of the book looks at the rules for how to use researched information within your papers. The book doesn't replace your instructor, of course, but it does help you become a more self-reliant writer by explaining the rules of college writing in a way you'll understand.

A. How the Handbook Works

The handbook teaches each rule three ways: definitions of *what* the rule is, examples that show *where* the rule applies, and explanations that walk you through *how* each example works.

1. Defining the Rules

The handbook introduces each concept with an explanation of the specific rule.

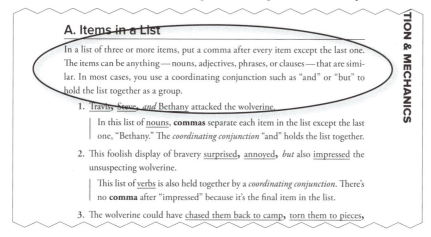

A. Items in a List

In a list of three or more items, put a comma after every item except the last one. The items can be anything—nouns, adjectives, phrases, or clauses—that are similar. In most cases, you use a coordinating conjunction such as "and" or "but" to hold the list together as a group.

1. <u>Travis</u>, <u>Steve</u>, *and* <u>Bethany</u> attacked the wolverine.

   In this list of <u>nouns</u>, **commas** separate each item in the list except the last one, "Bethany." The *coordinating conjunction* "and" holds the list together.

2. This foolish display of bravery <u>surprised</u>, <u>annoyed</u>, *but* also <u>impressed</u> the unsuspecting wolverine.

   This list of <u>verbs</u> is also held together by a *coordinating conjunction*. There's no **comma** after "impressed" because it's the final item in the list.

3. The wolverine could have <u>chased them back to camp</u>, <u>torn them to pieces</u>,

2. Giving Examples

The handbook then shows you where those rules apply in your writing by offering you practical examples of how those rules work in different situations.

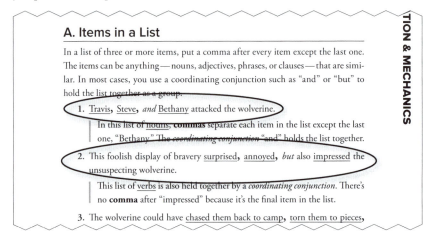

A. Items in a List

In a list of three or more items, put a comma after every item except the last one. The items can be anything—nouns, adjectives, phrases, or clauses—that are similar. In most cases, you use a coordinating conjunction such as "and" or "but" to hold the list together as a group.

1. Travis, Steve, *and* Bethany attacked the wolverine.

    In this list of nouns, **commas** separate each item in the list except the last one, "Bethany." The *coordinating conjunction* "and" holds the list together.

2. This foolish display of bravery surprised, annoyed, *but* also impressed the unsuspecting wolverine.

    This list of verbs is also held together by a *coordinating conjunction*. There's no **comma** after "impressed" because it's the final item in the list.

3. The wolverine could have chased them back to camp, torn them to pieces,

3. Explaining the Examples

Finally, the handbook shows you how to apply these rules with practical annotations. With bold, underlining, and italics, the handbook connects the explanation in the annotation back to the specific parts of the example sentence affected by the rules. Your sentences won't have this formatting, of course, but they'll follow the example in every other way.

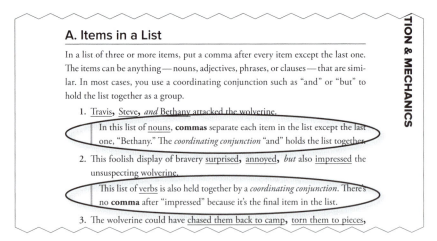

A. Items in a List

In a list of three or more items, put a comma after every item except the last one. The items can be anything—nouns, adjectives, phrases, or clauses—that are similar. In most cases, you use a coordinating conjunction such as "and" or "but" to hold the list together as a group.

1. Travis, Steve, *and* Bethany attacked the wolverine.

    In this list of nouns, **commas** separate each item in the list except the last one, "Bethany." The *coordinating conjunction* "and" holds the list together.

2. This foolish display of bravery surprised, annoyed, *but* also impressed the unsuspecting wolverine.

    This list of verbs is also held together by a *coordinating conjunction*. There's no **comma** after "impressed" because it's the final item in the list.

3. The wolverine could have chased them back to camp, torn them to pieces,

B. How to Find What You Need

The first way to get something out of this book is to find what you need. To help you do that, the handbook offers two tables of contents, chapter tabs, a glossary/index of commonly used technical terms, and an index of notes for multilingual writers.

1. Using Tables of Contents and Tabs

In the front of the handbook, a brief table of contents introduces you to the focus of each chapter. If you're not sure where to find something, this is a good place to start. Each page of each chapter has a tab with an icon that tells you which chapter you're in.

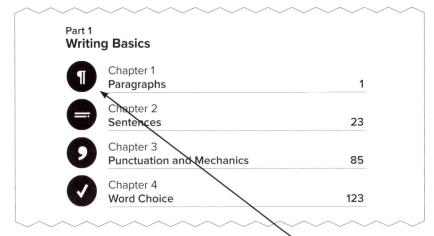

In the back of the handbook, an expanded table of contents presents the topics covered in every chapter. If you have a rough idea about what rules you need to learn, this will help you narrow your focus.

2. Using the Index/Glossary

The Chemeketa Handbook combines a glossary of key terms with an index that shows you where to find out more within the book:

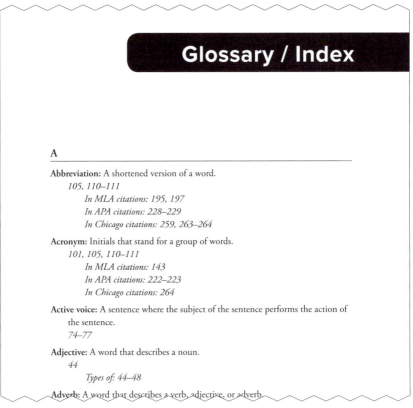

Glossary / Index

A

Abbreviation: A shortened version of a word.
105, 110–111
> *In MLA citations: 195, 197*
> *In APA citations: 228–229*
> *In Chicago citations: 259, 263–264*

Acronym: Initials that stand for a group of words.
101, 105, 110–111
> *In MLA citations: 143*
> *In APA citations: 222–223*
> *In Chicago citations: 264*

Active voice: A sentence where the subject of the sentence performs the action of the sentence.
74–77

Adjective: A word that describes a noun.
44
> *Types of: 44–48*

Adverb: A word that describes a verb, adjective, or adverb

3. Using the Index of Notes for Multilingual Writers

Finally, the handbook also offers an index of notes for multilingual writers that are spread throughout these chapters:

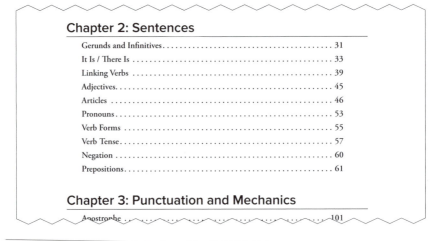

Chapter 2: Sentences

Gerunds and Infinitives 31
It Is / There Is 33
Linking Verbs 39
Adjectives. 45
Articles 46
Pronouns 53
Verb Forms 55
Verb Tense. 57
Negation 60
Prepositions. 61

Chapter 3: Punctuation and Mechanics

Apostrophe 101

C. How to Use What You Find

The second way to get the most out of this book is to read it carefully.

You don't have to read the whole book carefully. Just go to the parts that you need to read, and read *them* carefully. Your professor will tell you what those parts are. When you learn what to work on, go to the handbook and read about what rules you're expected to follow and how to apply them.

You'll understand the rules better if you also look at your own writing alongside the examples. Do your sentences look like the sentences in the examples? Are you putting commas in the same places as the examples and for the same reasons? This all takes practice, but it doesn't have to take *that much* practice when you read carefully and apply what you learn in the handbook.

Finally, to get more out of this book, ask questions about writing. If you read something in the handbook and it doesn't make sense, talk to someone who's spent more time with these rules. If you don't have a professor or writing tutor to talk to, you still have the Internet, and it is crawling with further examples and explanations of every topic in this book.

A lot of hard work goes into successful formal writing. It requires research and careful, honest thinking. When you have an idea to share, formal writing also requires you to understand and follow the rules for putting your ideas into sentences and documenting where your information came from.

None of that is beyond you. Writing is a skill you can improve, just like riding a bike or juggling butcher knives. You might not get it right the first time, but with the guidance of this handbook and your willingness to take your work seriously, your efforts will soon make you a more effective and more confident writer.

A Note to Faculty

Like most college textbooks, writing handbooks are more expensive than they should be. A bigger problem, however, is that most handbooks are written not to students who use them but to the instructors who order them. The elevated writing style and exhaustive breadth makes these handbooks challenging for students who haven't already mastered the basics of college writing. *The Chemeketa Handbook* addresses these problems by putting the focus back where it belongs — on the students.

A. What We've Done

The handbook is divided into two main sections: writing and research. It begins with paragraphs and steadily narrows its focus to sentences, punctuation and mechanics, and finally, individual word choice. In the second half, the handbook addresses the basics of research and provides explanations of the three most common documentation styles: MLA, APA, and Chicago.

From start to finish, the handbook uses accessible language, clear instructions, and practical examples. It doesn't attempt to be a rhetoric textbook and handbook rolled up into one. It's a companion that supplements your instruction. All this makes the handbook more effective for the students who need it and keeps the price low so that they are able to buy it.

The handbook supports classes ranging from developmental writing to upper-division research writing. Its usefulness also extends beyond the writing classroom. Any time students must demonstrate their understanding in writing, regardless of the discipline, this book offers the practical instruction they need to express their ideas clearly and correctly.

B. What You Can Do

How you use *The Chemeketa Handbook* depends on which classes you teach. With courses early in the composition sequence, you're likely to assign whole chapters from the first half of the book. With courses that have a research component, the chapters in the second half are more valuable.

For all faculty, however, the Common Problems sections at the end of the chapters are useful. Whenever you come across the lingering writing problems that follow many students to your classes, you can easily direct them to the targeted instruction they need. Similarly, we've embedded explanations of errors common to multilingual writers throughout the book to help you better support students fluent in languages other than English.

The most effective textbooks are the ones your students actually buy and read. *The Chemeketa Handbook* is an affordable and student-friendly handbook that will encourage them to do both. It may not be written *to* you as other handbooks are, but by writing to your students, it is definitely written *for* you.

PART ONE
Writing Basics

Paragraphs

A paragraph is a set of sentences that work together to present one main idea about something.

In the body of a formal paper, paragraphs present supporting ideas for the main idea of the paper. These might be examples or reasons or facts or definitions. They all help to explain and defend the main idea of the paper. Each paragraph has its own supporting idea to make, too, but that idea is a smaller part of the paper's main idea.

The opening and closing paragraphs also present one main idea. The opening presents the topic and then the main idea about that topic. The closing sends the readers off with the importance of the main idea—why it matters or what they should do about it.

To show readers where paragraphs begin and end, you have two choices. In most college papers, the conventional option is to indent the first line of a paragraph by a half inch. This paragraph and most of the paragraphs in this book use indentation. The indentation is a visual cue for readers that a new supporting idea is about to begin.

In some formal writing—such as business letters or reports—you have the option of adding a blank line between paragraphs to show where they begin and end. That's called block paragraphing. When you use block paragraphing, you don't indent. The next two paragraphs use block paragraphing.

See how a block paragraph works? See the space above and the space below? Now remember to not use a block paragraph for almost all of your college writing.

In this chapter, we'll look at how to write effective body, opening, and closing paragraphs. We'll end by looking at some common problems with paragraphs and how to fix them.

1. Body Paragraphs

In the body of a paper, each paragraph explains its one main idea in two ways. First, a topic sentence states the main idea directly. Second, the supporting sentences explain that idea in more detail. Transitional words and phrases help to guide readers along the way so that the idea is clear.

A. Topic Sentences

The topic sentence provides two main pieces of information—the topic of the paragraph and the author's main idea about that topic. This sentence is often the first or last sentence of the paragraph.

1. **One problematic lesson that Disney's *Cinderella* teaches is that physical beauty equates to moral goodness.** The title character has all the standard components of classic Disney beauty, including "clear skin, a thin waist, small feet, and slender limbs" (Willmore 108). Throughout the film, she exhibits moral goodness by serving her wicked stepmother and stepsisters with a dedicated selflessness. She never seeks revenge or even complains about her mistreatment. Conversely, Cinderella's stepsisters are ugly by Disney standards, exhibiting "big noses, broad faces, broad shoulders, thick waists, large feet, and dumpy hair" (Willmore 111). Far from being moral, the sisters are vain and rude, treating Cinderella with cruelty that neither she nor anyone else deserves. Beauty, this film seems to say, is an outward manifestation of inward goodness.

   In this **topic sentence**, the topic is the Disney movie *Cinderella*. The main idea about this topic is that the movie teaches that physical beauty equates to moral goodness.

2. **An even worse lesson from *Cinderella* is that people should passively accept whatever terrible treatment they receive.** As the heroine of this story, Cinderella herself illustrates the lesson. She begins as the beloved child of doting and well-to-do parents, but from that happy starting point, life gets steadily worse. First her mother dies. Then her father remarries a mean woman with two mean stepdaughters. Then her father dies, and her stepmother demotes Cinderella from daughter to servant, forcing her to live in the attic, cook all the food, clean all the dishes, and sweep up cinders. Mosher and Cox write that "Cinderella accepts this abuse passively by smiling and singing and making friends with the birds and rodents to whom she has been relegated" (89).

    > The topic of this **topic sentence** is the movie *Cinderella*. The main idea is that the movie teaches people to passively accept whatever terrible treatment they receive. The topic sentence also connects this idea to the ideas in prior paragraphs by saying that the lesson of passive acceptance is even worse than the other lessons the film teaches.

B. Supporting Sentences

The supporting sentences in a paragraph explain the topic sentence in more detail. They do so with additional information—examples, quotations, facts, and so on—and explanations of why that information is important.

Take another look at the first example paragraph and notice how all of the supporting sentences help to explain the idea in the topic sentence.

1. One problematic lesson that Disney's *Cinderella* teaches is that physical beauty equates to moral goodness.

    > This is the topic sentence. It introduces the general idea that this paragraph will present about beauty equating to goodness.

2. The title character has all the standard components of classic Disney beauty, including "clear skin, a thin waist, small feet, and slender limbs" (Willmore 108).

    > This supporting sentence provides a quotation that lists particular aspects of Cinderella's physical beauty.

3. Throughout the film, she exhibits moral goodness by serving her wicked stepmother and stepsisters with a dedicated selflessness.

    > This supporting sentence provides a summary of Cinderella's display of moral goodness. This shows the connection that Cinderella is physically beautiful and morally good.

4. She never seeks revenge or even complains about her mistreatment.

> This supporting sentence provides a second summary of how Cinderella never exhibits negative behavior — another sign of moral goodness.

5. Conversely, Cinderella's stepsisters are ugly by Disney standards, exhibiting "big noses, broad faces, broad shoulders, thick waists, large feet, and dumpy hair" (Willmore 111).

> This supporting sentence provides a quotation that lists particular aspects of the stepsisters' ugliness.

6. Far from being moral, the sisters are vain and rude, treating Cinderella with cruelty that neither she nor anyone else deserves.

> This supporting sentence provides a summary of how Cinderella's stepsisters display a lack of morals through their actions. This shows the connection that they are physically ugly and morally bad, as far as that sort of thing goes in Disney films.

7. Beauty, this film seems to say, is an outward manifestation of inward goodness.

> This final sentence analyzes the two connections the paragraph makes and offers an observation about why that might be.

Now take another look at the second example paragraph. Once again, notice how all of the supporting sentences help to explain the topic sentence idea.

8. An even worse lesson from *Cinderella* is that people should passively accept whatever terrible treatment they receive.

> The topic sentence introduces the general idea that the paragraph will present about passive acceptance. The topic sentence also connects this idea to the ideas in prior paragraphs.

9. As the heroine of this story, Cinderella herself illustrates the lesson.

> This supporting sentence follows up on the topic sentence by stating which character in the movie teaches this lesson. It narrows the focus of the paragraph to the title character.

10. She begins as the beloved child of doting and well-to-do parents, but from that happy starting point, life gets steadily worse.

> This supporting sentence provides a summary of what happens to Cinderella in the first part of the movie.

11. First her mother dies.

> This supporting sentence provides a fact about what happens to Cinderella.

12. Then her father remarries a mean woman with two mean stepdaughters.

> This supporting sentence provides another fact about what happens to Cinderella.

13. Then her father dies, and her stepmother demotes Cinderella from daughter to servant, forcing her to live in the attic, cook all the food, clean all the dishes, and sweep up cinders.

> This supporting sentence provides a long list of facts about what happens to Cinderella.

14. Mosher and Cox write that "Cinderella accepts this abuse passively by smiling and singing and making friends with the birds and rodents to whom she has been relegated" (89).

> This supporting sentence provides a quotation about how Cinderella responds to all these lousy facts.

C. Transitional Words and Phrases

Transitional words and phrases help readers see how the different supporting sentences are organized or how different ideas are related to each other.

1. **When** the king announces a royal ball, Cinderella's passive acceptance of her fate continues. She can't go to the ball **because** she has no suitable dress. **Though** she's an accomplished seamstress, she does nothing on her own behalf. **Instead**, her bird and rodent friends "reward her passive acceptance by making her a smart little dress while she does the bidding of her stepmother" (Mosher and Cox 90). **When** her stepsisters **then** tear the dress to shreds, Cinderella **again** does nothing for herself. She simply accepts the loss of the dress as another fitting part of her awful life. **However**, there is no need to worry **because** now a fairy godmother appears out of thin air to reward Cinderella's passivity by giving her an even better dress, a fancy carriage, and the horses to pull it. The lesson is clear that passive acceptance is not only expected from young girls but sure to be rewarded.

> These **transitional words** demonstrate how different ideas relate to each other. The "when" phrases and the word "then" show that two events are related in time. The "though" phrase shows that one idea is even more surprising because of another idea. "Because" shows that one idea is a reason for another idea. "Instead" and "However" show that one idea is in contrast with a previous idea. "Again" shows that one idea is a repetition of a previous idea.

You have many transitions to choose from. Here are just a few of your options:

To Show Relationships	To Show Organization
Addition: and, in addition to, also, too, moreover, additionally, furthermore, as well as	**Time:** before, later, after, then, next, in 1998, later that year, since November, when the king announces a royal ball
Contrast: but, however, not, unlike, albeit, otherwise, regardless, on the other hand, conversely, instead	**Rank:** the most important, also important, of less importance
Example: for example, one example of, one illustration is, namely, such as, in fact	**Location:** in Salem, near, next to, a little farther, beyond, among
Cause: because, it follows that, since, for, as a result, consequently	
Qualification: except for, although, unless, despite	
Agreement: similarly, likewise, as, like	

Students new to formal writing sometimes overuse transitional words and phrases in order to make sure their ideas are clear. However, the main way to make sure your readers can see how your ideas fit together is with clear organization. The transitions should provide secondary assistance. While transitional words and phrases *do* help readers to follow your thinking, too many of them will actually distract readers from your ideas. If readers already see how ideas are connected, the transitions will appear to be redundant or unnecessary.

D. Paragraph Groups

In the body of a paper, paragraph groups are sets of paragraphs that work together to present a more complex supporting idea. Each paragraph in the group still presents one idea of its own, but these ideas then work together to present the more complex paragraph group idea.

For example, if the essay's main idea is that the Disney movie *Cinderella* teaches children many harmful ideas, the body of the essay may be divided into several supporting paragraphs or paragraph groups for each of the harmful ideas that *Cinderella* teaches. Within each paragraph group, you then have two or more paragraphs that look more closely at different aspects of that big idea.

Paragraph Group Idea	*Supporting Paragraph Ideas*
Cinderella teaches that physical beauty is equal to moral goodness.	1. Cinderella provides a positive example by being beautiful and virtuous. 2. The stepsisters provide a negative example by lacking beauty and virtue.
Cinderella teaches children to passively accept anything bad that happens to you.	1. Cinderella illustrates this by passively accepting all the bad things that happen to her after her parents die. 2. Cinderella passively accepts all the bad things that happen before the ball and is rewarded. 3. Cinderella passively accepts all the bad things that happen after the ball and is rewarded.
Cinderella teaches that the only way for a woman to get out of a bad situation is to marry her way out.	1. As a woman, Cinderella is in a bad situation. 2. Cinderella does nothing to improve her situation or leave it. 3. The solution is for her to marry someone who will carry her away to her own happily ever after.

2. Opening and Closing Paragraphs

In addition to body paragraphs, formal papers use opening and closing paragraphs to introduce readers to the paper as a whole or to point to what comes next after the reader accepts the paper's main idea as true.

A. Opening Paragraphs

The primary job for the opening paragraph is to tell readers what to expect from the paper. The opening does this with three pieces of information:

- **Topic:** the subject of the paper as a whole

- **Focus:** the narrowed area of the topic that the paper will examine

- **Thesis:** the main idea that the paper explains, which is a reasonable idea that the author has about the focus

A secondary job for the opening is to engage the readers' interest so they will want to keep reading. In formal writing, this is less important because your readers — professors, scholarship committees, etc. — usually *have* to read what you have written whether you engage their interest or not. However, even with formal audiences, an engaging opening will make the paper more enjoyable and thus more effective.

You have many options for how to accomplish the work of the opening paragraph. What follows are just three of the most common approaches.

Moving from General to Specific

Moving from the general to the specific means starting with a broad topic and then narrowing down to the actual and much narrower focus of the paper. This shows readers some general context such as where the topic fits on the timeline of history or within some larger category.

1. Disney princesses are a prominent part of modern kid culture. As of 2017, there are eleven official Disney princesses in the Disney princess line, starting with Snow White from the 1937 film of the same name. By 2012, the princess line products alone generated over $3 billion for Disney (Vincent). The popularity of Disney princesses suggests that the ideas they embody are also valuable — or at least benign. However, there are increasing concerns that the values taught by Disney princess movies are quite *un*healthy (Coyne 23). Many of those concerns focus on the character of **Cinderella**, the star of the 1950 animated film produced by Walt Disney himself. In spite of her continuing popularity, **Cinderella** teaches so many unhealthy ideas that parents should be cautious about letting their children watch this movie.

The paragraph begins broadly with an introduction of Disney princesses — all eleven of them and how much money their products generate. The opening then narrows to focus on the ideas that these princesses teach and concerns that some of these ideas may be unhealthy. Then it narrows still more to the **topic** of the paper, the princess Cinderella. It closes with the paper's thesis, that parents should be cautious about letting this princess into their children's developing minds.

An Attention Grabber

An attention grabber is a statement that's designed to surprise, amuse, or possibly shock readers. This is found more commonly in informal writing — as seen in tabloid headlines or Internet clickbait, for example — but attention-grabbing will work in a formal paper if it's not too over-the-top and if you follow the attention grabber with a clear presentation of the topic, focus, and thesis of the paper.

2.   Disney princess movies are a cultural cancer. While educational programs like *Dora the Explorer* teach linguistics and geography and religious programs like *Veggie Tales* teach Christian values, Disney princess stories teach lessons that undermine and erode healthy cultural values with unrealistic definitions of beauty, regressive gender stereotypes, and many other problematic values. One of the worst offenders is ***Cinderella***, which Walt Disney himself produced in 1950. Because *Cinderella* teaches so many harmful ideas, parents should be cautious about letting their children watch this movie.

What grabs our attention here is how the author connects something so beloved as Disney princess movies with something so despised as cancer. That seems a little over-the-top, especially if you spent years of your young life watching princess DVDs. It makes you want to keep reading to see if the author is serious about this charge. The opening then moves on to clarify what the author means by "cultural cancer" and introduces the **topic** of the paper — *Cinderella*. It ends with a statement of its thesis, that parents should be cautious about letting their kids watch *Cinderella*.

An Engaging Anecdote

An anecdote is a short story — real or hypothetical — that illustrates a part of the topic and engages readers by inviting them to imagine what's happening. Again, you must then follow this up with a more direct introduction of the topic, focus, and thesis.

3. "I'm thirsty," my daughter Lucy said to Melanie, her five-year-old sister from our newly blended family. "Bring me some milk." Melanie asked her why. "Because," said Lucy, "you're just my mom's stepdaughter. I'm her real daughter." "Okay," said Melanie. I couldn't believe what I was hearing, but when I raced into the living room to get an answer, it all made perfect sense. They were watching *Cinderella*.

Increasing concerns about the values taught by Disney princess movies are well-founded (Coyne 23). Disney princess stories teach many lessons that undermine and erode healthy cultural values with unrealistic definitions of beauty, regressive gender stereotypes, and other problematic values. One of the worst of the princess movies is *Cinderella*, which Walt Disney himself produced in 1950. Because *Cinderella* teaches so many harmful ideas — including the horrifying idea that stepchildren aren't as important as birth children — parents should be cautious about allowing their children to watch this movie.

> The anecdote in the first paragraph provides readers with a story that is easy to visualize and thus engages their imaginations. It also introduces the **topic** of this paper — *Cinderella*. By itself, this paragraph is a good start for an opening, but formal writing requires more direct introduction of what to expect from the paper. That's where the second opening paragraph comes in. In the second paragraph, we get down to business. The paragraph presents the paper's focus on the problematic values taught by Disney princess movies. Then it presents the **topic** directly as the prime example of these values. It ends with the thesis, that parents should be cautious about letting their kids watch *Cinderella*.

B. Closing Paragraphs

The closing paragraph or paragraphs conclude the paper by doing two things. First, they remind readers about the thesis of the paper. Second, they point toward the future implications of that thesis being true. Once readers finish the paper, they will hopefully continue to think about the ideas the paper presented and perhaps do something because of those ideas. Just as with opening paragraphs, there are many possible strategies for effective closing paragraphs.

Doing Something about It

One option for the closing is to begin by presenting how the paper has defended its thesis and then giving readers some ideas about what they can do on their own.

1. <u>*Cinderella* is not a benign movie. It is filled with many lessons that are harmful for children to assimilate into their thinking. Once these ideas get into our children's heads, they are then difficult or impossible to get out. For those reasons,</u> **parents must use caution when it comes to *Cinderella.***

   Caution doesn't mean burning the *Cinderella* DVD or forcing your daughter to shift her pretend play from Cinderella to Ruth Bader Ginsburg. Caution means taking this potential threat seriously and acting appropriately. The first thing to do is watch the movie yourself first. Then decide if your child is old enough to watch the movie without being unduly frightened or confused. If not, then wait. Second, if your child is old enough to watch the movie, decide whether your child is old enough to talk about what's going on in the movie. If not, then wait. If so, then watch with your child and talk about the movie. Disarm the harmful lessons in the movie by bringing them out into the open.

   > The first paragraph of the closing summarizes the <u>evidence</u> from the body and then restates the **thesis** that the evidence supports. The author then assumes that because the paper has made a good case for this idea, readers will be open to putting it into action. The author then spells out what caution does and does not look like.

The Danger of Doing Nothing

A similar option is to present the potential cost of ignoring further action. Instead of showing readers what they can do with the idea, you warn them about what will happen if they do nothing.

2. **Parents must use caution when it comes to *Cinderella*** and the other Disney princess movies. Modern Disney princess movies offer more active princesses but still teach many or all of the same harmful lessons. If parents trust the warm, wholesome Disney brand and assume that Disney movies are

equally wholesome, their lack of caution will contribute to common problems in adolescence: poor self-esteem (Mosher and Cox 102), anxiety over body image (Rubens 22), eating disorders (Mosher and Cox 98), frustration with regressive gender stereotypes (Rubens 23), and distrust of parents (Largo). These are not benign movies, and as Coyne shows, once these ideas get into our children's heads, they are difficult or impossible to get out.

> This closing begins by restating the **thesis** that parents must use caution with *Cinderella* and adds that this extends to the other Disney princess movies as well. It then considers the consequences of doing nothing, which is a long list of fairly serious problems during adolescence. The paragraph ends by reminding readers about the evidence used to defend the essay.

Return to the Opening

If you began the paper with an anecdote, one way to end the paper is by following up on the anecdote.

3.   For parents, **the key is to use caution when it comes to *Cinderella*** or any other Disney princess movie, including the modern versions that may have more personally active princesses. These are not benign movies. They teach children harmful lessons that need to be avoided or disarmed with careful instruction.

My daughters Lucy and Melanie refused to give up on *Cinderella*. When I took their DVD away, they simply played out the roles on their own. It was too deeply a part of their culture of play. So I gave them back the DVD, and we watched the movie together. "Is it okay for those two sisters to treat their other sister like that?" I whispered at one point in the movie. "*No*," they said. "Is Cinderella a real daughter?" I asked. "*Mom*," Lucy said, "we understand." "Yeah," said Melanie "we're not *four-year-olds*." The point had been made. We'll work on age discrimination next.

> The first paragraph does the main work of the closing. It restates the **thesis** of the essay and then it reminds readers about the evidence from the body that explains why this thesis is valid. The second paragraph wraps things up by returning to an anecdote from the opening of the essay. The opening anecdote illustrates the problem with *Cinderella*. This follow-up anecdote illustrates the solution by showing how one parent exercised caution.

3. Common Problems

A. Unfocused Paragraphs

A paragraph is unfocused when it lacks a clear main idea. It may be that no topic sentence identifies a main idea, so readers aren't sure what the supporting sentences support. A more likely problem is that supporting sentences stray from their job of supporting the topic sentence. In some cases, all of the supporting sentences may be about the topic but not about the topic sentence idea.

Whatever causes the lack of focus, the problem is the same — readers become confused. They expect each paragraph to make a point, so when a paragraph doesn't do that, readers aren't sure what to think. This distracts them and makes them unsure about the meaning of the rest of the paper. If it happens in more than one paragraph, the readers may stop reading.

How to Fix Unfocused Paragraphs

The first thing to do is make sure *you* know what point the paragraph should make. You do that by identifying — or writing down — the topic sentence for that paragraph. Once you have identified this idea, you can check to see why the paragraph is unfocused and use the correct option to fix it.

Option 1: Add a Topic Sentence

If a missing topic sentence is what makes the paragraph hard to follow, the solution is straightforward — add a topic sentence.

1. **Problem:**

    In her first encounter with Drizella in the movie, Cinderella speaks with deference: "Good morning, Drizella. Sleep well?" Drizella replies with cruelty: "As if you care. Take that ironing and have it back in an hour. One hour, you hear?" It's similar with Anastasia. Cinderella greets her politely, and her stepsister responds severely, treating Cinderella as a servant: "Well, it's about time. Don't forget the mending. Don't be all day getting it done, either." By accepting this treatment with a simple "Yes, Drizella" and "Yes, Anastasia," it suggests that Cinderella agrees with them about her status.

    > These supporting sentences all work together to capture a single moment from early in the film. They do that clearly, but what isn't clear is what idea this scene illustrates. The last sentence hints that is has something to do with status, but that's all we have to go on. Without a clear main idea, the paragraph remains unfocused.

Solution:

Neither Cinderella nor the stepsisters view Cinderella as an equal sister. In her first encounter with Drizella in the movie, Cinderella speaks with deference: "Good morning, Drizella. Sleep well?" Drizella replies with cruelty: "As if you care. Take that ironing and have it back in an hour. One hour, you hear?" It's similar with Anastasia. Cinderella greets her politely, and her stepsister responds severely, treating Cinderella as a servant: "Well, it's about time. Don't forget the mending. Don't be all day getting it done, either." By accepting this treatment with a simple "Yes, Drizella" and "Yes, Anastasia," it suggests that Cinderella agrees with them about her status.

> Now that the paragraph has a **topic sentence**, it's clear that these supporting sentences are illustrating the idea that none of the sisters look at Cinderella as an equal.

That was an easy fix. However, if the problem is found in the supporting sentences, your work will be a little more challenging. Consider the following options.

Option 2: Remove or Revise Unrelated Supporting Sentences

If the paragraph already has a clear topic sentence, you can see which idea the paragraph needs to explain. Now check the supporting sentences to make sure that each sentence helps to explain the topic sentence's idea.

2. **Problem:**

Cinderella is the object of others' actions rather than the source of her own actions. For example, the birds and mice do all the work on her first gown for the ball. She is busy while the animals do their work. Later, Cinderella's fairy godmother provides the second gown for the ball. Cinderella doesn't call for her fairy godmother's help. She waits for the fairy godmother to come to her. **The fairy godmother should have shown up a few years earlier and done something about Cinderella's stepmother and stepsisters. It is odd that the women in this movie only get excited about dresses.**

> The **unrelated sentences** don't contribute meaning to the topic sentence about Cinderella being an object rather than an actor. Another sentence sounds unrelated, but the idea could be used to help explain the topic sentence's idea.

Solution:

Cinderella is the object of others' actions rather than the source of her own actions. For example, the birds and mice do all the work on her first gown for the ball. She is busy while the animals do their work, but even that activity is not her doing. It was all given to her by her stepmother. **When her**

stepsisters see the refurbished dress, they also make Cinderella the object of their actions by ruining it. After that disaster, Cinderella does nothing but accept her fate. However, once again someone else makes her the object of their actions. This time, her fairy godmother provides the second gown for the ball. Cinderella doesn't call for her fairy godmother's help. She waits for the fairy godmother to come to her. **After the ball, when the prince is looking for the foot that fits the slipper, he too is the one who does all the work for Cinderella. She doesn't come to him.**

> Now all the sentences are focused on the topic sentence idea about Cinderella being an object rather than an actor. The <u>potentially unrelated sentence</u> now connects to that idea as a supporting clause in a more focused sentence. By removing the unrelated sentences, there is also more room to add **additional examples** of this idea, which make the paragraph even more effective.

Option 3: Separate Ideas and Expand

You may find that part of the paragraph helps to support the topic sentence and the rest presents a second idea. If that's the problem, the solution is to divide that paragraph into two—one paragraph for each idea. Make sure each paragraph has a clear topic sentence. If necessary, you can then expand each paragraph with additional supporting sentences to present its topic sentence idea.

3. **Problem:**

   Another harmful lesson from *Cinderella* is that stepchildren are not as valuable as birth children. This is demonstrated by how Lady Tremaine and her birth daughters treat Cinderella. They don't allow her to eat with them, live in the best rooms with them, or wear nice clothes. They also force her to do all the housekeeping and cooking for them. <u>Cinderella's only friends are birds and mice. A young woman needs to have more going on in her life than cooking and cleaning and talking to animals. She needs meaningful relationships. She needs adult interaction.</u>

   > The paragraph begins with a **topic sentence** that presents an idea about another harmful lesson from *Cinderella*. The three sentences that follow provide some supporting evidence for that idea. However, the paragraph then shifts direction to discuss another <u>loosely related idea</u>, that a "young woman needs to have more going on in her life than cooking and cleaning and talking to animals." This shift in focus makes the purpose of the paragraph unclear. It also means that the paragraph fails to fully explain either idea in sufficient detail.

Solution:

Another harmful lesson from *Cinderella* is that stepchildren are not as valuable as birth children. This is demonstrated by how Lady Tremaine and her birth daughters treat Cinderella. While Cinderella says good morning to her stepmother early in the film, Lady Tremaine answers, "Pick up the laundry and get on with your duties." After one of Cinderella's mice accidentally turns up, Lady Tremaine loads on more work as punishment:

> Time for vicious practical jokes? Perhaps we can put it to better use. Now, let me see . . . There's the large carpet in the main hall. Clean it! And the windows, upstairs and down. Wash them! Oh, yes. And the tapestries and the draperies. Do them again! And don't forget the garden. Scrub the terrace. Sweep the halls and the stairs. Clean the chimneys. And, of course, there's the mending and the sewing and the laundry.

Meanwhile, Lady Tremaine's birth daughters aren't given even the smallest chore. This inequity in labor is a clear indication of inequity in value.

> The first step to solving this problem is giving the first main idea its own paragraph and explaining it with additional supporting sentences that make the point much clearer. Some of the support comes in the form of a block quotation in the middle of the paragraph.

Cinderella's low status as a stepchild is also seen in her segregation from the others in the family. While Drizella and Anastasia practice music upstairs, Cinderella cleans downstairs. While the stepmother and stepdaughters prepare for the ball, she retires to her room with her animal friends and then goes back to cleaning. The majority of Cinderella's time — including the first six scenes of the movie — is spent in the company of animals instead of people. In the rare instances when Cinderella enters the living space when others are present, she does so as a servant. As Mosher and Cox point out, "Cinderella is old enough to leave this house and find a new life of her own, but she has internalized her stepmother's segregations so deeply that now she believes this separate space is where she belongs as a lesser member of this family" (105).

> The revised **topic sentence** of this paragraph introduces the idea that Cinderella is segregated from her sisters. It more clearly connects this paragraph to the one before it and thus the idea that this movie teaches that stepchildren are not equal to birth children. By focusing just on segregation, the paragraph can bring in more supporting sentences to illustrate that idea. Nice.

B. Disorganized Paragraphs

Disorganized paragraphs do not arrange their supporting sentences according to a clear pattern of organization. In some cases, the supporting sentences may be arranged according to a pattern or organization, but the readers are unable to recognize that pattern because of a lack of transitions.

When readers don't see how the sentences of a paragraph work together, they struggle to figure out what point the paragraph is trying to make. This also makes it harder for them to move from paragraph to paragraph and make sense of the paper as a whole.

How to Fix Disorganized Paragraphs

Readers more easily see how the supporting sentences work together when the sentences are better organized, such as in a chronological pattern or a pattern of ranking from most important to least important. You can do two things to make sure that sentences are organized and that the organization is easy to see.

Step 1: Organize a Disorganized Paragraph

If no organizational pattern is present in a paragraph, the solution is to add one and use it to organize the sentences.

1. **Problem:**

    > Cinderella can't go to the royal ball because she has no suitable dress. Though she's an accomplished seamstress, she does nothing on her own behalf, even after her stepsisters tear to shreds the dress made for her by her bird and rodent friends. **This is another example of her passive acceptance of her fate.** Cinderella simply accepts the loss of the dress as another fitting part of her awful life. There's no need to worry. Her friends first "reward her passive acceptance by making her a smart little dress while she does the bidding of her stepmother" (Mosher and Cox 90). Then a fairy godmother appears out of thin air to reward Cinderella's passivity by giving her an even better dress, a fancy carriage, and the horses to pull it. The lesson is clear that passive acceptance is not only expected from young girls but sure to be rewarded.

    > This paragraph has a **topic sentence**, but it's buried in the middle of the supporting sentences. The quotation is wedged in where it doesn't quite belong, and while the supporting sentences all help to explain the topic sentence's idea, they are presented in a random order. This means the reader has to mentally rearrange them to see the whole idea — kind of like solving a puzzle, only not any fun.

Solution:

> **Cinderella's passive acceptance of her fate continues.** She can't go to the royal ball because she has no suitable dress. Though she's an accomplished seamstress, she does nothing on her own behalf, so her bird and rodent friends "reward her passive acceptance by making her a smart little dress while she does the bidding of her stepmother" (Mosher and Cox 90). Her stepsisters tear the dress to shreds, and Cinderella again does nothing for herself. She simply accepts the loss of the dress as another fitting part of her awful life. There's no need to worry because a fairy godmother appears out of thin air to reward Cinderella's passivity by giving her an even better dress, a fancy carriage, and the horses to pull it. The lesson is clear that passive acceptance is not only expected from young girls but sure to be rewarded.

> With the revised **topic sentence** at the start of the paragraph, readers have an easier time seeing the main point right away. Just as importantly, the supporting sentences are now organized in a generally chronological pattern: 1) the announcement of the ball; 2) her animal friends' efforts to prepare her for the ball; 3) her stepsisters' efforts to undermine her attendance; and 4) her fairy godmother's magical intervention just before the ball was to begin. The quotation is better integrated, too. Finally, separating and organizing the events by time also makes it clearer that Cinderella displayed passivity on two different occasions before the fairy godmother showed up.

Step 2: Add Transitions to Point Out Organization

Sometimes a paragraph is organized, but readers don't really notice the organization. The result can be similar as if it were actually disorganized—they get confused. In that case, fix the problem with transitions that make the organization obvious.

2.   **When the king announces a royal ball**, Cinderella's passive acceptance of her fate continues. She can't go to the ball because she has no suitable dress. Though she's an accomplished seamstress, she does nothing on her own behalf. Instead, her bird and rodent friends "reward her passive acceptance by making her a smart little dress while she does the bidding of her stepmother" (Mosher and Cox 90). **When** her stepsisters **then** tear the dress to shreds, Cinderella again does nothing for herself. She simply accepts the loss of the dress as another fitting part of her awful life. However, there is no need to worry because **now** a fairy godmother appears out of thin air to reward Cinderella's passivity by giving her an even better dress, a fancy carriage, and the horses to pull it. The lesson is clear that passive acceptance is not only expected from young girls but sure to be rewarded.

Because this paragraph uses chronological order, these **transitional words and phrases** show readers where each sentence fits on a timeline. In addition, other transitional words show a second level of organization, the contrast between Cinderella's initial passivity and the subsequent activity of the others in her life.

C. Clichéd Opening Paragraphs

A cliché is an initially colorful phrase like "at the end of the day" or "walk the talk" that has been used so many times that it has now become dull and boring.

A clichéd opening employs a strategy that has been used so many times it too has become boring. Here are just a few opening strategies that no longer effectively engage readers:

- **Dictionary definitions:** "According to Merriam-Webster's dictionary, 'princess' is defined as . . ."

- **Excessively general openings:** "Since the beginning of time, princesses have been . . ."

- **Boring questions:** "Have you ever wondered why princesses . . . ?"

- **Announcing your intention:** "In this paper, I will attempt to explain why princesses . . ."

How to Fix Clichéd Opening Paragraphs

There's no way to fix a clichéd opening. Don't even try.

The only thing you can do is shake your head sadly, remove the cliché, and add one of the effective openings from this chapter.

Sentences

A sentence states an idea with two main ingredients — a noun and a verb.

Noun	Verb
Marjorie	smiled.
Rain	fell.
She	frowned.

The noun names or describes the subject of the idea, so this half of the sentence is called the subject. The verb describes the subject or tells us what the subject does. This half of the sentence is called the predicate, and it's usually longer than a single verb because our ideas tend to be more complex than that.

Subject	Predicate
My dear Aunt Marjorie	smiled happily to herself.
The afternoon rain	fell like tears from Heaven.
The gentle woman	stopped while she admired her colorful way with words.

At an early age, you learned how to combine subjects and predicates without learning any of the terms or the rules that apply to them. You just started talking and kept talking (and talking) until now you can create sentences intuitively. That's all you need for conversation and informal writing such as texts, emails, and passive-aggressive notes of complaint on the refrigerator.

However, formal writing—school papers, job applications, legal papers, business plans, and so on—expects you to explain yourself precisely and carefully. In other words, it expects you to use sentences that consistently follow the formal rules of grammar, not just the informal rules that apply to conversation. If you ignore that demand, two things will happen. First, your writing won't be as effective as it should be. Second, and perhaps worse, your ideas won't be taken as seriously as they deserve.

To show you how sentences work in formal writing, this chapter will look at the three main ingredients in sentences:

- **Clauses** are groups of words that contain a subject and predicate. The examples on the previous page are all clauses, and so is "while she admired her colorful way with words," which also contains a subject ("she") and predicate ("admired her colorful way with words").

- **Phrases** are groups of words that together add up to a single unit. "My dear Aunt Marjorie," for example, is a noun phrase because all four words help to describe a single thing—or person, actually, in this case.

- **Parts of Speech** are the seven main types of words—noun and verb are two types. Each part of speech has to be used in certain ways in order for your ideas to make sense.

We'll end the chapter with a look at some of the common sentence problems that college writers run into and how to solve them.

1. Clauses

Clauses present ideas within sentences. Every clause consists of two main ingredients—a subject and a predicate. The subject is a noun phrase that presents the topic of the idea. The predicate is a verb phrase that states your idea about that topic.

If a clause makes sense all by itself, it's a main clause (also known as a sentence). If it doesn't make sense all by itself, it's a dependent clause that presents a supporting idea within a sentence.

A. The Main Clause

The main clause states the main idea of a sentence. It's also known as an independent clause because it is a complete idea all by itself, just like you are independent when you pay for your food and electricity and shoes all by yourself.

1. **She** lied.

   Sometimes the **subject noun phrase** and predicate verb phrase are single words.

2. **The tall woman** lied about her height.

   Usually, though, other words and phrases describe the **subject** and predicate more precisely.

3. **The tall woman from Albany** lied when I asked her about her height.

   Here's another **subject noun phrase** and predicate verb phrase.

4. **I** was shocked at her lie because I could see with my own eyes that she was at least as tall as my uncle, who is six foot seven.

   Here's one more **subject noun phrase** and predicate verb phrase.

   In English, the subject of a clause usually comes first and is followed by the predicate. However, we can also introduce a clause by shifting part of the predicate to the beginning:

5. When I asked her about her height, **the tall woman from Albany** lied.

   If you do move part of the predicate to the beginning of a clause like this, separate it from the **subject** with a comma.

6. However, **she** was polite about it.

   If you put a transitional word like "however" before a clause, separate it from the **subject** with a comma, too.

B. Dependent Clauses

Dependent clauses present supporting ideas that help to describe the subject or the predicate of a main clause. They still have a subject and a predicate, but for one reason or another, they depend on a main clause to make sense.

Example 3 on the previous page has a dependent clause in the predicate:

when **I** <u>asked her about her height</u>.

This clause doesn't make sense on its own, even though it has a **subject** and <u>predicate</u>. It only makes sense when it's helping the main clause by explaining when the woman lied. Example 4 above has several dependent clauses in it:

because **I** <u>could see with my own eyes</u>

> This clause explains *why* I was shocked at her lie.

that **she** <u>was at least as tall as my uncle</u>

> This clause explains *what* I could see with my own eyes.

who <u>is six foot seven</u>

> This clause explains how tall my uncle is. He's *really* tall, but he's starting to stoop a little.

As you can see, none of these dependent clauses makes sense on its own. Each only makes sense when it helps to explain some other verb or noun. Each depends on that main clause to make sense.

C. Types of Dependent Clauses

Dependent clauses can help to explain main clauses in many different ways, and they fall into several categories that are each punctuated differently.

Subordinate Clauses

Subordinate clauses consist of the usual subject and predicate, but a subordinating conjunction joins this dependent clause to the main clause of a sentence and shows us how the subordinate clause helps to explain the main clause.

1. I like ice cream *if* **it** <u>is just a little bit soft</u>.

    > This <u>subordinate clause</u> begins with the *subordinating conjunction* and then adds the supporting idea with its supporting **subject** and predicate. The main clause is "I like ice cream," and the <u>subordinate clause</u> explains a condition that has to be true for the main clause to be true.

2. I like ice cream *even though* **it** <u>is so bad for me</u>.

    > Sometimes a *subordinating conjunction* consists of two words working together.

3. I like ice cream *because* **ice cream** is part of my self-image.

> You'll notice that there's no comma before the *subordinating conjunction*. Even if you hear a pause, don't use a comma to separate a subordinate clause from the main clause.

4. *Although* **you** may be surprised at this, I like ice cream.

> If the sentence begins with a subordinate clause, however, you do separate it from the subject of the main clause with a comma.

Relative Clauses

Relative clauses also have a subject and predicate. They usually support the main clause by providing more information about a noun. Relative pronouns—"that," "who," "which," or "whose"—connect the relative clause to that other noun.

Consider this main clause:

> **The road** is full of potholes.

We can add more information to the **subject** and predicate with relative clauses.

1. The road **that** runs past my house is full of potholes.

> This relative clause describes the subject noun, "road." The **relative pronoun** is the subject of the relative clause.

2. The road is full of potholes **that** are killing my car.

> This relative clause describes the noun "potholes." The **relative pronoun** is the subject of the relative clause.

If you think that the information from the relative clause is essential to the meaning of your sentence, then you use a restrictive relative clause, and you don't separate it from the main clause with any commas. Whenever you use "that" to start a relative clause, you've decide that the information is essential.

If the information in the relative clause is not essential to the meaning of the sentence, then you can use a nonrestrictive relative clause:

3. The road, **which** runs past my house, is full of potholes.

> Nonrestrictive relative clauses are considered interruptions or asides within the main clause, so you separate them from the main clause with commas.

Using restrictive or nonrestrictive relative clauses changes the meaning of the sentence slightly.

4. The road **that** runs past my house is full of potholes.

> I'm talking about the road that runs past my house—not any other roads.

5. The road, **which** runs past my house, is full of potholes.

> You already know which road. By the way, it also runs past my house.

6. The road is full of potholes **that** <u>are killing my car</u>.

  | These are really bad potholes.

7. The road is full of potholes, **which** <u>are killing my car</u>.

  | You already understand how bad the potholes are. By the way, they are killing my car.

If the noun phrase you want to describe is a person, use the relative pronoun "who":

8. I'm cooking this hamburger for the professor **who** <u>gave me a D</u>.

  | Omitting the comma makes this a <u>restrictive relative clause</u> and shows that I have many professors. This *E. coli* burger is for the only one who gave me a D.

9. I'm cooking this hamburger for the professor**,** **who** <u>gave me a D</u>.

  | Using a **comma** makes this a <u>nonrestrictive relative clause</u> and shows that there is only one professor, and she gave me a D.

Noun Clauses

Noun clauses operate as noun phrases within a main clause, but they also contain their own subject and predicate. They begin with a word like "that," "how," "whatever," or "whether" or a phrase like "whether or not."

1. **Whatever you want to order** <u>is fine with me</u>.

  | This noun clause is the **subject** of the main clause. It is the thing that the <u>predicate verb phrase</u> describes.

2. **Whether or not you order French fries** <u>makes no difference to me</u>.

  | Here's a similar example. This noun clause is **subject** that makes no difference to me.

3. I <u>know</u> **that the French fries will give you a heart attack**.

  | This noun clause is an **object** for the <u>verb</u> from the main clause. It is the thing that I know.

4. However, I <u>support</u> **whatever you decide to do**.

  | This noun clause is also an **object** for the <u>main verb</u>. It is the thing that I support.

Even though you sometimes hear a pause before or after a noun clause, it's an essential part of the main clause. Don't use a comma to separate it from the rest of the main clause.

SENTENCES
Dependent Clauses

2. Phrases

Phrases are groups of words that operate as a unit to present one part of an idea. There are three main types of phrases in English sentences—noun phrases, verb phrases, and prepositional phrases.

A. Noun Phrases

The words of a noun phrase work together to name or describe a person, place, thing, or idea. They consist of a proper noun (such as "Bobby"), a common noun (such as "accountant"), or a pronoun (such as "she"), along with any other words that describe that noun. The order in which these elements are arranged is remarkably consistent, as you can see in this table of noun phrases:

Adjectives	Noun or Pronoun	Prepositional Phrases	Relative Clauses
	Bobby		
	Bobby	from Klamath Falls	
the	accountant		
the old, mean	accountant	at my office	who looks like a cat
my	cat		
the pretty	cat		that Mom stole
	she		
	she		who watches

Gerunds and infinitives transform verbs into noun phrases so that we can talk about doing those actions in the same way we talk about physical objects and places and ideas.

Gerund Phrases

To create a gerund, you take the base form of any verb and add "–ing." "Complain," for example, becomes "complaining." Gerund phrases are structured more like verb phrases, which are described later in this chapter, but you can also use adjectives to describe the gerund. The following table shows how gerunds are structured.

Adjectives	Gerund	Object Noun Phrases	Other Stuff
	babysitting		
	babysitting	your hamster	
	babysitting	your hamster	while you were in Sun River
my recent	babysitting		of your hamster

Use gerund noun phrases wherever you would use other noun phrases.

1. **Babysitting your hamster** made me realize the importance of friendship.

   > This gerund phrase is the **subject** of the sentence. It's the thing that made you realize the importance of friendship.

2. I truly <u>loved</u> **babysitting your hamster**.

   > This time, the gerund phrase is the **object** of the <u>main verb</u> in this sentence, the thing that you truly loved.

3. I even wrote a poem <u>about</u> **babysitting your hamster**.

   > The gerund is the **object** of a <u>preposition</u>. It's what the poem was about.

Infinitive Phrases

An infinitive phrase is the preposition "to" followed by the base form of any verb — "to be," for example, or "to go" or "to complain" or "to babysit." An infinitive phrase consists of an infinitive like these and then any other optional words that help to describe it. This table shows how infinitive phrases are structured.

Infinitive	Object Noun Phrases	Other Stuff
to count		
to count	my toes	
to count		on my sister
to count	sheep	when I need to fall asleep

Use infinitive phrases wherever you would use any other noun phrase.

1. **To count sheep when I need to fall asleep** <u>is a waste of time</u>.

   > This infinitive phrase is the **subject** of this sentence. It is the thing that the <u>predicate verb phrase</u> describes.

2. My mother always <u>said</u> **to count sheep when I need to fall asleep**.

   > This time the infinitive phrase is the **object** of the <u>main verb</u> in this sentence, the thing that your mother always said.

3. My mother always said to count sheep <u>when I *need* **to fall asleep**</u>.

   > There's also an infinitive phrase inside the <u>dependent clause</u> that begins with "when." It's the **object** of the *verb* in that clause, the thing that I need to do.

Gerunds and Infinitives

Multilingual writers may be understandably confused by gerund phrases, which some languages don't use at all, and infinitive phrases. These two verb-like noun phrases do the same job. They both present an action as a noun phrase within a sentence.

In English, gerunds sound more natural as subjects and complement noun phrases:

1. **Adopting this cat** <u>was a big mistake</u>.

   > The gerund is the **subject noun phrase** of the sentence. The <u>predicate</u> provides an idea about that subject.

2. **My mistake** was <u>adopting this cat</u>.

   > The gerund in this sentence is a **complement noun phrase** that helps to describe the **subject**.

When it comes to object noun phrases, however, the main verb usually determines whether you should use a gerund or infinitive phrase. That means that you have to learn which verbs go best with gerund phrases and which go best with infinitive phrases.

Verbs That Prefer Gerunds

Verb	*Example*
advise	Allison advised against citing Dr. Oz in a paper.
appreciate	Jeremy appreciates hearing her side of the story.
consider	Maria considered telling him about my toenail fungus.
dislike	Shannon dislikes waking up before six in the morning.
enjoy	Alexis enjoys hearing your unending criticisms.
finish	At midnight, Denise finally finished telling me about her last boyfriend.
mind	Most times, Don doesn't mind cleaning the bathroom.
miss	Chrys misses feeling the soft caress of her cat against her leg.
practice	Jan practices listening to her daughter.
quit	One day, Eva will quit trying so hard.
recall	Donna recalled loaning the book to her brother-in-law.
spend (time)	Jill spent the day painting her hall closet a vibrant brown.
suggest	Brian suggested meeting another day when he's not so preoccupied with his sick dachshund.

Verbs That Prefer Infinitives

Verb	Example
agree	Karl agreed to babysit the hamster.
appear	Vinod appears to enjoy his job at Subway.
be able	We were able to contribute a little more to the shelter this year.
choose	Kim chose to skip her Monday class.
continue	Kevin continues to pine for his boss's daughter.
decide	Tammy decided to go to the coast again.
get	Matthew will soon get to quit his other jobs.
like	Sara would like to know if she can count on Jose for help.
mean	Steve means to give Ron a raise.
need	He needs to be patient, though.
say	LeAnna said to wait another couple of days before contacting her.
try	Maggie tried to get tickets to the symphony.
use	Justus used to cry about everything.

B. Noun Phrases in Sentences

Within a sentence, noun phrases have four different jobs to do. They can be subjects, objects, complements, or appositives.

Subjects

The subject is the star of the sentence. The predicate either tells us what the subject does, or it describes the subject. Either way, it's the subject's show.

1. **My uncle** <u>lost</u> his phone.

   > The **subject** of this sentence did something. What he did is explained by the <u>predicate</u>.

2. **His phone** <u>was a brand new iPhone</u>.

   > The <u>predicate verb phrase</u> describes the **subject** of this sentence.

3. **The poor man** <u>put</u> it on top of his car.

   > In English, the **subject** usually comes first in a sentence and is followed by the <u>verb</u>.

4. <u>Then</u> **he** drove out of the parking lot.

   > However, sometimes an introductory <u>adverb</u> comes before the **subject**.

5. <u>As you might have guessed</u>, **the phone** slid off and smashed against the pavement.

> If the sentence begins with a transitional word or introductory phrase or clause, put a comma between the <u>introduction</u> and the **subject**.

6. *Losing this phone* made my uncle reflective about how we are slaves to our possessions.

<u>To lose this phone</u> made my uncle reflective about the nature of possessions.

> *Gerund phrases* sound more natural as **subjects** than <u>infinitive phrases</u>.

It Is / There Is

Sometimes we want to state that something is happening or that something exists. Some languages allow writers to simply use a noun phrase for this:

1. Raining outside!

> This is a gerund noun phrase that describes something that is happening. There is no subject or verb, however, so this is not a grammatical sentence.

2. Important to breathe oxygen.

> This is an adjective that describes an infinitive noun phrase. The verb "breathe" is in the infinitive noun phrase, but the main clause does not have a verb. This is not a grammatical sentence, either.

3. Cats on the window sill.

> This is a regular noun phrase that describes a thing. There is no verb, however, so this is not a grammatical sentence.

4. Problem to avoid.

> This is a regular noun phrase, too. The verb "avoid" is inside an infinitive phrase that describes what kind problems, but the main clause does not have a verb.

English requires that sentences have subjects and verbs, but it also provides two easy ways to add a subject and verb to statements like "raining outside" or "cats on the windowsill."

It + To Be

When you want to state that something is happening add the pronoun "it" and the verb "to be" to a gerund noun phrase.

5. **It** <u>is</u> raining outside.

This is now a grammatical sentence because we have a **subject** and <u>verb</u>.

6. **It** <u>is</u> important to breathe oxygen.

> This is now a grammatical sentence because we have a **subject** and <u>verb</u> to introduce the adjective an infinitive phrase.

The pronoun "it" in these examples doesn't refer to any previous noun phrase. This is just a way that English allows us to present a gerund noun phrase or adjective with a subject and verb.

7. **Breathing oxygen** <u>is</u> important.

> You can also use a gerund phrase in place of the infinitive phrase and link it to the adjective with the verb "to be." It's good to have options. To put it another way, having options is good.

There + To Be

To state that something exists, add the adverb "there" and the verb "to be" to a regular noun phrase.

8. **There** <u>are</u> cats on the window sill.

> This is now a grammatical sentence because we have a **subject** and <u>verb</u>. The adverb "there" doesn't really refer to any particular place most of the time. This is just a way that English allows us to focus on the noun phrase and still have a complete sentence.

9. **There** <u>is</u> a problem to avoid.

> This is now a grammatical sentence because we have a **subject** and <u>verb</u>. The adverb "there" doesn't refer to any particular place where the problems exist.

One thing to keep in mind is that the verb form should match the noun phrase that follows it. If the noun phrase is plural, use a a plural verb. If a noun phrase is singular, use a singular verb.

Objects

Objects are noun phrases that are affected by verbs or that prepositions connect to the rest of the sentence. One type of object noun phrase is the direct object. This is the thing that the verb directly affects. If you kick a window, for example, the window is the object of your kick.

1. My uncle lost **his phone** again.

> The **direct object** is the thing that my uncle lost. This time he left it on a table at a restaurant.

2. He asked **me** to call my aunt.

> I am the **direct object** being asked — again.

3. I don't enjoy **making excuses for my uncle**.

| Gerund phrases can be **direct objects**.

4. I don't want **to make my aunt mad**.

| Infinitive phrases can also be **direct objects**.

Another type of object is the **indirect object**. This is a noun phrase that the verb affects—but not directly. When you throw a can of beets, the can is the direct object of the throw. If you throw a can of beets at your brother, your brother is the indirect object. You don't throw him, but the can that you do throw hits him on the side of the head. See how that works?

5. My uncle paid <u>me</u> **twenty dollars** to call my aunt and tell her about the phone.

He paid **twenty dollars** to <u>me</u> to call her and tell her about the phone.

| The **direct object** isn't necessarily the noun phrase immediately after the verb. It all depends on how you phrase the sentence. An <u>indirect object</u> might come first, or it might come later.

6. She asked <u>me</u> **a question**.

She asked **a question** of <u>me</u>.

7. I told <u>her</u> **the truth**.

I told **the truth** to <u>her</u>.

| The truth was "twenty dollars."

8. She just laughed.

| Some verbs (like "laugh") don't usually take any object, direct or indirect. They just happen.

A third type of object is the **object of a preposition**. This is any noun phrase that's connected by a preposition to another noun, verb, or adjective.

9. My aunt's laughter sounded *good* <u>to</u> **me**.

| I am the **object** of the <u>preposition</u>. This phrase describes an *adjective*.

10. I *laughed* <u>with</u> **my aunt**.

| This <u>preposition</u> connects the **object noun phrase** to a *verb*.

11. Then it was *quiet* <u>for</u> **a minute**.

| This <u>preposition</u> connects the **object noun phrase** to an *adjective*.

Complements

A complement noun phrase completes the meaning of a sentence by providing necessary information about either the subject or object of the sentence.

1. <u>My heart</u> *is* **an ocean of emotion**.

   <u>You</u> *might be* **my closest friend**.

   > When a **complement** noun phrase describes the <u>subject</u> of a sentence, a *linking verb* connects the two noun phrases. In this case, "my closest friend" is necessary information about what I mean when I say "you."

2. However, you just called <u>me</u> **a fool**.

   > A **complement** noun phrase can also rename or describe a <u>direct object</u>. In this case, "fool" is describing "me." Actually, that's true in most cases.

3. That makes <u>my heart</u> **a raging sea**.

   > **Complement** noun phrases always follow the <u>direct object</u>. What's "a raging sea"? "My heart" is a raging sea. No wonder I don't have many friends.

Appositives

An appositive noun phrase is an interruption of a sentence that renames or describes the noun phrase right before it.

1. <u>Potatoes</u>, **my vegetable of choice**, are so starchy that I get fat just looking at them.

   > The **appositive** must follow immediately after <u>the noun phrase that it renames or describes</u>.

2. <u>My second favorite vegetable</u>, **the tomato**, is more of an unpleasant fruit than a vegetable.

   > Because **an appositive** is an interruption of the main sentence, you separate it from the main sentence with commas.

3. I refuse to eat <u>Brussels sprouts</u>, **the so-called king of vegetables**.

   > If the **appositive** comes at the end of the sentence, you only need to separate it from <u>the noun phrase it describes</u> with a single comma.

C. Verb Phrases

The words in a verb phrase tell us something about the the subject of the sentence. When using an action verb, they tell us what the subject does. With linking verbs, they give us more information about the subject. Although the verb phrase usually begins with a verb, the structure isn't as regular as it is with noun phrases.

With Action Verbs

Let's suppose that the subject of our sentence is "the cell phone." Here are different ways to create verb phrases for that subject using the word "ring."

Verb(s)	Other Stuff	Notes
rings **rang** <u>is</u> **ringing** <u>has been</u> **ringing** <u>will</u> **ring**		A verb phrase can consist of a single **main verb** or a set of <u>helping verbs</u> and a main verb that explains what the subject does. Different forms of the verb show when the action happens.
rings	loudly in the morning for two minutes	Usually, though, adverbs and prepositional phrases provide more information about the **main verb**.
is ringing	even though I told my boyfriend I'd be home in ten minutes	Subordinate clauses provide supporting ideas about the **main verb**.
<u>never</u> **rings**		You can change the meaning of the **verb** to mean the opposite with a <u>negative adverb</u>.
did <u>not</u> **ring** is <u>not</u> **ringing**		<u>Negative adverbs</u> need to come before the **main verb**.

With Linking Verbs

Linking verbs link the subject to additional information about the subject. Let's say that the subject is "my sister-in-law." Here are different ways to use linking verbs to describe her:

Linking Verb	Other Stuff	Notes
seems **appears**	<u>friendly</u> to most people <u>polite</u> before you get to know her	The **linking verb** can connect an <u>adjective</u> to describe the subject noun phrase.
was **is** **is**	<u>from L.A.</u> <u>between jobs</u> because of attitude issues <u>in the bathroom</u> again	You can also link <u>prepositional phrases</u> back to the subject.
looks **smells** **sounds**	under the weather foul tired	Linking verbs are also sometimes related to our five senses: look, smell, sound, feel, and taste. When using these as linking verbs they are about perception, not action.
has been **became**	<u>a dedicated Cleveland Browns fan</u> <u>my nemesis</u> for the past three years	With <u>complement noun phrases</u>, the **linking verb** shows that the subject is or has been one of these things.
is <u>not</u> **was** never **will** <u>never</u> **be**	funny on time a gentle soul	<u>Negative adverbs</u> with a linking verb tell readers that the following descriptions do not apply to the subject.

Linking Verbs

Linking verbs will understandably be challenging for writers fluent in languages that don't have any linking verbs.

1. **Problem:**

   My brother <u>sweaty</u> and <u>out-of-breath</u>.

   > "My brother" is the **subject** of the sentence. The rest of the sentence is a list of <u>adjectives</u> that describe him. But there's no verb, so it's not a grammatical sentence in English.

   Solution 1:

   My brother *is* <u>sweaty</u> and <u>out-of-breath</u>.

   > Now the sentence is grammatical because it has a *verb*. The *linking verb* "is" connects the **subject** and the <u>adjectives</u> that describe it.

   Solution 2:

   My brother *smells* <u>sweaty</u> and *sounds* <u>out-of-breath</u>.

   > Now the sentence is grammatical because it has a linking *verb* for each <u>adjective</u>. The *linking verbs* connect the **subject** to the <u>adjectives</u> that describe it.

2. **Problem:**

   Your room <u>a mess</u>.

   > "Your room" is the **subject** of the sentence. The rest of the sentence is a <u>noun phrase</u> that describe your room. There's no verb, howeer, so it's not a grammatical sentence in English.

   Solution:

   Your room *was* <u>a mess</u>.

   > Now the sentence is grammatical because a *linking verb* connects the **subject** and the <u>complement noun phrase</u> that describe it.

D. Prepositional Phrases

Prepositional phrases consist of a single preposition—such as "on" or "to" or "from"—and a noun phrase. Within a sentence, they describe verbs and nouns, often explaining where something is or when it is happening.

As Adjectives

Within noun phrases, prepositional phrases always follow the noun they describe, and they are never separated from that noun with commas.

1. The tattoo <u>parlor</u> **on the corner** seems pretty sketchy.

   > The **prepositional phrase** explains where the <u>noun</u> is located.

2. The <u>customers</u> **in the window** appear to be dangerously angry.

   > This **prepositional phrase** identifies which <u>nouns</u> look angry.

3. <u>Anyone</u> **in their right mind** would check out the reviews first.

   > Sometimes a **prepositional phrase** helps to define the boundaries of a <u>noun</u>. Anyone who is *not* inside this boundary will walk on in.

4. However, a <u>friend</u> **of mine** just walked right in.

   > A **prepositional phrase** can also show that a <u>noun</u> belongs to another noun.

5. He wanted a <u>tattoo</u> **of Justin Bieber on his forehead**.

   > You can use more than one **prepositional phrase** to describe a <u>noun</u>. "Of Justin Bieber" is one phrase and "on his forehead" is the other. You still don't add any commas in there.

6. He wanted a <u>tattoo</u> **in green ink of Justin Bieber on his forehead**.

   > However, more than two **prepositional phrases** after the <u>noun</u> are hard to follow.

As Adverbs

Within verb phrases, prepositional phrases always follow the main verb that they describe. They are not separated from that verb with commas because they are considered essential information about that verb.

1. I <u>was playing</u> **in the street**.

   > This **prepositional phrase** explains where the <u>verb</u> takes place.

2. I <u>was hit</u> **by a car**.

   > This **prepositional phrase** explains how the <u>verb</u> happened.

3. Fortunately, I <u>was</u> **inside a bigger car**.

   > With linking verbs, the **prepositional phrase** describes the subject noun phrase, but it still follows the <u>verb</u>.

4. My mom's car is where I <u>play</u> **with my toys**.

   This **prepositional phrase** is inside a dependent clause, but it still follows the <u>verb</u> there, too.

5. She always <u>parks</u> **in the street** *because it's easier than parking at the curb*.

   Prepositional phrases follow the <u>verb</u> and come before any *dependent clauses*.

6. Maybe she will <u>try</u> *harder* **after this**.

   Only *adverbs* can slip in between the <u>verb</u> and a **prepositional phrase**. *Adverbs* go wherever they want, basically. There's no stopping them.

As Introductions and Transitions

Although you often hear pauses before and after prepositional phrases when speaking, they're almost always essential parts of a noun phrase or verb phrase, so don't separate them from the rest of the clause with commas. Resist the temptation.

However, there are two exceptions. When prepositional phrases are used as introductions or transitions, separate them from the rest of the sentence with commas.

1. **In the morning**, <u>my cat</u> eats Cheerios.

   Because this **prepositional phrase** comes before the <u>subject</u> of the sentence, we separate it from the subject of the sentence with a comma.

2. <u>Cats</u>, **in my opinion**, <u>should not be limited to the "cat food" imposed on them by corporations</u>.

   This **prepositional phrase** is a transition that interrupts the <u>main clause</u>, so we separate it from the main clause with a comma on either side.

3. **In my opinion**, <u>people</u> should not be limited to eating corporation-defined "people food," either.

   If a transitional **prepositional phrase** introduces a sentence, separate it from the <u>subject</u> of the sentence with a comma.

3. Parts of Speech

The words in any language belong to different categories, and each category has at least one job to do. Noun, for example, is one category, and it's job is to name a person, place, thing, or idea.

These word categories are called parts of speech. In English, there are seven main parts of speech:

- **Nouns** (like "Salem" or "broccoli") name places, people, things, or ideas.

- **Adjectives** (like "crowded" or "green") describe nouns.

- **Pronouns** (like "she" or "we") refer to nouns so that we don't have to repeat the noun several times in a row.

- **Verbs** (like "stares" or "go") name different things that nouns can do.

- **Adverbs** (like "very" or "smoothly") describe verbs.

- **Prepositions** (like "to" or "with") show relationships between nouns and other parts of a sentence.

- **Conjunctions** (like "and" or "because") connect words or phrases together.

As a speaker of a language, you've learned through practice how to use these different parts of speech correctly. It's automatic and unconscious. As a writer, however, you have to understand what you're doing more consciously in order to correctly structure and punctuate your sentences.

To talk about that, we rely on technical terms like these for the parts of speech, so here's a closer look at what the parts of speech are in English and the jobs they perform in our sentences.

A. Nouns

Nouns name a person, place, thing, or idea. Common nouns are nouns that could apply to any of several people, places, or things. Proper nouns are the official names for specific people, places, or things. Because they're so proper, we capitalize them.

1. A **director** makes **movies**.

    | These are **common nouns** because they apply to any director or movie.

2. Errol Morris is a **director**.

    | This proper noun is the official name for one particular director. "Director" is a **common noun** for the job he does.

3. Errol Morris sometimes gets on my **nerves**.

These are specifically my nerves, but this is still a **common noun** because I don't have pet names for each of my individual nerves.

4. His **films** show in lots of **theaters**.

   These are **common nouns** that name groups of things. No specific names are used.

5. However, his **films** seldom come to Salem Cinema.

   This proper noun is the name of one particular theater.

Most nouns can name either a single thing or many things. If a noun names a single thing, it's called a **singular noun**. If it names many things, it's a **plural noun**. In most cases, you turn a singular noun into a plural noun by adding the letter "s" to the end of the word.

6. If you like cats, you'll like my **cat**.

   To turn this **singular noun** into a plural noun, you just add an "s."

7. If you like flies, you'll like my **fly**.

   Singular nouns that end with a "y" often need to replace "y" with "ies" when they become plural nouns.

8. I'll trade you one big **toy** for three little toys.

   However, if there's another vowel before the "y," like with this **singular noun**, you just add an "s" to make it a plural noun.

9. The **glass** on the **couch** distinctly reminds me of other glasses on other couches.

   With **singular nouns** that end in an "s" or similar sound, add "es" to create a plural noun.

10. The **tooth** on that **goose** is just like the teeth on those geese.

    Yikes. With some older **singular nouns**, the old-fashioned plural noun spellings persist. You'll have to memorize these exceptions. A dictionary will help you out.

11. Your one **child** is chasing my three children.

    Here's another old-fashioned plural noun.

A few nouns can't be turned into plural nouns because they name things that can't be divided into separate units and counted—nouns like "salt" or "happiness" or "advice." These are called **mass nouns**.

B. Adjectives

Adjectives are words that describe nouns and pronouns. They can describe nouns and pronouns with many characteristics, such as by quantity ("three," "many"), by characteristics ("angry," "ugly," "soft"), by ownership ("my," "her"), and more.

Descriptive Adjectives

The most common type of adjective is the one that describes a noun's characteristics.

1. The **thirteenth** <u>floor</u> does not exist in my building.

   | This **descriptive adjective** tells us the position of the nonexistent <u>noun</u>.

2. <u>Wasps</u> *are* always **angry**.

   | The **adjective** describes the emotional state of the <u>noun</u>, "wasps." Notice that this adjective is connected to the noun by the *linking verb*. Not all adjectives can do that, but descriptive ones can.

3. Wasps are probably angry about all the **rotten**, **stinking** <u>food</u> they eat.

   If I were a wasp, *I* would also be **angry**, **aggressive**, and **relentless**.

   | You can list **descriptive adjectives** before or after a <u>noun</u> or *pronoun*.

4. I have a **wasp** <u>mindset</u>.

   | Not to confuse things, but nouns can sometimes be used as **descriptive pronouns** to describe other <u>nouns</u>. "Wasp" was our noun in the two sentences above and now here it is as an adjective that describes "mindset."

Participle verb forms can also be used as descriptive adjectives. Present participles add an "-ing" to the verb. This form describes the effect that a noun has on something else.

5. This **tsunami** is <u>boring</u> to *me*.

   | In this case, the **noun** creates the effect that the <u>adjective</u> describes. It has that effect on *something else*. In this case, the effect is that a life-threatening tidal wave bores you.

Past participles add an "-ed" to the verb form. This form of the verb is used to describe how the noun was affected by something else.

6. **I** was <u>bored</u> by the *tsunami*.

   | The past participle form of "to bore" is now an <u>adjective</u> that describes how the **subject noun phrase** was affected by *something else*. What doesn't bore you, exactly?

Quantity Adjectives

Quantity adjectives describe the number of a noun. Numbers tell us exactly how many of the noun there are. Indefinite adjectives give a sense of how many there are, but they don't provide a specific number.

1. I would like **three** cheeseburgers.

   | The **number** tells us exactly how many of the noun you would like to eat.

2. I would like **some** cheeseburgers.

   | This **indefinite adjective** tells us that you would like more than one but not necessarily a lot of the noun.

3. I would like **no** cheeseburgers.

   | This **indefinite adjective** tells us that you've finally come to your senses. Cheeseburgers are not very good for you.

Adjectives

In Spanish, descriptive adjectives also show whether the noun being described is singular or plural. In English, they don't.

1. **Problem:**

   I have **helpfuls** friends.

   | "Helpful" is a **descriptive adjective** that describes the noun "friends." Descriptive adjectives in English are always singular, so the "s" here is incorrect.

   Solution:

   I have **helpful** friends.

   | Now that the **descriptive adjective** is singular, the sentence is grammatical.

2. **Problem:**

   The girl wears **greens** bracelets

   | The writer has added an "s" to the **descriptive adjective**. Even though the noun is plural, the **descriptive adjective** cannot be plural.

   Solution:

   The girl wears *five* green bracelets.

   | "Five" is a *quantity adjective* that better describes the number of the **noun** that this girl wears, but you still don't add an "s" to it. The **descriptive adjective** does not change, either.

Determiners

Determiners show which noun we mean. When they show up in a noun phrase, they're always the first words used.

Articles are a type of determiner that show whether we mean one particular noun or one among several possible nouns.

1. **The** thirteenth <u>floor</u> does not exist in my building.

   | The **definite article** "the" shows that we mean one particular <u>noun</u>.

2. This is **a** hard <u>concept</u> for my guests to understand.

   | The **indefinite article** "a" shows that we mean one of several possible <u>nouns</u> that the guests could struggle with.

3. I need to get **an** <u>apartment</u> in another building.

   | If the word immediately following the **indefinite article** "a" starts with a vowel sound — as this <u>noun</u> does — use "an" instead of "a."

Articles

Many languages don't use articles with singular noun phrases, but English does. Consider this problem sentence:

I gave her **flower**.

English offers two solutions:

1. I gave her <u>a</u> **flower**.

   | Use the <u>indefinite article</u> "a" when you mean one singular **noun** out of many possible nouns — in this case, one out of many possible flowers.

2. I gave her <u>the</u> **flower**.

   | Use the <u>definite article</u> "the" when your reader already knows which **noun** you are talking about.

How can you know if your reader knows which noun you are talking about? A few nouns like "sun" are universal because there is only one. Most of the time, however, you know that your reader understands which noun you mean because you've mentioned it.

3. This morning I bought <u>a</u> **flower** for my mother. When I came home, I gave her *the* **flower**.

   | In this case, the <u>indefinite article</u> shows this just one of many possible **nouns** you could bought for your mother. The *definite article* shows that this is definitely the same **noun** you mention earlier.

Demonstrative adjectives also show which noun we mean by showing whether a noun is associated with us or not.

1. **This** <u>pimple</u> is distracting me.

   The **demonstrative adjective** "this" suggests that a singular <u>noun</u> is close at hand—that it's my pimple.

2. **These** <u>pimples</u> are distracting me.

   The **demonstrative adjective** "these" suggests that a plural <u>noun</u> is close at hand.

3. **That** <u>pimple</u> is driving me crazy.

   The **demonstrative adjective** "that" suggests that a singular <u>noun</u> is not close at hand—that it's someone else's pimple.

4. **Those** <u>pimples</u> are distracting me.

   The **demonstrative adjective** "those" suggests that a plural <u>noun</u> is not close at hand.

Possessive adjectives are versions of pronouns or noun phrases that show that a noun belongs to some other noun.

1. **My** <u>uncle</u> owns a gas station.

   The **possessive adjective** is a pronoun that shows the <u>noun</u> belongs to me.

2. **My** *three unfortunate* <u>cousins</u> work at **his** *gas* <u>station</u>.

   If you use a **possessive adjective**, it must come before the <u>noun</u> and any *quantity* or *descriptive adjectives*.

3. **Their** *entire* <u>salary</u> consists of candy bars and chili dogs.

   That's really not fair to them, but it does illustrate how the **possessive adjective** comes before the *descriptive adjective*.

4. **My uncle's** <u>children</u> deserve better than this.

   You can create a **possessive adjective** with many noun phrases by adding an apostrophe and "s" to the end of it.

5. They can't stand the **chili dogs'** bitter <u>flavor</u>.

   If the noun is plural and has an "s" at the end already, you just add an apostrophe to create a **possessive adjective**.

Adjective Order

English has developed some patterns for organizing a set of adjectives around a common noun. These patterns are usually intuitive and thus invisible for many who grow up speaking English, but if you try rearranging this order in a noun phrase, you'll see that it's been quietly guiding your noun phrases all this time.

	Example 1	Example 2	Example 3	Example 4
Determiner	the	my	a	
Quantity	three			some

Descriptive Adjectives

	Example 1	Example 2	Example 3	Example 4
Judgment		beautiful	clever	hip
Size	little			
Age		old	five-year-old	young
Shape				
Color	brown		golden	
Material		bronze		
Proper				Salem
Purpose		magnifying		graphic
Noun	bears	glass	retriever	designers

SENTENCES
Adjectives

C. Pronouns

A pronoun stands in for a noun that's been used in a previous sentence or an earlier part of the same sentence. They come in many varieties — personal, relative, interrogative, demonstrative, indefinite, possessive, and reflexive.

Personal Pronouns

Personal pronouns usually refer to actual people, but they can also refer to things. There are three categories of personal pronouns in English:

- **First person:** "I" and "we"
- **Second person:** "you" (either a single person or several)
- **Third person:** "he," "she," "it," and "they"

The examples above show you what each pronoun looks like when it is used as the subject of a sentence. The word form usually changes when a pronoun is used as an object noun phrase:

- **First person:** "me" and "us"
- **Second person:** "you"
- **Third person:** "him," "her," "it," and "them"

The noun that a pronoun refers to is called the **antecedent** of the pronoun.

1. The toaster is broken. **It** won't toast my bread.

   > "It" is a third-person singular **pronoun**. The antecedent is in the previous sentence.

2. My sister and I went to a toaster store. **We** couldn't believe the cost to repair **it**.

   > "We" is a first-person plural **pronoun** and the subject of this sentence. The antecedent is in the prior sentence. "It" is still a third-person singular **pronoun** that refers to the toaster.

3. **They** wanted to *charge* **us** $100.

   > "They" is a third-person plural **pronoun**. The antecedent is the people at the toaster store. "Us" still refers to my sister and me, but now this first-person plural **pronoun** is an **object** noun phrase for the *verb*.

4. **You** wouldn't *pay* **them** $100, would **you**?

   > "You" is a second-person **pronoun** that might be singular (if there is one of you reading this) or plural (if you are reading this together with friends). "Them" refers to the jerks at the toaster store, but because they are now the object of the *verb*, the wording changes for this third-person plural **pronoun**.

Possessive Pronouns

Possessive pronouns come in two flavors. The first is the possessive adjective that is presented in the adjectives section. Because it is a type of personal pronoun, it comes in the same three categories:

- **First person:** "my" and "our"
- **Second person:** "your"
- **Third person:** "his," "her," "its," and "their"

The second type of personal pronoun stands on its own and means "the thing that belongs to me" — or you or him or her:

- **First person:** "mine" and "ours"
- **Second person:** "yours"
- **Third person:** "his," "hers," and "theirs"

1. **Your** <u>books</u> are used, but **his** <u>books</u> are new.

   "Your" and "his" are both examples of the possessive-adjective type of **pronoun** that tells us who owns the <u>nouns</u>.

2. **Yours** didn't cost as much as **his**.

   "Yours" and "his" are now personal **pronouns** that stand on their own as noun phrases. They refer to "your books" and "his books." You were the smart shopper.

3. **My** <u>car</u> is valuable, but **yours** is just expensive.

   "My" refers to me, the author of this sentence. It is a possessive-adjective type of **pronoun** that identifies the <u>noun</u> that is valuable. "Yours" refers to you again and means "your car," which I'm sure is very nice.

Reflexive Pronouns

Reflexive pronouns refer to nouns or pronouns that immediately precede or follow them. Because this is a type of personal pronoun, it comes in the same three categories:

- **First person:** "myself" and "ourselves"
- **Second person:** "yourself" and "yourselves"
- **Third person:** "himself," "herself," "itself," and "themselves"

1. We have nothing to fear but <u>fear</u> **itself**.

   "Itself" is a **reflexive pronoun** that refers to the <u>noun phrase</u> immediately before it.

2. However, I **myself** am afraid of more than just fear.

   | Doing this adds emphasis to that <u>noun</u>.

3. For example, <u>my dad</u> accidentally nailed **himself** to the roof with his nail gun.

   | "Himself" is a **reflexive pronoun** that refers to the subject <u>noun phrase</u> of the same sentence. We use it because the <u>antecedent</u> is doing something to the <u>antecedent</u>. Dad is both nailing and being nailed, which has to hurt.

4. <u>My brother</u> was also working on the roof. Dad accidentally nailed **him** to the roof, too.

   | In this case, we don't use a **reflexive personal pronoun** because the *subject* of the sentence is not the <u>antecedent</u> to the **pronoun**.

5. So in addition to fear **itself**, my dad scares *me*.

   | Do you see why one **pronoun** is reflexive and the *other* is not?

Demonstrative Pronouns

Demonstrative pronouns refer to noun phrases that are closer or farther in distance or time:

- **Closer:** "this" and "these"
- **Farther:** "that" and "those"

These are called "demonstrative" because they demonstrate or point out another noun phrase.

1. **This** is for your heartache, and **these** are for your runny nose.

   | "This" is a **demonstrative pronoun** that refers to a single noun like "book of poetry," and "these" is another **demonstrative pronoun** that points out a plural noun like "tissues."

2. **That** is for your heartache, and **those** are for your runny nose.

   | "That" and "those" are **demonstrative pronouns** that point out the same noun phrases. They suggest that those things aren't as close as they were in Example 1.

3. **This** is Joe, and **that** is the mess he made.

   | The **pronoun** "this" refers to Joe, who is standing right beside us, and the **pronoun** "that" suggests that his mess is farther away.

Indefinite Pronouns

Indefinite pronouns don't refer directly to an antecedent noun phrase. One type doesn't refer to any specific noun phrase:

- anybody, anyone, anything
- everybody, everyone, everything
- nobody, none, no one, nothing
- somebody, someone, something

1. **Everybody** <u>is</u> going to miss me.

   | This category of pronoun always takes a <u>singular verb</u>.

2. **Someone** probably <u>misses</u> me.

3. **No one** <u>misses</u> me.

   | Seriously? I miss you.

The other type of indefinite pronoun refers to a specific noun phrase, but it doesn't clearly define what portion of that noun phrase is included:

- **Plural:** all, most, many, several, some, few, both
- **Singular:** either, neither, one, none

4. The people here are friendly. **Several** <u>have invited</u> me to dinner.

   | If this type of **indefinite pronoun** refers to more than one thing, it takes a <u>plural verb</u>.

5. **One** <u>has given</u> me cupcakes.

   | If this type of **indefinite pronouns** refers to a single noun, use a <u>singular verb</u>.

6. **None** <u>has abandoned</u> me emotionally like **either** of you <u>has</u>.

   | "None," "either," and "neither" are also considered singular, even though it sounds a little weird sometimes.

Interrogative Pronouns

Interrogative pronouns help us ask questions. There are only five — "who," "whom," "whose," "what," and "which."

1. **Who** ate one of my cupcakes?

2. **What** were they thinking?

3. Oh. These aren't my cupcakes. **Whose** are they?

Pronouns

Many languages don't use pronouns. Others use pronouns but don't change the form of the pronoun for gender or number or when the pronoun is used as an object noun phrase.

In English, pronouns are used a lot, and the form of the pronoun has to match person, gender, number, and how the pronoun is used in a sentence. Pronouns must also be used instead of a noun phrase and not right next to it.

1. **Problem:**

   My brother works hard <u>because knows it will pay off</u>.

   > "My brother" is the **subject** of this sentence and of the <u>dependent clause</u>. However, English requires us to use a pronoun for "my brother" within the <u>dependent clause</u>, and that pronoun is missing in this sentence.

   Solution:

   My brother works hard because <u>he</u> knows it will pay off.

   > The <u>pronoun</u> in the dependent clause refers to the **subject** of this sentence. Now readers know that my brother works hard and that he knows it will pay off.

2. **Problem:**

   My sister likes <u>his</u> job.

   > The gender of the **subject** noun phrase, "my sister," is female. The gender of the <u>possessive pronoun</u> that refers to the subject is male. They don't match.

   Solution:

   My sister likes <u>her</u> job.

   > "Her" is the <u>possessive pronoun</u> for females, so now the **subject** and the <u>pronoun</u> match. I'm glad the job is going well.

3. **Problem:**

   After **Layli's parents** left, Layli missed <u>him</u>.

   > In this case, the **antecedent noun phrase**, "Layli's parents," is a **plural noun phrase**. "Him" is a singular <u>pronoun</u>. They don't match.

   Solution:

   After **Layli's parents** left, Layli missed <u>them</u>.

   > "Them" is a plural <u>pronoun</u> that matches the **plural noun phrase**.

4. **Problem:**

Layli loves **they**.

> "They" is a <u>pronoun</u> that refers to more than one person—in this case, Layli's parents. However, "they" should only be used as the subject of the sentence. In this example, the pronoun is the object of Layli's love, so we need to use the object form of the pronoun.

Solution:

Layli loves <u>them</u>.

> "Them" is an object form of the <u>pronoun</u>. Now it is correct.

5. **Problem:**

My brother <u>he</u> is the troublemaker in the family.

> One last thing—don't repeat a **noun phrase** by putting a <u>pronoun</u> right after the **noun phrase** that it refers to.

Solution 1:

My brother is the troublemaker in the family.

Solution 2:

<u>He</u> is the troublemaker in the family.

> With either solution, you have just one subject noun phrase for the verb. With the second solution, however, we have to know who you mean by "he." You would have to mention your brother in the sentence or two before this one.

D. Verbs

Verbs tell us about the subject of a sentence or clause. Active verbs like "kick" and "narrate" tell us what the subject is doing. Linking verbs like "is" or "has" describe the subject by linking the subject to descriptive information.

Verb Forms

When it comes to how a verb is spelled in a sentence, regular verbs all follow the same general rules. Irregular verbs don't follow those same rules very well. They are usually older verbs that are still following outdated grammar rules from *Game of Thrones* days. The rules for verb forms depend on three main characteristics—number (singular or plural), person, and tense.

Number and Person

Just like with nouns, verbs have singular and plural forms. And just like with pronouns, they also come in first-, second-, and third-person forms. You can see how this works most clearly with the irregular verb "to be."

	Singular		*Plural*	
Person	noun	verb	noun	verb
First Person	I	am	we	are
Second Person	you	are	you	are
Third Person	he, she, it	is	they	are
	Jojo the dog		the gerbils	

Number and person are less obvious but still present with a regular verb like "to look."

	Singular		*Plural*	
Person	noun	verb	noun	verb
First Person	I	look	we	look
Second Person	you	look	you	look
Third Person	he, she, it	looks	they	look
	Jojo the dog		the gerbils	

For regular verbs, then, the main rule is that you add the letter "s" to the verb when the subject is a third-person singular noun phrase like "it" or "the dog" or "Jojo." Otherwise, leave it alone.

Verb Forms

Many languages have only one verb form. Other languages have multiple verb forms but those forms don't change for person or number. With English, however, the person and number of the subject determine the form of the verb. Multilingual writers must pay close attention to the person and number of the subject noun phrase when choosing which verb form to use in a sentence.

Verb Tense

Verb tense shows us when something happens. English changes the spelling of the verb and sometimes adds helping verbs to show readers whether something happened in the past, is happening in the present, or will happen in the future. Here are some of your options:

Tense	Time	Irregular Verb	Regular Verb
Present	**It happens now.**	**She sings.**	**We listen.**
Present Progressive	It is in the process of happening at this moment.	She is singing.	We are listening.
Present Perfect	It began in the past and ended now or recently.	She has sung.	We have listened.
Past	**It happened before now.**	**She sang.**	**We listened.**
Past Progressive	It began, continued for a while, and ended recently.	She was singing.	We were listening.
Past Perfect Progressive	It began, continued, and ended in the past.	She had been singing.	We had been listening.
Future	**It will happen later.**	**She will sing.**	**We will listen.**
Future Progressive	It will begin and con-tinue for a while in the future.	She will be singing.	We will be listening.
Future Perfect	It will begin and end in the future.	She will have sung.	We will have listened.

Present tense is also used for most statements of fact, regardless of time.

1. I **am** a great friend.

   This is a **present tense verb**, but this is not only true at this exact moment. It was true three weeks ago, and it will be true for years to come.

2. On page 236 of *Jane Eyre*, the governness **says**, "What could possibly go wrong if I enter my master's bedroom at two in the morning?"

   Jane Eyre was originally published on October 16, 1847, but we use a **present tense verb** to talk about what happens in the novel. At least, we do in MLA style. In APA, use a past tense verb.

Verb Tense

Some languages do not use verb tenses at all, so multilingual writers will sometimes use only the base form of a verb and put other information into the sentence to explain when something happened. In English, the verb must use the right tense for when something happened. This is true even if other information in the sentence also explains when something happened.

1. **Problem:**

   Damon **go** to the doctor <u>next week</u>.

   > The sentence says <u>when the doctor appointment will happen</u>, but the **verb** is only the base form of "to go." It doesn't show the verb tense.

   Solution:

   Damon **will go** to the doctor next week.

   > Now the **verb** is in the future tense. That matches the other information about <u>when the appointment will happen</u>.

2. **Problem:**

   Damon **go** to the doctor <u>this week</u>.

   > The **verb** is just the base form of "to go." It does not show the verb tense.

   Solution:

   Damon **goes** to the doctor <u>this week</u>.

   > Now the **verb** is in the present tense. That matches the other information about <u>when the appointment happens</u>.

   Multilingual writers sometimes rely on simple present tense verbs because they are the first ones learned and become familiar. However, using only present tense verbs tells readers that everything is happening in this exact moment. To correctly express your ideas, use whichever verb tense is correct for when something happened, happens, or will happen.

3. **Problem:**

   Damon **goes** to the doctor <u>last week</u>.

   > The sentence says that <u>when the doctor appointment happened</u> is in the past. However, the **verb** is the present tense form of "go." It does not match when this happened.

   Solution:

   Damon **went** to the doctor last week.

   > The sentence says the appointment happened in the past. Now the **verb** is in the past tense form of "go." That matches the other information about when the appointment will happen.

Helping Verbs

Helping verbs, also known as auxiliary verbs, combine with an active verb to provide additional information about that action. These helping verbs always come before the main active verb, but sometimes adverbs will also slip in between them.

Be, Has, and Will

These helping verbs help to show when something happens.

1. A grand piano **will** <u>fall</u> from the sky.

   > This **helping verb** shows us that the <u>main verb</u> will happen in the future.

2. A grand piano **will** *probably* <u>fall</u> from the sky.

   > *Adverbs* also affect the meaning of the <u>main verb</u>, but they aren't **helping verbs**. They're just *adverbs*, and *adverbs* go anywhere they want.

3. A grand piano **has** <u>fallen</u> from the sky twice in my lifetime.

   > This **helping verb** and the form of the <u>main verb</u> show that this action has happened in the past.

4. A grand piano **is** <u>falling</u> from the sky at this moment.

   > This **helping verb** and the form of the <u>main verb</u> show that this action is happening now.

5. A grand piano **will** *not* **be** <u>falling</u> from the sky at this moment.

   > *Negations* before the <u>main verb</u> come after the first **helping verb**.

Do

The helping verb "do" adds extra emphasis to the main verb or allows you to negate the meaning of the main verb.

1. A falling grand piano <u>destroys</u> the car it lands on.

   > Here's a <u>main verb</u> without any added emphasis.

2. A falling grand piano **does** <u>destroy</u> the car it lands on.

   > The **helping verb** asserts the <u>main verb</u> more strongly—just in case anyone has any doubts about this idea.

3. A falling grand piano **does** *not* <u>destroy</u> the car it lands on.

   > If there aren't any other helping verbs present, you can negate the meaning of a <u>main verb</u> with this **helping verb** and the *adverb* "not."

4. A falling grand piano destroys *not* the car it lands on.

   > Without the helping verb, your *negation* make you sound like you're giving a speech two hundred years ago.

Modals

Modal verbs change what's called the "mood" of the verb. They make the main verb conditional, possible, or necessary in some way. You have several modal verbs to choose from — "can," "could," "may," "might," "shall," "should," "will," "would," and "must." Each puts a slightly different spin on the meaning of the main verb.

1. He **should** <u>move</u> his car before the grand piano destroys it.

   > The **modal helping verb** shows that it would be a good idea for the <u>main verb</u> to happen.

2. He **might** <u>move</u> his car before the grand piano destroys it.

   > The **modal helping verb** shows that it is a possibility that the <u>main verb</u> will happen.

3. He **can** <u>move</u> his car before the grand piano destroys it.

   > The **modal helping verb** shows that the subject is capable of doing the <u>main verb</u>.

4. He **may** <u>move</u> his car before the grand piano destroys it.

   > The **modal helping verb** shows that the subject has the choice to do the <u>main verb</u>.

5. He **may** *not* <u>move</u> his car before the grand piano destroys it.

   > As with all the other helping verbs, *adverbs* can also slip in between the **modal helping verb** and the <u>main verb</u>, but they are still *adverbs*, not helping verbs.

SENTENCES
Verbs

E. Adverbs

Adverbs are versatile words that describe verbs, adjectives, and even other adverbs. Their most common job is to provide more information about the main verb of the sentence or clause — usually by explaining how, when, where, or why that verb happens.

1. Kim <u>complained</u> **loudly** about the onions on her salad.

   | This **adverb** explains how the <u>main verb</u> happened.

2. **Tonight**, Kim <u>complained</u> about the onions on her salad.

   | This **adverb** explains when the <u>main verb</u> happened. Notice that it comes before the subject. Adverbs can slip into many different places in a sentence.

3. In fact, Kim *is* **still** <u>complaining</u> about the onions on her salad.

   | This **adverb** also explains when the <u>main verb</u> happens. It has slipped in between the *helping verb* and the <u>main verb</u>.

4. **Later,** Kim <u>complained</u> **loudly** about the lack of onions.

   | You can pile on the **adverbs**, too. <u>Main verbs</u> can take it.

One thing to remember about adverbs is that you can usually make your writing more effective by not using them. Instead, choose more precise verbs or nouns that already include information the adverb provides:

> Kim railed against the lack of onions.
> Kim bemoaned the lack of onions.
> Kim decried the lack of onions.

Negation

In Spanish, "no" is the equivalent of the English adverb "not." In English, "no" and "not" are two different words and are used differently.

1. **Problem:**

   They **no** argue.

   Solution:

   They <u>do</u> **not** argue.

   | In English, you show negation by placing the **adverb** "not" after a <u>helping verb</u>. You don't negate the verb itself.

F. Prepositions

Prepositions are words that show the relationship of one noun phrase to a verb or another noun phrase. When the noun phrases are tangible things, the prepositions almost always refer to the actual location of the object.

1. Jan keeps her cello **inside** a case.

   | This **preposition** indicates the actual location of the cello.

2. She stores the case **under** her bed

   | This **preposition** indicates the actual location of the case.

However, prepositions can also be used to make intangible connections between noun phrases and verbs or other noun phrases.

3. Jan *practices* cello **for** <u>two hours a day</u>.

   | The **preposition** connects <u>a length of time</u> to the *verb*.

4. She *has been practicing* **since** <u>May 1962</u>.

   | This **preposition** connects <u>a starting point</u> in time to the <u>verb</u>. That's a lot
   | of practice, by the way.

5. Jan *practices* **for** <u>the love of music</u>.

   | This **preposition** connects <u>an intangible motive</u> to the *verb*.

Prepositions

Using prepositions correctly in English is not usually a problem for native English speakers because they have learned how to use them through long years of speaking, reading, and listening. Prepositions in English, however, are used differently than their translations in other languages. That means that multilingual writers must learn both the correct word in English and how it is or is not used in different situations. It may take years of practice to learn all of these rules for using different prepositions. However, there are some common errors that are easier to correct.

From and Of

The word *de* in Spanish means "of" and "from." In Spanish, those words can be used interchangeably. In English, they are used differently.

1. He was **from** <u>Oregon</u>.

   | Use this **preposition** <u>with a single place</u>.

2. He was from <u>the west side</u> **of** Oregon.

   Use this **preposition** when talking about <u>a part of a place</u> but not when talking about the whole place.

At, In, and On—with Places

In English, you generally use "at" for a specific place. Use "in" for an enclosed space. Use "on" for a surface.

1. Jan's concert was held **at** <u>the Silverton Palace of Music</u>.

   This **preposition** is used with <u>a specific place or location</u>.

2. Jan was so nervous that she vomited **in** <u>the Palace of Music bathroom</u>.

   This **preposition** is used with <u>an enclosed space</u>.

3. The Silverton Palace of Music is **in** <u>Silverton, Oregon</u>.

   This **preposition** is used with <u>cities</u>, too. Cities are considered enclosed spaces because they have boundaries. You also use this preposition with states, countries, and other geographically enclosed spaces.

4. Jan played her cello **on** <u>the stage</u>.

   This **preposition** is used with <u>a surface</u>, such as a stage.

At, In, and On—with Time

1. Jan's concert began **at** 7:30 p.m. She threw up **at** 7:15 p.m.

   Jan hadn't performed for others **in** three years.

   Jan's concert was **on** Friday. Her next concert will be **on** May 19.

   In English, you generally use "at" for a specific time. Use "in" for months, years, or other long periods of time. Use "on" for days and holidays.

G. Conjunctions

Conjunctions connect words, phrases, or clauses within a sentence. Coordinating conjunctions connect words, phrases, or clauses of equal importance to create a list of two or more equal and similar items. Correlative conjunctions also connect words, phrases, or clauses of equal importance, but they do so with a pair of words. Subordinating conjunctions connect a dependent clause to a main clause.

Coordinating Conjunctions

The coordinating conjunctions are "for," "and," "nor," "but," "or," "yet," and "so." You can remember this by remembering the otherwise meaningless acronym "FANBOYS." Although each coordinating conjunction creates a slightly different relationship between whatever items it connects, the implication is that those items are equally important.

1. <u>I don't like cake</u>, **and** <u>I don't like ice cream</u>.

   > This **coordinating conjunction** links two <u>independent clauses</u> to create a compound sentence.

2. I don't like <u>cake</u> **or** <u>ice cream</u>.

   > This **coordinating conjunction** links two <u>noun phrases</u> to create a compound noun phrase of things I don't like.

3. I like <u>donuts</u>, <u>fig bars</u>, and <u>coffee</u>, **but** not <u>ice cream</u>.

   > This **coordinating conjunction** links four <u>noun phrases</u> to create an even longer compound noun phrase of things I do or do not like.

4. Ice cream <u>gives me gas</u> **but** <u>makes me happy</u>.

   > This **coordinating conjunction** links two <u>verb phrases</u> to create a compound predicate that describes the two equally important but contradictory things that ice cream does to me.

Correlating Conjunctions

Like coordinating conjunctions, correlating conjunctions connect equally important words, phrases, or clauses. The difference is that they do this as a team of two words. The first word comes before the first item, and the second comes before the last item.

1. **Either** <u>your dog goes</u>, **or** <u>I go</u>.

   > This set of **correlating conjunctions** links two <u>independent clauses</u> to create a very difficult choice.

2. **Neither** <u>my dog</u> **nor** <u>you</u> are going anywhere.

   > This set of **correlating conjunctions** links two <u>noun phrases</u> to create a definite compound subject.

3. Your dog is **both** <u>stupid</u> **and** <u>ugly</u>.

   > This set of **correlating conjunctions** links two <u>adjectives</u> that describe the poor, soon-to-be-going dog.

Subordinating Conjunctions

Subordinating conjunctions connect two unequally important clauses—a more important main clause and a less important dependent clause. Once connected to the main clause, the dependent clause takes on a supporting role, helping to explain something about the main clause.

You have many subordinating conjunctions to choose from, including:

- **Cause:** as, because, in order that, since, so that

- **Concession:** although, even though, while

- **Condition:** even if, if, in case, unless

- **Place:** where, wherever

- **Time:** after, as soon as, before, until, when, while

1. I went to the bathroom **before** <u>you arrived</u>.

   The **subordinating conjunction** connects "you arrived" to the rest of the main clause, creating a <u>dependent clause</u>. Notice that the **conjunction** becomes part of the <u>dependent clause</u>.

2. We should leave soon **because** <u>it's a long drive</u>.

   The **subordinating conjunction** connects "it's a long drive" to the rest of the main clause, creating a <u>dependent clause</u> that explains why we should leave soon.

3. <u>We should also leave in an hour</u> **if we want to avoid rush-hour traffic**.

   There's no comma between the **dependent clause** and the rest of the <u>main clause.</u> That's because dependent clauses like these are considered essential parts of the main clause. Even if you hear a pause when reading it out loud, you don't separate them with a comma.

4. **Although it's a long drive**, <u>I</u> will stop **if you need to go to the bathroom**.

   Both **dependent clauses** help to explain about why I might stop on this long drive. Because the first comes before the <u>subject</u> of the main clause, it's separated from the subject by a comma.

4. Common Problems

A. Sentence Fragments

A sentence fragment is a phrase or dependent clause that is punctuated as if it were a complete, independent sentence.

1. *Fragment:* Because that truck is not worth the money.

   Complete Sentence: <u>You shouldn't buy Kevin's truck</u> **because that truck is not worth the money**.

   > The first "sentence" is a **dependent clause**. A **dependent clause** only makes sense when it's helping to explain the idea of an <u>independent clause</u>.

2. *Fragment:* Which is not my definition of true love.

   Complete Sentence: The feelings we have for puppies are based on <u>a hormonal reaction</u>, **which is not my definition of true love**.

   > The first "sentence" is a **relative clause**. A **relative clause** only makes sense when it's used to further explain a <u>noun phrase</u> in the main clause.

3. *Fragment:* Venturing out late into the night on a mission of mercy.

   Complete Sentence: **Venturing out late into the night on a mission of mercy** <u>is dangerous</u>.

   > The first "sentence" is a **gerund noun phrase**, a thing you might do if you are brave or foolish enough, but it's not a complete thought. In the second actual sentence, the **gerund noun phrase** now makes sense as the subject of an independent clause because a <u>predicate verb phrase</u> completes the thought.

Sentence fragments usually happen within paragraphs of several sentences when a supporting clause or phrase within one sentence is separated from the rest of that sentence and punctuated as if it made sense on its own.

4.   Another example of how Rick avoids the truth comes when he goes into the kitchen. He stares sadly at a picture of the two of them hanging on the fridge. **Coming as close to actually facing his feelings as he will get in this story.** However, instead of facing the fact that she simply left, he continues to believe Bigfoot stole his wife. He can face that she is gone, but he cannot face the real reason for her going.

   > The sentence fragment in this paragraph is a **gerund noun phrase** that follows up on the previous sentence with a closely related observation about the significance of that prior sentence. It doesn't make sense on its own, but within the flow of the paragraph's ideas, it blends right in.

When you read your own work, it's hard to spot a sentence fragment because the flow of ideas in a paragraph makes sense as a whole. However, if you take the time to read a paragraph backward, sentence by sentence, it becomes easier to check that each sentence makes sense on its own.

He can face that she is gone, but he cannot face the real reason for her going.

| This sentence makes sense as a complete thought.

However, instead of facing the fact that she simply left, he continues to believe Bigfoot stole his wife.

| This one makes sense, too. Well, the grammar makes sense, anyway.

Coming as close to actually facing his feelings as he will get in this story.

| Uh-oh. Taken outside of the flow of the paragraph, it's easier to see that this sentence doesn't make sense on its own.

He stares sadly at a picture of the two of them hanging on the fridge.

| This is a complete sentence, and it's the one the fragment above should be connected to, using one of the solutions described below.

Another example of how Rick avoids the truth comes when he goes into the kitchen.

| This sentence is fine.

Sentence fragments are a problem because readers expect each sentence to provide a complete idea. A sentence fragment doesn't deliver that complete idea, so readers have to step back, look at the paragraph as a whole, and figure out what idea you are trying to explain with the sentence fragment. This makes your writing less effective, even if readers are able to eventually figure out your idea.

How to Fix Sentence Fragments

To fix sentence fragments, you can either reconnect them to the main idea they should help to explain, or you can rephrase them as independent clauses.

Option 1: Reconnect to a Main Clause

If the sentence fragment isn't meant to be a complete idea of its own, the better solution is to reconnect it to the idea it was meant to explain.

1. **Problem:**

   He stares sadly at a picture of the two of them hanging on the fridge. **Coming as close to actually facing his feelings as he will get in this story.**

   | This sentence fragment is a **gerund noun phrase** that explains what happens when he stares.

Solution 1:

Coming as close to actually facing his feelings as he will get in this story, he stares sadly at a picture of the two of them hanging on the fridge.

> If his staring at the photo is the important idea, the better option is to reconnect the **dependent clause** as an introductory clause for the main clause.

Solution 2:

He stares sadly at a picture of the two of them hanging on the fridge, **coming as close to actually facing his feelings as he will get in this story.**

> The **dependent clause** can also follow the rest of the main clause.

2. **Problem:**

The taco truck's chicken tacos have extra cilantro. **Which is my favorite.**

> This sentence fragment is a **relative clause** that is meant to add a side comment about a noun in the previous sentence.

Solution:

The taco truck's chicken tacos have extra cilantro, **which is my favorite**.

> Because this clause is an aside, the better solution is to reconnect it to the main clause as a **nonrestrictive relative clause**, using a comma to show that it's not essential information.

3. **Problem:**

This kale provides all the nutrients I need. **And tastes like nutrients, too.**

> This sentence fragment is a **verb phrase** with a coordinating conjunction. It doesn't make sense on its own because it refers back to the subject of the previous sentence.

Solution 1:

This kale provides all the nutrients I need **and** tastes like nutrients, too.

> Because this phrase refers to the previous sentence, one way to reunite it is to use the **coordinating conjunction** to create a compound predicate.

Solution 2:

This kale provides all the nutrients I need, **and** it tastes like nutrients, too.

> Another fix is to join the fragment to the previous sentence with the **coordinating conjunction** and then add a second subject noun phrase. That creates a compound sentence—two closely related and equally important ideas.

Option 2: Rephrase as a Complete Sentence

If the sentence fragment was intended to be a complete idea of its own, then rephrase the fragment so that the idea has a subject and predicate that present a complete idea.

1. **Problem:**

   He stares sadly at a picture of the two of them hanging on the fridge. **Coming as close to actually facing his feelings as he will get in this story.**

   > This sentence fragment from earlier is still just a **gerund noun phrase**.

   Solution:

   He stares sadly at a picture of the two of them hanging on the fridge. **This** is as close to actually facing his feelings as he will get in this story.

   > In this solution, we keep the two related sentences loosely connected by making the subject of the second sentence a **demonstrative pronoun** that refers back to what he does in the first sentence. The rest of the fragment becomes the predicate verb phrase of the second sentence.

2. **Problem:**

   This kale provides all the nutrients I need. **And tastes like nutrients, too.**

   > The sentence fragment from earlier is still just a **predicate verb phrase** without a subject. However, maybe they aren't as closely related as I thought.

   Solution:

   This kale provides all the nutrients I need. **It** tastes like nutrients, too.

   > Now each of these related sentences have a **subject** and predicate verb phrase of its own. Presenting them separately shows that they are separate ideas. Presenting them next to each other shows that they are loosely connected.

3. **Problem:**

   The feelings we have for puppies are based on a hormonal reaction. **Which is not my definition of true love.**

   > This sentence fragment is a **relative clause** that adds an aside about the nature of puppy love.

   Solution 1:

   The feelings we have for puppies are based on a hormonal reaction. **That** is not my definition of true love.

   > If you think this aside should stand on its own in your paragraph, rephrase it by replacing the relative pronoun "which" with a **demonstrative pronoun** as the subject of the new sentence. The rest of the relative clause becomes the predicate verb phrase of the second sentence.

Solution 2:

The feelings we have for puppies are based on a hormonal reaction. **A hormonal reaction** is not my definition of true love.

> You could also replace "which" with a **regular noun phrase** and have the rest of the relative clause act as the predicate verb phrase.

B. Run-On Sentences

Run-on sentences are two or more independent clauses that are either punctuated as if they were a single main idea or connected with the wrong sort of punctuation.

1. Run-on: You looked, I panicked.

   > This type of run-on sentence is called a "comma splice" because it combines or splices two independent clauses with a single **comma**. Even if it's only four words long, it's still a comma splice.

2. Run-on: It rained it poured.

   > When two independent clauses are connected by nothing, it's called a "fused sentence."

Length has nothing to do with this, by the way. As you see, run-on sentences can be very short. That's because it's a problem of having too many main ideas in the sentence, not with wordiness.

3. **One of the many problems with so many of the sentences in so many of the college textbooks that a student reads in the course of a year** is that the sentences in these books employ far more words and phrases and dependent clauses than are actually necessary for the presentation of even the simplest of ideas.

   > This long sentence has a single **subject noun phrase** and a single predicate verb phrase, so it stands on its own as an independent clause with one main idea. It's a boring sentence because it's long-winded, but at least it's grammatical.

Run-on sentences are a problem because they confuse readers. Readers expect each sentence to provide a single, complete idea. When a run-on sentence gives readers more than one idea at once, they have to step back, look at the sentence, and separate the two ideas from that single sentence. This delay in understanding your ideas makes the paper as a whole less effective.

How to Fix Run-On Sentences

There are several ways to fix run-on sentences. With every option, the solution requires you to use the right punctuation to give your readers one complete idea at a time.

Option 1: Separate the Independent Clauses with a Period

If the two ideas in the run-on sentence are not very closely related, or if you don't want to emphasize how the two ideas are related, you should present them separately.

1. **Problem:**

   I adore pie, it goes well with a cup of coffee.

   > This is a comma splice because it splices two independent clauses together with a **comma**.

   Solution:

   I adore pie. It goes well with a cup of coffee.

   > If you replace the comma with a **period**, you make each independent clause its own sentence.

2. **Problem:**

   My cat's whiskers are long, they tickle my ears when she climbs on my head.

   > This is another comma splice. Each independent clause presents an idea about your cat's disgusting whiskers. The **comma** splices these two ideas together as if they were one sentence.

   Solution:

   My cat's whiskers are long. They tickle my ears when she climbs on my head.

   > These are related ideas, so you might want to find a different way to combine them, but if you want each idea to stand on its own, replace the comma with a **period**.

3. **Problem:**

   The rest stop smelled like urine it had a beautiful view.

   > This is a fused sentence because two independent clauses are jammed together with nothing between them.

   Solution:

   The rest stop smelled like urine. It had a beautiful view.

   > These ideas are so different from each other that they really need to be punctuated as separate ideas. Nothing says "the end of one idea" like a **period**.

Option 2: Use a Coordinating Conjunction to Create a Compound Sentence

If the two ideas in your run-on are equally important, you can connect them with a coordinating conjunction such as "and," "or," "but," or "so." This creates a compound sentence.

1. **Problem:**

   I adore pie, it goes well with a cup of coffee.

   > This is still a comma splice made of two independent clauses joined together with a single **comma**.

   Solution:

   I adore pie, *and* it goes well with a cup of coffee.

   > The *coordinating conjunction* shows that these two independent clauses are equal and related, but that's all. You'll notice that the **comma** remains.

2. **Problem:**

   I'll buy anything on sale, last week I bought a rest stop.

   > Here's another comma splice with two independent clauses and a single **comma**.

   > **Solution:** I'll buy anything on sale, *so* last week I bought a rest stop.

   > This *coordinating conjunction* shows that the first independent clause is a reason or condition that leads to the second, equally important independent clause.

3. **Problem:**

   The rest stop smelled like urine it had a beautiful view.

   > This is still a foul-smelling fused sentence made of two independent clauses with nothing between them.

   > **Solution:** The rest stop smelled like urine, *but* it had a beautiful view.

   > This *coordinating conjunction* shows that the first independent clause contrasts with the second, equally important independent clause. Notice that you have added a comma before the coordinating conjunction.

When you fix a run-on sentence in this way, you keep the comma before the coordinating conjunction because this is a compound sentence.

Option 3: Use a Subordinating Conjunction to Create a Complex Sentence
If one idea is more important than the other, you should use a subordinating conjunction such as "because," "if," "although," or "when." This combines the two ideas into a single main idea with a dependent clause that helps to explain it.

1. **Problem:**

   I adore pie**,** it goes well with a cup of coffee.

   > Yes, we've heard about your pie thing. This is a comma splice. Independent clauses do not go well together with just a **comma** between them.

   Solution 1:

   I adore pie *because* it goes well with a cup of coffee.

   > The *subordinating conjunction* shows us that the second clause is a reason for the first one. In this revision, that reason has become a dependent clause that only makes sense when it's explaining the first and more important idea.

   Solution 2:

   Because it goes well with a cup of coffee, I adore pie.

   > You can use the dependent clause as an introduction to the main clause, too.

2. **Problem:**

   You make me so angry I love you so much.

   > These are two closely related independent clauses, but because there is nothing between them, they become a fused sentence.

   Solution 1:

   Even though you make me so angry, I love you so much.

   > The *subordinating conjunction* turns the first idea into a dependent clause that now introduces the main clause. This solution decides that love is the more important of the two ideas.

   Solution 2:

   I love you so much *even though* you make me so angry.

   > This works, too. If you read it out loud, you'll hear a pause before the *subordinating conjunction*. However, don't add a comma because this is a dependent clause now. It's an essential part of the predicate verb phrase, so no comma should come between a dependent clause and its verb.

3. **Problem:**

   I'll buy anything on sale**,** I'll buy a used rest stop.

   > Ah, you're a collector. This is a comma splice because a **comma** joins the two independent clauses.

Solution:

I'll buy anything on sale *if* I'll buy a used rest stop.

> The *subordinating conjunction* turns the second idea into a dependent clause that presents a condition that would make the first and more important idea true. Again, don't separate the dependent clause from the rest of the predicate with a comma. It's just not done.

Option 4: Use a Semicolon to Show a Very Close Relationship

If you want to emphasize that the two ideas in the run-on are very closely related, you can join them with a semicolon and keep them as a single sentence.

1. **Problem:**

You make me so angry I love you so much.

> Have you two considered counseling? This is still a fused sentence.

Solution 1:

You make me so angry; I love you so much.

> By adding a **semicolon**, you tell the reader that these two independent clauses are so closely related that you can't bear to put even a period between them.

Solution 2:

You make me so angry; *therefore,* I love you so much.

> You can also add a *transitional word or phrase* after the **semicolon** to suggest the relationship of the two independent clauses. Put a comma after the *transition* because it's an introduction.

2. **Problem:**

The rest stop smelled like urine it had a beautiful view.

> This is a foul-smelling fused sentence composed of two independent clauses.

Lousy Solution:

The rest stop smelled like urine; it had a beautiful view.

> This is a lousy solution because it takes two unrelated independent clauses and joins them with a **semicolon**. This is grammatically correct, but it suggests to the reader that the two ideas are very closely related when they aren't. So don't do this, in other words.

C. Passive Voice

Passive voice, also known as "passive sentence structure" or "passive construction," disconnects a verb from the noun that is doing that verb. In this way, passive sentence structure obscures or deemphasizes who or what is acting in the sentence.

Formal writing prefers active voice because it makes a clear connection between the action and the actor in a sentence. With active voice, the subject of a sentence is the doer, and the main verb is the action.

1. **Andrea** slept on my couch.

   > The **subject** is the noun phrase that does something, and the main verb is what the **subject** does.

2. **The UPS driver** rang the doorbell seventeen times.

   > The **subject** does the verb.

3. **The doorbell** woke Andrea.

   > You get the idea.

When linking verbs are involved, the rest of the predicate stays focused on the subject of the sentence.

4. **Andrea** is *unhappy*.

   > The linking verb connects an *adjective* to the **subject**.

5. **The UPS driver** has been *a bit of a turd lately*.

   > In this case, the linking verb connects the **subject** to a *complement noun phrase* that describes our annoying UPS driver. Someone really needs to talk to his supervisor.

Passive structure, on the other hand, focuses on the verb and the thing that is affected by that verb. The subject of the sentence is not the doer of the verb anymore.

6. **My couch** was slept on by *Andrea*.

   > The **subject** is now the **noun phrase** affected by the verb. The *doer* of the verb is removed from the action in a prepositional phrase.

7. **My couch** was slept on.

   > The *doer* of the verb isn't even in this sentence.

8. **The doorbell** was rung seventeen times by *the UPS driver*.

   > Again, the **subject** is what is affected by the verb. The *doer* of the verb is tucked away in a prepositional phrase.

9. **The doorbell** was rung seventeen times.

   > Who was ringing my doorbell? All we have now are the verb and the **noun phrase** affected by the verb. Anyone could have been ringing it.

Sometimes Passive Voice Isn't a Problem

If you don't know who or what did the verb, then passive voice makes a lot of sense. It still allows you to state that something has happened.

1. **My car** <u>was broken into</u> last night.

   > You don't know who did the <u>verb</u>, so it makes sense to make the affected noun phrase the **subject**.

2. **My cassette tapes** <u>were stolen</u>.

   > We don't know who did this <u>verb</u>, either, but we do know what **noun phrase** was affected.

3. **Cassette tapes** <u>can't be replaced</u>.

   > That might not be the worst thing.

Sometimes you may know who or what is doing the verb, but that information isn't important or is implied by the context.

4. **The park** <u>was rumored</u> to be haunted.

   > The key idea is that the <u>verb</u> is happening and clouding the reputation of the **subject**. The doers responsible for the <u>verb</u> don't matter as much.

5. **The rumors** <u>were</u> widely <u>thought</u> to be false.

   > The unnamed doer of this sentence is an implied consensus of everyone who has heard the rumors.

6. **Our thinking** <u>was changed</u> by *the jogging ghost of Bush's Pasture Park*.

   > Finally, we have the *doer* of the <u>verb</u>, but focus of the sentence remains on the **subject** and how it's been affected by the <u>verb</u>.

Passive Voice Is Usually a Problem

One simple reason that passive voice is usually a problem is that it requires more words than active voice to state the same information.

1. *Active:* Andrea slept on my couch.

   Passive: My couch was slept on by Andrea.

   > This passive sentence uses seven words to present the same information.

2. *Active:* The UPS driver rang the doorbell seventeen times.

   Passive 1: The doorbell was rung seventeen times by the UPS driver.

   > Two more words.

   Passive 2: The doorbell was rung seventeen times.

   > Yes, the second passive sentence used two *fewer* words, but it's shorter because it removes the doer of the verb entirely. It's not the same information, so it's not really shorter, is it?

A more important problem with passive voice is that it obscures the subject of the verb, which justifiably raises questions for readers.

3. The dishes have been washed.

> Who washed the dishes? They didn't wash themselves—though that would be nice.

4. The robber was apprehended.

> By whom? The police? A citizen militia? The League of Dishwashers?

When the doer is important to the idea and missing from a sentence, passive voice makes readers wonder about the full meaning of the sentence. That moment of distraction makes your writing less effective. However, even if you include the doer later in the sentence, passive sentence structure still disconnects the subject from the verb.

5. *Passive:* **Chemicals** <u>were released</u> into the water supply late last night by *the Corporation for Corporate Freedom.*

> This sentence names the *doer* of the <u>action</u>, but this sentence tucks that information away at the end of the sentence, far from the <u>verb</u>. It makes the *doer* seem less guilty.

Active: **The Corporation for Corporate Freedom** <u>released</u> chemicals into the water supply late last night.

> Do you see how much worse the action seems when the doer of the <u>verb</u> is the **subject** of the sentence?

6. *Passive:* **This call** <u>is being recorded</u> for quality assurance.

> This idea seems harmless enough. With passive structure, the **subject** is what is affected by the <u>verb</u>, not who is doing it.

Active: **The Corporation for Corporate Freedom** <u>is recording</u> this call for quality assurance.

> Not them again! The idea is more alarming when active structure makes the doer the **subject** of the <u>verb</u>.

The final problem with passive sentence structure, then, is that it can deliberately hide the doer of the verb in order to purposely confuse or withhold important information from readers. That makes for good advertising but dishonest writing.

How to Fix Passive Voice

When the subject next to the verb isn't the doer of the verb, you probably have passive verb structure. If that's a problem—as it usually is—then fixing the problem is straightforward: make the doer of the verb the subject of the sentence.

1. **Problem:**

   Snails <u>are considered</u> a delicacy by *the French*.

   > The **subject** of this sentence is not the thing that does the <u>verb</u>. The *doer* of the verb comes at the end of the sentence.

   Solution:

   The French <u>consider</u> snails a delicacy.

   > In this active sentence structure, the doer of the <u>verb</u> is now the **subject**.

2. **Problem:**

   Oxygen <u>was discovered</u> in 1774.

   > The **subject** of this sentence is not the thing that did the <u>verb</u>. So the doer of the <u>verb</u> is missing, and that information seems to be important.

   Solution:

   Joseph Priestly <u>discovered</u> oxygen in 1774.

   > In this active sentence structure, the doer of the <u>verb</u> is now the **subject** of the sentence. (Thank you, Wikipedia.)

3. **Problem:**

   Sales in the Northwest Region <u>were observed</u> to be 10 to 30 percent higher than last month.

   > The **subject** of this sentence is what the <u>verb</u> observed, not the doer of the <u>verb</u>.

   Solution 1:

   I <u>observed</u> sales in the Northwest Region to be 10 to 30 percent higher than last month.

   > In this active sentence structure, the doer of the <u>verb</u> is now the **subject** of the sentence. However, it's not a great solution. The important information in this sentence is what you observed, not that you were observing.

   Solution 2:

   Sales in the Northwest Region <u>increased</u> 10 to 30 percent from last month.

   > What matters is what you observed, and now that's the **subject** of this sentence's <u>verb</u>. The problem with "I" is that its use draws readers away from the more important information.

4. **Problem:**

Mistakes <u>were made</u>.

Solution:

I <u>made</u> mistakes.

> Okay, fine. It was me. I am the **subject** of this, the doer of this <u>verb</u>.

D. Faulty Parallelism

In writing, parallelism means using the same grammatical patterns to demonstrate that things or actions or ideas are similar in nature and importance. Just like two parallel lines head in the same direction forever without crossing, parallel structure keeps your ideas separate while emphasizing the relationship between them. This often shows up in lists:

1. Last night, I **studied for my classes, chatted with friends**, and **played video games online**.

> In this case, you want to do three similar and equal actions, so you use the same grammatical pattern—**verb phrase**—to present each of those actions.

2. I love to eat **apples, oranges, mangos**, and **bananas**.

> You love to eat four similar and equal things, so you use the same grammatical pattern—**noun**—to present those things.

You can also use parallelism with clauses that present similar and equally important main or supporting ideas.

3. I like Esther **because she listens to me, because she respects me**, and **because she loans me money**.

> In this case, you present three equal and similar reasons why you like Esther with three **dependent clauses** that all focus on what Esther does.

4. **Give me liberty**, or **give me death**.

> In this case, you are Patrick Henry, and you have two opposite but equally important demands for the Virginia House of Commons. You demonstrate this with two similar **independent clauses** in a compound sentence.

Faulty parallelism happens when you present things that are similar in nature and importance with grammatical patterns that are *not* similar.

5. Last night, I **studied for my classes**, <u>chatting with friends</u>, and **played video games online**.

> You did the same three actions as before, but for two of those things you use a **verb phrase** and for one you use a <u>gerund phrase</u>. The three actions are no longer parallel.

6. I like Esther <u>for the way she listens to me</u>, **because she respects me**, and **because she loans me money**.

> You still present three equal and similar reasons why you like Esther, but now two are presented as **dependent clauses** and one as a <u>prepositional phrase</u>. They are no longer parallel reasons.

The main problem with faulty parallelism is that you lose the effectiveness of parallelism, which makes your ideas clearer and more memorable. It can also distract your readers when they notice that one of these things is not phrased like the others.

How to Fix Faulty Parallelism

The first step to fixing faulty parallelism is to identify the similar and equally important things, actions, or ideas you want to present. The second step is to use the same grammatical pattern for those things.

1. Problem:

In her anatomy class, Alexis learned **to dissect a pig's heart** and <u>all the bones in the skull</u>.

> Alexis learned two similar and equally important things, but this isn't parallel because one grammatical pattern is an **infinitive phrase** and the other is a <u>noun phrase</u>. Even worse, there's some unintended parallelism that actually confuses the intended meaning.

Worse Problem:

In her anatomy class, Alexis learned to dissect **a pig's heart** and **all the bones in the skull**.

> Here you see that similar grammatical patterns — the two **noun phrases** that follow "dissect" — suggest that Alexis learned to dissect two similar things. But she didn't learn how to dissect the bones in the skull. That's only taught in the advanced class.

Solution:

In her anatomy class, Alexis learned **to dissect a pig's heart** and **to identify all the bones in the skull**.

> Now the two similar things that Alexis learned are presented in parallel with two **infinitive phrases**.

2. Problem:

Steve **opened** the car door and <u>was watching</u> Gracie struggle with her seatbelt.

> This sentence presents two similar and equal things that Steve did, so it wisely uses one verb phrase for each action. However, the **verb** in the first verb phrase is in **past tense**. The <u>verb</u> in the second verb phrase is <u>past progressive</u> (note the "ing"). That's not parallel.

Solution:

Steve **opened** the door and **watched** Gracie struggle with her seatbelt.

> Now both **verbs** are in **past tense**. This is parallel. It's also kind of mean to just stare at the kid while she struggles. Come on, Steve. You're better than that.

3. **Problem:**

Cordon is looking for a drummer **who is dependable**, <u>punctual</u>, and **who can keep a steady beat**.

> Cordon is looking for a drummer with three similar and equal qualities that are almost impossible to find in a drummer. This is not parallel, however, because two of those qualities are presented as **relative clauses** and one is presented as an <u>adjective</u>.

Solution 1:

Cordon is looking for a drummer **who is dependable**, **who is punctual**, and **who can keep a steady beat**.

> Now all three **qualities** Cordon is looking for are presented with **relative clauses**. This is now parallel.

Solution 2:

Cordon is looking for a drummer **who is dependable**, **punctual**, and **rhythmic**.

> This is also parallel. All three **qualities** Cordon are presented as **adjectives** within a single relative clause. It doesn't really matter, though, because Cordon is going to have to stick with his brother-in-law, Apollo, who is at least punctual — most of the time.

4. **Problem:**

After **he slipped on the ice**, <u>sprained his ankle</u>, and **his car was buried in a snowbank**, Ronald elected to stay indoors for the rest of the day.

> This sentence presents the three similar and equally important events that made Ronald give up on the day. However, it's not in parallel because two of the items are **clauses** and one is a <u>verb phrase</u>. Another problem is that "sprained his ankle" only makes sense when it's clearly connected to the prior "he," and it's not.

Solution:

After he **slipped on the ice, sprained his ankle,** and **buried his car in a snowbank**, Ronald elected to stay indoors for the rest of the day.

> Now each event is present as a **verb phrase**, so the sentence is parallel. All is well except for Ronald's ankle and car. Elevate that ankle, Ronald, and have some cocoa.

5. **Problem:**

Pediatrics is <u>a branch of medicine that focuses on children</u>. **The branch of medicine that focuses on feet** is <u>podiatry</u>.

> These two sentences present two similar and equal ideas about two branches of medicine and the focus of each. However, the sentences are not parallel because the **subject noun phrases** and <u>complement noun phrases</u> describe different things.

Solution:

Pediatrics is <u>a branch of medicine that focuses on children</u>. **Podiatry** is <u>a branch of medicine that focuses on feet</u>.

> Now the **subject noun phrases** and <u>complement noun phrases</u> describe the same type of thing, so the sentences are parallel and the comparison is much clearer. You're less likely to take your aching feet to a pediatrician now.

E. Subject-Verb Disagreement

When a sentence's subject and verb agree, the number (singular or plural) of the subject matches the number of the verb. For example, if your sentence has a singular subject like "the dog," its verb needs to be written in the singular form, too. If you don't make them match, then the subject and verb disagree with each other.

Disagreement usually happens when the number of the subject becomes unclear for some reason. This can happen when you join multiple singular subjects with "and."

1. *Disagreement:* **Damon and Walnut the dog** <u>is</u> beginning to look alike.

> The <u>verb</u> is a singular form of the verb "to be." Damon is a singular noun phrase, and Walnut the dog is a singular noun phrase, but when you join them together with "and," you have a **plural subject noun phrase** that requires a plural form of the <u>verb</u>.

Agreement: **Damon and Walnut the dog** <u>are</u> beginning to look alike.

> "Are" is the third person, plural form of the <u>verb</u> "to be" and agrees with the **plural subject**.

Disagreement can happen when you join multiple singular subjects with "or."

2. *Disagreement:* **Rae or Dusty** <u>mention</u> this to Damon every day.

> When you join two singular noun phrases with the coordinating conjunction "or," the **compound subject** is considered singular and requires a singular <u>verb</u>. This <u>verb</u> is a plural form of "to mention."

Agreement: **Rae or Dusty** <u>mentions</u> this to Damon every day.

> Now the <u>verb</u> is the third person, singular form of the verb "to mention" and agrees with the **singular compound subject**.

3. *Disagreement:* **Rae or his other coworkers** <u>mentions</u> this to Damon every day.

> When you join a singular noun phrase and plural noun phrase with the coordinating conjunction "or," the <u>verb</u> has to agree with the noun phrase in the **subject** that is closest to the <u>verb</u>. In this case, "Damon's coworkers" is a plural noun phrase and "mentions" is the singular form of the <u>verb</u>. We can't have that.

Agreement: **Rae or his other coworkers** <u>mention</u> this to Damon every day.

> Now the <u>verb</u> is the third person, plural form of "to mention" and agrees with the closest noun phrase in the **compound subject**.

The number of your subject can get confusing when you have interruptions between the subject and its verb.

4. *Disagreement:* **Neither Damon nor his coworkers**, *who see him almost every day*, <u>seems</u> to care.

> When interruptions like this *relative clause* come between the **subject** and the <u>verb</u>, it can be hard to keep track of subject and verb agreement. In these cases, read the sentence without the interruption.

Agreement: **Neither Damon nor his coworkers**, who see him almost every day, <u>seem</u> to care.

> "Seem" is the third person, plural form of the <u>verb</u> and agrees with the plural noun phrase that is closest to the verb in the **compound subject**.

Here's another one: use singular verbs after each, either, everyone, everybody, neither, nobody, none, and someone.

1. **Problem:**

Everybody else who knows Damon <u>care</u> a lot. He is starting to shed and might have fleas.

> Even though "everybody" sounds like a lot people, it is considered a **singular noun**. That doesn't agree with "care," which is a plural form of the <u>verb</u>.

Solution:

Everybody else who knows Damon <u>cares</u> a lot. He is starting to shed and might have fleas.

| The **plural noun** agrees with the <u>plural verb</u>.

Subject-verb disagreement is a problem because it confuses your reader. They can easily lose track of information that you're trying to get across.

How to Fix Subject-Verb Disagreement

The trick is to read carefully every time, no matter what. You have to think about whether a subject is plural or not. As the examples show, that can be hard sometimes. You have to know the singular and plural verb forms so that you can match that subject.

However, a little awareness goes a long way with this problem. If you know that this is a problem for you, taking some time to stop and think about the subject and the verb will help you to make sure they agree most of the time. As you continue to take time to consider subject-verb agreement, this will become a more automatic part of your writing practice.

Punctuation and Mechanics

With informal writing, punctuation is often used to create sound effects. Commas create, the sound, of pauses. Ellipses create the sound . . . of a voice . . . trailing away. . . . That's fine for notes to friends and gut-wrenching poetry. However, with formal writing, punctuation and mechanics are only used to present ideas more clearly. There are no sound effects.

Punctuation clarifies the ideas within a sentence. It shows readers how the parts of a sentence are organized and connected to each other. It separates the items in a list. It identifies any words that you're quoting directly from outside sources. In this way, punctuation helps readers see how the phrases and clauses of a sentence work together to create the main idea of the sentence.

Mechanics focus mostly on the meanings of words and phrases within a sentence. Capitalization, for example, distinguishes between the official names of specific things and the general names for types of things. Italics add emphasis to important terms and identify the titles of creative works. In this way, mechanics show your readers exactly what you mean by the words or phrases in your sentences.

The more complex your ideas become, the more carefully you must use punctuation and mechanics to show readers exactly what you mean. In this chapter, we will start by looking at the main rules that guide punctuation:

- ending punctuation
- commas
- semicolons
- colons
- apostrophes
- quotation marks
- other punctuation marks

Then we'll look at some important guidelines for sentence mechanics:

- capitalization
- abbreviations
- italics
- hyphens

We'll end by looking at some common errors and how to fix them.

1. Ending Punctuation (. ? !)

All writing requires complete sentences, and complete sentences require some form of ending punctuation before a new sentence can begin. Ending punctuation tells readers that a sentence has ended in one of three ways—a statement (.), a question (?), or a shout (!).

A period is the most common ending punctuation mark. It tells a reader that this sentence is a statement of an idea or information. A question mark indicates that the sentence asks a question. Finally, an exclamation point signals a level of surprise or excitement that warrants a shout.

1. Here is a sentence that ends in a period.

   It's a statement of fact.

2. The first known use of the period is thought to be in a cave painting in Mongolia circa 25 B.C.

   This may not actually be a fact. However, notice that the sentence ends with the abbreviation "B.C.," which itself uses **periods**. When a sentence ends with a period as part of an abbreviation, use only the single period to also end the sentence.

3. When should a sentence end in a question mark**?**

   ❚ That's the question, which always ends with a **question mark**.

4. Should all sentences end in question marks**?**

   ❚ No—only the questions.

5. That's remarkable**!**

   ❚ It's just a basic rule of punctuation. There's no need to shout.

6. I never realized just how stimulating it is to use an exclamation point properly**.**

   ❚ Yes, it's quite a revelation.

2. Commas (,)

Commas divide, and with formal writing, that's all they do. You may have been taught to "put a comma where you hear a pause," but that sound-based tip is only good with informal writing. It doesn't work well in the idea-based world of formal writing. In your college papers, you should only put a comma where a comma rule applies to the ideas in the sentence.

A. Items in a List

In a list of three or more items, put a comma after every item except the last one. The items can be anything—nouns, adjectives, phrases, or clauses—that are similar. In most cases, you use a coordinating conjunction such as "and" or "but" to hold the list together as a group.

1. <u>Travis</u>**,** <u>Steve</u>**,** *and* <u>Bethany</u> attacked the wolverine.

   ❚ In this list of <u>nouns</u>, **commas** separate each item in the list except the last one, "Bethany." The *coordinating conjunction* "and" holds the list together.

2. This foolish display of bravery <u>surprised</u>**,** <u>annoyed</u>**,** *but* also <u>impressed</u> the unsuspecting wolverine.

   ❚ This list of <u>verbs</u> is also held together by a *coordinating conjunction*. There's no **comma** after "impressed" because it's the final item in the list.

3. The wolverine could have <u>chased them back to camp</u>**,** <u>torn them to pieces</u>**,** *and* <u>eaten them</u>.

   ❚ Here's a list of three <u>verb phrases</u> in the past tense. Do you notice how the items in the list all use the same verb tense (past)? All the items in the list are the same type of grammatical thing. This is called parallelism, and it makes your idea more memorable.

4. The wolverine could have <u>screamed in terror</u>, <u>run away</u>, <u>climbed a tree</u>, *or* <u>simply died of fright</u>.

> This is a list of four <u>verb phrases</u>. You can see how the rule still applies, even when the number of items in the list increases.

5. The wolverine could have hidden under <u>the branches of a tree</u> *or* <u>a rotten log</u> *or* <u>a couch</u>.

> Here's a comma-free variation to the rule. Here we have a list of three <u>noun phrases</u> where the wolverine might hide. However, we have a *coordinating conjunction* between each <u>noun phrase</u>, so no commas are required.

6. The <u>ferocious</u>, <u>unpredictable</u>, <u>sneaky</u> creature simply laughed.

> This is a variation without the use of a conjunction. With a list of adjectives before a noun, we still put a **comma** after each <u>adjective</u> (except the last one), but we don't need a coordinating conjunction to hold the list together. Why no coordinating conjunction? We don't know. That's just the way it is.

7. The wolverine then <u>smiled to herself</u> *and* <u>trotted away</u>.

> This list of <u>verb phrases</u> is held together by a *coordinating conjunction*, but there are only two items in this list, so we don't use any commas here.

You may have been taught to omit the comma that comes after the next-to-last item in the list and before the coordinating conjunction. This next-to-last comma goes by many names—such as Oxford comma and serial comma—and its use is the subject of one of grammar's most contentious and nerdy debates. If you were taught to use it, your teacher was probably taught the same as a student.

In your own college writing, you will often get to decide whether you use the serial comma or not. As long as you use it (or not) consistently in your paper, you should be fine. However, there are rare situations where the absence of the Oxford comma creates confusion, suggesting the final two items in the list describe the first item.

Consider how the meaning of this sentence changes when we remove the Oxford comma:

8. I admire my parents, God, and Carrie Underwood.

> This makes sense. All three items in the list seem admirable.

9. I admire my parents, God and Carrie Underwood.

> Now the meaning is unclear. This *might* mean the same idea as the first sentence, but without the Oxford comma to clearly divide the items in this list, it might mean that your parents are God and Carrie Underwood.

10. The donor pledged her support**,** financial assistance and time.

> Is the donor pledging three things (support, financial assistance, and time) or just two forms of support (financial assistance and time)?

11. The donor pledged her support, financial assistance**,** and time.

> With the **Oxford comma**, it's now clear that in addition to financial assistance and time, you can count on the donor's support. Maybe she'll introduce you to her rich friends.

B. Clauses in Compound Sentences

A compound sentence is a list of two or more independent clauses — ideas that could stand on their own as complete sentences. Treat a compound sentence like any other list by putting a comma after each independent clause except for the last one. The only difference is that you use a comma even if there are only two independent clauses in the list. A coordinating conjunction such as "and" or "but" holds the compound sentence together.

1. I like the accordion**,** *and* the accordion likes me.

> In this compound sentence, a **comma** separates the first independent clause from the second one. The *coordinating conjunction* holds the sentence together.

2. A lot of people don't like the accordion**,** *but* a lot of people are wrong.

> This example works just like the first example. Both clauses could stand alone as complete sentences. This *coordinating conjunction*, however, shows that the ideas contrast.

3. Accordion music is fun to listen to**,** accordion music is fun to make**,** *but* accordion music does cause hair loss.

> Here we have a list of three independent clauses that are separated by **commas** and held together by a *coordinating conjunction*.

4. Accordions are not cheap**,** *and* accordion lessons are not cheap**,** *but* I really want to play this beautiful instrument**,** *so* I plan to spend the money

> This list of four independent clauses are separated by **commas**. In this example, the relationship between independent clauses keeps changing, so we use more than one *coordinating conjunction*.

Technically, you can use the list rule to create a grammatical compound sentence with any independent clauses. However, just like with any other list, it should be a list of *similar* items. In other words, the independent clauses should be closely related.

5. My new accordion is beautiful, *but* the music I make with it is pretty ugly.

> The two underlined independent clauses here are focused on the same topic and have a clear, contrasting relationship that the *coordinating conjunction* captures.

6. I will soon learn to make beautiful accordion music, *and* my foot itches.

> This sentence is a compound sentence, but in spite of the *coordinating conjunction*, these two independent clauses don't seem to have anything in common. This should not be a compound sentence.

C. Introductory Words or Phrases

Use a comma to separate any introductory words or phrases from the subject of the sentence.

1. In the morning, *my homework* is due.

> In this sentence, the introductory phrase tells us when the main idea happens. The **comma** separates that introduction from the *subject* of the main sentence — my homework.

2. However, I have not yet started my homework.

> There are many ways to introduce the main clause. This introduction is a transitional word that connects this sentence to a previous sentence. It tells us this is a contrasting idea.

3. Because I care about my education, my homework is important.

> This introduction is a dependent clause that provides a supporting reason for the main idea of the sentence.

4. Unfortunately, I had to work all afternoon in the dining hall.

> This introduction is an adverb that tells us what the author thinks about the main idea — in this case, it was unfortunate.

5. My dear professors, you need to understand that I have an actual life outside your classrooms.

> Here the introduction is a direct address that tells the readers this sentence is directed at them. Directly addressing the reader is okay with informal writing but not with formal writing. It's also kind of whiny in this case. Nobody likes a whiner.

6. In fairness to me, however, *the homework* was only assigned this morning.

> If there's more than one introduction before *the subject* of the sentence, put a **comma** after each introduction.

7. <u>Then</u> *I* went right to work.

> Here's an exception to the rule. With many single, time-related adverbs like "now," "then," or "today," you don't separate the <u>introduction</u> from the *subject* of the main sentence. That's because adverbs don't follow rules. They just do whatever they want.

The key with this rule is being able to identify the subject of the main sentence. So who or what is doing something or being described by this sentence? That thing is usually the subject of the sentence. If any words or phrases—other than time-related adverbs—come before that subject, this rule applies.

D. Interruptions to the Main Clause

Writers often interrupt their sentences to add additional information or transitions that refer back to prior sentences. Use commas to separate the main clause from this additional information or transition.

1. Standardized testing**,** <u>however</u>**,** is not an accurate measure of knowledge.

> The <u>interruption</u> is a transitional word. Because this comes in the middle of the main sentence, **commas** come before and after it. Notice that if you cut out the interruption, the sentence still makes sense. That will be true for all interruptions.

2. Standardized testing**,** <u>which was first used in 1682</u>**,** is not an accurate measure of knowledge.

> The <u>interruption</u> here is a clause that provides nonessential information about the subject. Notice the **commas**.

3. Standardized testing**,** <u>my child</u>**,** is not an accurate measure of knowledge.

> This <u>interruption</u> is a direct address to the reader. This is too informal for college writing, though. Don't try this at home. Actually, you can try it at home, but don't try it at school.

4. Standardized testing**,** <u>tragically</u>**,** is not an accurate measure of knowledge.

> This <u>interruption</u> is a judgment of the main idea of the sentence that it interrupts. It's not essential information for this idea.

5. Standardized testing**,** <u>unlike individualized testing</u>**,** is not an accurate measure of knowledge.

> The <u>interruption</u> is a negation of the term that comes before it. It highlights that term but isn't essential for explaining the main idea.

6. Standardized testing is not an accurate measure of knowledge**,** <u>however</u>.

> When the nonessential information or transition comes at the end of the main sentence, you still separate the <u>interruption</u> from the main sentence with a **comma**, but you don't put a comma after the <u>interruption</u>. Use ending punctuation instead.

7. Standardized testing is not an accurate measure of knowledge**,** <u>is it</u>?

> This type of <u>interruption</u> is called a tag question. It refers back to the main idea and asks the reader to consider it, but it doesn't add new information to that main idea. With tag questions, the ending punctuation is determined by the question, not the statement it is asking you to consider.

8. Standardized testing is not an accurate measure of knowledge **,** <u>which makes many scholars question its use</u>.

> This <u>interruption</u> adds a follow-up observation about the entire main idea.

E. Direct Quotations and Attributions

Use commas to separate direct quotations from attributions, which are statements that identify the source of the quotation.

1. *William Shakespeare writes***,** "<u>All the world's a stage, and all the men and women merely players</u>."

> In this example, the *attribution* comes first, then the **comma**, and then the <u>direct quotation</u>.

2. "<u>All the world's a stage, and all the men and women merely players</u>**,**" *writes William Shakespeare.*

> The *attribution* can also follow the <u>direct quotation</u>, but that's more common in informal writing. Notice how in this case the **comma** goes inside the second quotation mark.

3. "<u>All the world's a stage</u>**,**" *according to William Shakespeare***,** "<u>and all the men and women merely players</u>."

> The *attribution* can also interrupt the <u>direct quotation</u>. In that case, the interruption rule applies, so you put a comma before and after the interruption. Pay attention to the **comma** placement.

4. Shakespeare says the world is like "<u>a stage</u>."

> However, when the <u>direct quotation</u> is just a word or phrase and is needed to complete the sentence's idea, this comma rule doesn't apply.

F. Multipart Numbers and Nouns

Commas also separate the parts of multipart nouns—things like "Portland, Oregon," or the number 10,000—that are made up of more than one thing. This helps readers to keep those parts straight while reading.

Numbers

With large numbers, separate every three digits with a comma.

1. I won $10,000 at the casino.

   > With large numbers, use a **comma** to separate the number after <u>every three digits</u>.

2. I had <u>100,000,000</u> ideas about how to spend my winnings.

   > This rather large number has <u>three sets of three digits</u>, so it requires two **commas**.

3. Then I lost $<u>11,800</u> at the casino.

   > Bummer.

4. I had to borrow $<u>1200</u> from my mom to make rent.

   > With <u>four-digit numbers</u>, the **comma** is optional.

Cities

Use commas to separate contextual information that is closely related to a particular city.

1. Powell's Books is located in <u>Portland</u>, *Oregon*.

   > Use a **comma** to divide the name of the <u>city</u> from its *state*.

2. <u>Portland</u>, *Oregon*, is also where my cat now lives.

   > When the <u>city</u> is in the beginning or middle of the sentence, put a **comma** before and after the *state*.

3. My cat and I often visited <u>Washington</u>, *D.C.*

   > The contextual information isn't limited to states. Here the city is listed with the district where it's located.

4. <u>Seattle</u> was just okay as far as cats are concerned.

   > When there's only one well-known <u>city</u> by that name, you don't need to include the contextual information.

5. <u>Paris</u>, *France*, was a virtual paradise for cats.

   > This differentiates it from Paris, Texas, or Paris, Kentucky, or for older readers, Paris Hilton.

Addresses

Use commas to separate the main parts of an address.

1. You can mail my check to <u>Chemeketa Community College</u>, <u>4000 Lancaster Drive NE</u>, <u>Salem</u>, <u>Oregon 97305</u>.

> Use a **comma** to divide the <u>name</u>, <u>street address</u>, <u>city</u>, and <u>state</u>. However, you *don't* need a **comma** to separate the zip code from the state.

People

Use commas to separate the name of a person from any degrees, titles, or other suffixes that are closely connected to their name.

1. Have you ever read the work of <u>Kurt Vonnegut</u>, *Jr.*?

> This works with names like it did above with cities. You separate the *suffix* from the <u>name</u> with a **comma**.

2. <u>Kurt Vonnegut</u>, *Jr.*, used to be my favorite author.

> When the <u>name</u> is used in the beginning or middle of the sentence, use **commas** before and after the *suffix*.

3. Then I discovered <u>James Jones</u>, *Jr.*, *MBA*, *PhD*, *LMT*.

> When there is more than one *suffix* for a <u>name</u>, separate each with **commas**.

Dates

When you use the full date as a noun, use commas to separate the year from the rest of the date.

1. My uncle moved to Tigard on <u>March 22</u>, *1958*.

> Separate the *year* from the <u>date</u> with a **comma**.

2. On <u>March 22</u>, *1958*, Tigard only had eight hundred people living in it.

> When the <u>date</u> is used in the beginning or middle of the sentence, use **commas** before and after the *year*.

3. <u>March 22</u> was the spring equinox that year.

> If you don't provide the year, don't use commas with the <u>date</u>.

4. Tigard has grown more than 5,000 percent since <u>March 1958.</u>

> Likewise, if the <u>date</u> consists of just the month and year, don't separate the year from the month with commas. It feels like you should, but here's one more example where your feelings are trying to betray you.

G. To Avoid Confusion

There are times when the phrases within a sentence look awkward or confusing when placed side by side with other parts of a sentence. When that happens, you can separate one part from another with a comma. However, you may be better off simply rephrasing the sentence to avoid the awkward structure in the first place.

1. <u>Whatever will be</u>, will be.

   In this case, the <u>subject</u> ends with a verb, and that looks weird when it's placed next to the main verb, so we separate the two verbs with a **comma**.

2. <u>Many people who like to sing</u>, sing while in the shower.

   Here's another example of the same problem. You can also reword this: "Many people who like to sing do so while in the shower."

3. <u>What I think it is</u>, is a moth.

   Here's another example. How about rephrasing it to "I think it is a moth"? Isn't that better?

3. Semicolons (;)

Semicolons have two regular uses in formal writing: They join two complete sentences to indicate a close relationship between the ideas, and they separate items in a list when one or all of the items contain commas.

A. Join Independent Clauses

Semicolons join two or more closely related independent clauses to form a more complex idea. Adding a transitional word or phrase like "however," "therefore," or "on the other hand" will show readers how these two independent ideas are related.

1. <u>The professor was late to class</u>; <u>the students waited outside the door</u>.

   Here we have two <u>independent clauses</u>. There's an implied cause-and-effect relationship here, so joining the two clauses together makes sense. The <u>independent clause</u> after the **semicolon** is not capitalized.

2. <u>The professor was late to class</u>; *however*, <u>she had a good reason</u>.

   Here, a *transitional word* after the **semicolon** shows the relationship between the two <u>independent clauses</u>. A comma separates the introductory transition from subject of the second <u>independent clause</u>.

3. <u>Dustin was also late to class</u>; <u>his excuse</u>, *however*, <u>was obviously a lie</u>.

> In this example, the *transitional word* occurs in the middle of the second <u>independent clause</u>. The **semicolon**, however, must always go where the two <u>independent clauses</u> meet.

4. <u>Dustin's excuses for tardiness are usually lies</u>; *for example*, <u>he once claimed he had been detained by Martians</u>.

> These <u>independent clauses</u> are related, as the *transitional phrase* indicates, so a **semicolon** is okay. However, they aren't that closely related, so a semicolon is probably not the best option.

5. <u>Dustin's excuses for tardiness are usually lies</u>. *For example*, <u>he once claimed he had been detained by Martians</u>.

> Letting each <u>independent clause</u> stand as separate sentence allows each idea to be considered on its own.

B. Separate Multipart Items in a List

Semicolons also separate multipart items in a list when one or more of those items already contains commas.

1. Over the years, I have lived in <u>Springfield, Oregon</u>; <u>Springfield, Kentucky</u>; <u>Springfield, Georgia</u>; and <u>Springfield, Vermont</u>.

> The <u>multi-part items</u> in the list are a series of cities and states that are already separated by commas. The **semicolons** work just like the commas in Comma Rule A. They show you that I've lived in four places and not eight.

2. Over the years, I have lived in <u>Springfield, Oregon</u>; <u>Springfield, Kentucky</u>; <u>Springfield, Georgia</u>; *Paris*; and <u>Springfield, Vermont</u>.

> Not all the items in the list need to be <u>multipart nouns</u> for **semicolons** to apply. It can be a mix of *single nouns* and <u>multipart nouns</u>.

3. The family reunion included <u>my uncle, Homer Simpkins, a retired vet</u>; <u>my aunt, Marge Simpkins, a retired nurse</u>; <u>my cousin, Lisa Andres, a doctor</u>; and <u>her brother, Bartholomew Simpkins, a pathologist</u>.

> Each <u>item</u> in this list consists of three parts, and each part is separated from the others by commas. Without **semicolons** to separate these items, readers have a hard time sorting out who is who.

4. The picnic table was packed with <u>kids eating cake</u>, <u>parents wiping cake off of the kids' clothes</u>, and <u>grandparents laughing knowingly</u>.

> Notice how no semicolons are used here? That's because the <u>items</u> in the series don't include commas.

4. Colons (:)

The colon is a bridge between an independent clause and a list, definition, explanation, quotation, or some other elaboration of the opening statement. They tend to emphasize the follow-up elaboration. In addition to this use in sentences, colons also have some technical duties to perform.

A. Introduce Elaborations

When a statement introduces a more detailed elaboration of that same idea, use a colon as a bridge between the idea and the elaboration. The statement before the colon must always be an independent clause because it must always be a complete idea. The words after the colon can be anything from a noun phrase to a complete sentence.

1. For some, <u>the definition of love is simple</u>: *unconditional sacrifice.*

   The **colon** here is a bridge between the <u>independent clause</u> and a short *definition* that elaborates upon that first idea. Notice how the **colon** focuses attention on that definition.

2. <u>Others see love as a composite of three necessary qualities</u>: *empathy, passion, and just a little lunacy.*

   This **colon** here introduces a *list* of three "necessary qualities." The list provides details about the <u>independent clause</u>.

3. <u>No one needs to live without love</u>: *Healthy, enriching relationships are available to all who seek them sincerely.*

   The **colon** introduces a *restatement* of the first <u>independent clause</u>. Because the *restatement* is also a complete idea, it's capitalized.

4. <u>My uncle has his own idea about love</u>: "It ain't a bowl of jellybeans on a Sunday afternoon. It's damned hard work."

   In this sentence, the **colon** introduces a quotation that elaborates on the <u>independent clause</u>. The quotation marks show readers that these are your uncle's actual words.

B. Technical Clarity

Colons also have smaller and more technical roles to play in formal writing, usually with the goal of clarifying the meaning.

1. Dear Mrs. Steuck**:**

   Here the **colon** comes after the greeting in a formal letter. It becomes a bridge to the body of the letter.

2. This letter is in reference to your recent order of the book *Batboys***:** *The True Story of Baseball's Unsung Heroes.*

   The **colon** divides the <u>main title</u> from the *subtitle*, which is an elaboration of the <u>main title</u>.

3. At 4**:**30 p.m. yesterday, your bank informed us that your ratio of debt to credit is 4**:**1.

   The **colon** separates the <u>hour</u> from the *minutes*. It also shows the relationship of two numbers. Poor Mrs. Steuck.

5. Apostrophes (')

Apostrophes have three specific functions in formal writing. They show that some letters or numbers are missing, they help to create possessive adjectives, and on extremely rare occasions—occasions so rare that many live their whole lives without experiencing one—they help to resolve confusion when letters become plural nouns.

A. Missing Words or Numbers

An apostrophe shows readers that letters or numbers have been removed from a word. The resulting word is called a contraction because the word contracts into a shorter version of its formerly expansive self.

1. I <u>didn't</u> answer your phone call last night.

   This is a <u>contraction</u> of the words "did" and "not." Because the "o" is omitted, the **apostrophe** goes between the "n" and the "t."

2. To get me to answer, <u>you'll</u> need to call before midnight.

   This is a <u>contraction</u> for "you" and "will." The **apostrophe** shows where "wi" has been removed.

3. I **won't** bother to explain why midnight is too late for a phone call.

   This is a <u>contraction</u> for "will" and "not." The **apostrophe** represents the missing "o" from "not." "Willn't" never really caught on, so for some reason, we instead say "won't."

4. You can reach me any time before ten **o'clock**.

   > This is an old <u>contraction</u> for "of the clock." In this case, the **apostrophe** shows where whole words have disappeared from the original phrase.

5. **It's** also fine to email me.

   > This <u>contraction</u> is commonly misused as a possessive adjective. Anytime you write "it's," substitute the words "it is" or "it has" in your head as a test. If that makes sense, use the **apostrophe**.

6. I prefer email because I am not stuck in the **'80s** like some people I know.

   > The full word for this <u>contraction</u> is "1980s." The **apostrophe** indicates that "19" has been omitted.

7. How **'<u>bout</u>** you stop <u>whinin'</u> **'<u>bout</u>** it?

   > You can also use **apostrophes** to create informal <u>contractions</u> that sound like a spoken dialect. This is an informal style of writing, though, so don't use it in a formal paper.

Contractions make your writing sound more like spoken language, so they tend to be less appropriate for formal papers. It's like wearing sweatpants on a date. Yes, sweatpants are more comfortable—everyone knows that—but taking the time to get dressed up for someone sends a message that he or she is important. Writing out the full phrase shows the same kind of respect for the readers of a formal paper.

B. Possessive Adjectives

Apostrophes also show ownership or close association between two noun phrases by turning one of the noun phrases into a possessive adjective for the other.

Singular Noun Phrases

With singular noun phrases, add an apostrophe and "s" to the end of a noun phrase to convert it into a possessive adjective.

1. I approve of <u>my sister's</u> *husband*.

   > By adding an **apostrophe** and "s" to "my sister," it becomes a <u>possessive</u> <u>adjective</u> that describes who owns the *noun phrase*. It tells us the husband belongs to my sister. Kind of.

2. I borrowed <u>my brother-in-law's</u> *truck* for the week.

   > With a compound noun like "brother-in-law," add an **apostrophe** and "s" to the end of the last word to create a <u>possessive adjective</u> that now describes who owns the *noun phrase*. You wouldn't write "brother's-in-law."

3. I borrowed <u>James</u>'s *truck*, in other words.

> Even if a singular noun ends with an "s," you add an **apostrophe** and "s" to create a <u>possessive adjective</u>.

4. Technically, it became <u>my sister and James</u>'<u>s</u> *truck* when they married.

> With a compound noun phase like "my sister and James," add an **apostrophe** and "s" to the end of the whole noun phrase to create a monster <u>possessive adjective</u> that now describes who owns the *noun phrase*.

5. Technically, <u>my sister and James</u> both owned the *truck* when they married.

> If a complicated possessive adjective becomes too hard to follow, however, you can rephrase the idea to show that a *noun phrase* belongs to a <u>compound noun phrase</u> without using a possessive adjective.

6. They have a cat named Socrates, so they are also <u>Socrates</u>' *owners*.

> When the noun phrase doing the owning is a proper noun, ends in "s," and is more than one syllable long—which is an admittedly rare event—you only need to add the **apostrophe** to create a <u>possessive adjective</u>.

Plural Noun Phrases

With plural noun phrases, you have two options for creating possessive adjectives. When the main plural noun ends with an "s," as most do, add an apostrophe after the "s." When it ends with another letter, add an apostrophe and an "s."

1. <u>Dogs</u>' *best friends* are not people.

> When the <u>plural noun phrase</u> ends in "s," just add the **apostrophe** without the additional "s" to show who owns the *noun phrase*.

2. However, <u>my friends</u>' *dogs* sure act like they are.

> Adding the **apostrophe** without the additional "s" tells readers that you have more than one friend who own the *noun phrase*. If you mean the dogs of one friend, you would use "friend's" as the <u>possessive adjective</u>.

3. <u>The men</u>'<u>s</u> *room* is off limits to dogs.

> When the plural noun doesn't end in "s," add the **apostrophe** and "s" to create a <u>possessive adjective</u> for the *main noun*.

C. Plural Letters

You can also use an apostrophe and "s" to make a word plural, but you only do that when the word is a single letter and only when it helps to avoid confusion. This is rare.

1. *Correct:* I got straight A's this term.

   Confusing: I got straight <u>As</u> this term.

   > Use an **apostrophe** and "s" to make a single letter a <u>plural noun</u> when the absence of an apostrophe would cause confusion. Leaving out the **apostrophe** here makes the <u>plural noun</u> confusing because it looks like a different word.

2. It's harder to get good grades now than it was in the <u>1990s</u>.

   > However, don't use an apostrophe to make a <u>number plural</u>. Just add the "s" because this is not confusing.

3. I don't have time to listen to <u>CDs</u> or watch <u>DVDs</u>.

   > Just add the letter "s" to make an acronym a <u>plural noun</u>, too.

4. Last week, I studied with my friends, the <u>Woffords</u>.

   > Do not use **apostrophes** to turn last names into <u>plural nouns</u>. People love to do that on charming little signs that welcome you to their homes, but it's still a mistake.

Apostrophe

Spanish does not use the apostrophe. Many native Spanish speakers are understandably confused by its use, particularly when it comes to using an apostrophe with the letter "s" for singular and plural possession.

Pay close attention to the rules to learn to correctly use apostrophes.

6. Quotation Marks (" ")

In formal writing, quotation marks primarily show readers that a set of words in your writing come from someone else. They also are used to talk about words as words, to set off the titles of short works, and to act like air quotes to make a word or phrase ironic.

A. Direct Quotations

Quotation marks show readers that the words between the first and second quotation mark come from a source outside the formal paper. When a word or phrase that requires quotation marks is used within a set of quotation marks, the interior quotation marks change from double to single quotation marks.

1. Koeby said, "Public speaking is a lost art."

   The **quotation marks** go at the beginning and end of the quotation. Capitalize the first letter inside of **quotation marks** when the quotation is a complete sentence (or longer). Place the ending punctuation for the main sentence inside of the second set of **quotation marks**.

2. Holly said that the country needed "another Martin Luther King, Jr."

   Do not capitalize the first letter inside of the **quotation marks** when the quotation is a word or phrase that completes the rest of the sentence.

3. Shaeny agreed: "I love that speech!"

   If the quotation is a question or exclamation, the punctuation mark goes inside the **quotation marks**.

4. Is Shaeny being honest when she says, "I love that speech!"?

   If the quotation is part of a larger question or exclamation, the ending punctuation marks go outside the **quotation marks**.

5. Torrey replied, "She is. The repetition of 'I have a dream' really got her."

   When a word or phrase that requires quotation marks goes inside a larger quotation, use **single quotation marks** for the inner quotation.

B. Words as Words

Quotation marks also show readers that you are writing about words as words and not as the things that those words represent.

1. One of my favorite words is "sluice."

   > The **quotation marks** show that you are talking about a word and not an actual sluice, whatever that is.

2. I hate to use the word "hate."

   > The first "hate" is you being a hater. The **quotation marks** show that the second "hate" is a word that you maybe don't hate as much as you think.

3. A common error is the use of "anxious" to mean "eager."

   > Again, the **quotation marks** show that we're talking about how to use two words, not the emotions they represent.

C. Titles of Shorter Works

Quotation marks also signal the beginning and end of titles for shorter works – works that are usually parts of some larger work. There is a hierarchy to formatting correctly.

Books	Anthologies	Periodicals	TV Shows	Websites	Albums
"Chapters"	"Short Stories," "Poems," or "Articles"	"Articles"	"Episodes"	"Articles" or "Pages"	"Songs"

Books are made up of chapters. Television shows are made up of episodes. Albums are made up of songs. The smaller work published within the larger work should be within quotation marks.

1. Conrad's favorite song on the album *Let It Be* is the song "Let It Be."

   > **Quotation marks** set off the title of a shorter work within an *album*.

2. Caelin read "Where the Sidewalk Ends" from Shel Silverstein's *Where the Sidewalk Ends*.

   > **Quotation marks** set off the title of a shorter work within a *book*.

3. "Which Rock Star Will Historians of the Future Remember?" is a fascinating article in this week's *New York Times Magazine*.

   > **Quotation marks** set off the title of this shorter work within a *magazine*.

D. Ironic Meaning

Quotation marks can also work like air quotes to show that a word or phrase is being used ironically. Formal writing doesn't do a lot of this, but some "scholars" can't help themselves.

1. I really **"**love**"** working in the lab all weekend.

   > The **quotation marks** show that the literal meaning of the <u>word</u> has been reversed. I hate working on the weekends actually.

2. Sure, I have a **"**goal**"** in life — to avoid anything involving responsibility.

   > These **quotation marks** overturn the conventional meaning of the <u>word</u>, as if to say, "That's your word, not mine."

3. *Nietzsche*'s idea of **"**superman**"** is super overrated.

   > With formal writing, **quotation marks** can show readers that this is an important <u>word or phrase</u> from an *outside source*. The **quotation marks** also tend to challenge the validity of that term.

7. Other Punctuation Marks

A. Parentheses ( )

Parentheses work as a team of two to enclose information that is not part of the main clause but is still relevant and good to know.

1. *Standardized testing* (<u>first used in 1682</u>) *has never been an accurate measure of knowledge.*

   > The **parentheses** show that the <u>enclosed information</u> is related to the *main clause* but not a direct part of that idea.

2. I read about it in a journal (*Childhood Education*) my teacher assigned.

   > The <u>information</u> inside the **parentheses** adds detail to the main clause that is not essential to that main idea.

3. The author teaches at a small college in Springfield (<u>Illinois</u>).

   > The <u>information</u> inside the **parentheses** clarifies which Springfield we're talking about. It is not a necessary part of the *main clause*.

4. I can't remember the name of the article because the *dek* (<u>the subtitle that comes after the main title</u>) was very long and stuffed with fancy words.

   > **Parentheses** can also provide a short <u>definition</u> of a *word* that is likely to be unfamiliar to the readers.

5. Graydon works for the *Downtown Emergency Service Center* (<u>DESC</u>).

> **Parentheses** can provide an <u>acronym or abbreviation</u> for a *longer term*. You can then use the abbreviation in future sentences.

6. I gave Graydon *four hundred dollars* (<u>$400</u>) as a charitable donation.

> You can clarify a *written number* by adding the <u>numerals</u> in **parentheses**.

B. Dash (—)

Dashes can separate, introduce, interrupt, or omit words, phrases, and clauses within a sentence. They can do just about anything, in other words. However, all of those jobs are done more precisely by other punctuation marks, so in formal writing, which requires precision, you should avoid dashes. The only exceptions to that rule are for introductions or interruptions that require extra—some would say dramatic—emphasis.

Dramatic Introduction

Use a dash to separate an introductory noun phrase from an idea about that noun phrase.

1. <u>Unconditional sacrifice</u>— for some, this is the definition of love.

> The **dash** separates an important <u>introductory noun phrase</u> from the full idea about that noun phrase.

2. <u>Love, love, love</u>—I am sick to death of reading examples about love.

> The **dash** can also separate a list of important <u>introductory noun phrases</u> from the full idea about them.

Dramatic Interruption

Use dashes to add extra emphasis to an interruption to the main clause. This is more typical in informal writing, so only do this when the interruption really needs to stand out. Otherwise, use commas or parentheses to separate the interruption.

1. *Standardized testing*— <u>first used in 1682</u>— *has never been an accurate measure of knowledge.*

> The **dashes** before and after the <u>interruption</u> make it clear that this is not part of the *main clause*. The extra emphasis also suggests that this side fact is important. If it's not, then use commas to separate the <u>interruption</u>.

2. *Louis Armstrong's claimed date of birth*— <u>July 4, 1900</u>— *is probably untrue.*

> When there are commas within an <u>interruption</u>, the **dashes** are better than commas at separating the <u>interruption</u> from the *main clause*. If the interruption isn't worthy of extra emphasis, use parentheses instead.

3. *I prayed*— but dared not hope — *that this day would come.*

> The **dashes** indicate a sudden interruption of thought in the middle of the *main clause*. Dashes make more sense with informal sentences like this one.

C. Ellipses (. . .)

Ellipses are a series of three successive periods that indicate the author has removed words from a direct quotation. They replace words from the original text that the author doesn't believe are relevant to the purpose of the quotation. They thus make the quotation easier to understand.

1. Professor Slemenda maintains that "The Rabid Bats are . . . well on their way to the highest levels of rock status."

> The **ellipses** indicates an omission of words within a direct quotation.

2. Slemenda claims that the band "will break even newer ground if rumors pan out about . . . a virtual reality interaction . . . technology, called 'Bats in Your Brain'."

> You are welcome to use more than one set of **ellipses** in a single quotation as long as it doesn't change the meaning of the sentence.

3. Slemenda claims that the band "will break even newer ground" with new technology.

> When you omit words before the quotation, don't add ellipses.

4. Slemenda also observes, "The Bats have long been popular among the young . . . . Now that their earliest fans are old, they appeal to all ages."

> If the omitted words include the ending punctuation of a sentence within the quotation, add an extra period to the **ellipses**—but only one, even if more than one sentence is omitted.

5. Slemenda concludes, "This is just one example of the sort of dangerous showmanship that . . . suggests that the Rabid Bats are no mere flash in the pan . . . ."

> If you end a quotation before the sentence you're quoting is complete, add an **ellipsis** to the ending punctuation to indicate the author's words continue in the original.

8. Capitalization

Capitalization means putting an upper case or capital letter at the beginning of a word. Capitalization also helps readers distinguish between proper nouns and common nouns.

A. The First Word of a Sentence

1. **The** White House is a white house.

   | Capitalize the **first word** of every sentence.

2. My uncle always says, "**You** could live in the White House some day."

   | Capitalize the **first word** of <u>a complete sentence within quotation marks</u>.

3. My uncle says that I have "<u>the mind of **President Lincoln**</u>."

   | If <u>part of a sentence</u> is within quotation marks, only capitalize **words that are capitalized in the original**.

4. However, I don't want to live in the White House: **White** <u>is a boring color for a house</u>.

   | Capitalize the **first word** of a complete sentence that follows a colon.

B. Proper Nouns

Capitalize the official name of any person, place, thing, or idea.

1. The **White House** is a white house.

   | Capitalize the **official name** of a specific place.

2. People who live in **Oregon** are called *Oregonians*.

   | Capitalize the **names** of cities, states, countries, and regions of a country. Also capitalize any *word that is formed from that name*.

3. **Aunt Ali** said she was my *aunt*, but **Mom** and **Doctor Dye** both said that she was actually my *grandmother*.

   | Capitalize the **names of people**. Capitalize the titles of people when they're used as part of a **name** or in place of a **name**, but don't capitalize them when they are used as a *common noun*.

4. I suffer from **Trabue Syndrome**, a *syndrome* that includes a grave fascination with whales.

   | Capitalize the **official name** of any particular thing. Don't capitalize a *common noun*.

5. I live in **Southern Oregon**, which is *north* of **Northern California** but still part of the **West**.

> Capitalize directions when they are used as a **name** or as a part of a **name** but not when they are used as a *general term*.

6. The **State of Jefferson** is not an actual state, but it too is part of the **West**.

> However, do not capitalize <u>short prepositions</u>, <u>conjunctions</u>, or <u>articles</u> within a **name**.

C. Major Words in Titles of Created Works

Capitalize the first word and other major words in the titles of songs, books, articles, films, and other created works.

1. I was listening to Joni Mitchell's "*Wild* **Things** <u>Run</u> *Fast*" on the Canadian oldies station.

> Capitalize all the **nouns**, <u>verbs</u>, and *adjectives* or *adverbs* in titles.

2. That song reminds me of *The Wind* ***in*** *<u>the</u>* *Willows*.

> Don't capitalize **prepositions**, <u>articles</u>, or conjunctions unless one is the first word of the title. Always capitalize the first word of a title.

D. Days, Months, and Holidays

Always capitalize the names of days, months, and holidays, but only capitalize seasons if you are talking about a specific season in a given year.

1. Next **Monday**, I plan to spend most of the day planning out what to do on **Tuesday**.

> Capitalize **days** of the week.

2. I plan to spend most of **October** planning for **Halloween**.

> Capitalize **months** and **holidays**.

3. The **spring** is a great time for planning, but when I look back at all the planning I've done, <u>Spring 2005</u> stands out as the best of all time. That's not weird, is it?

> Don't capitalize the names of **seasons** unless you refer to a <u>specific season</u>.

E. The Pronoun "I"

For some reason, always capitalize the pronoun "I."

1. **I** don't understand why **I** can't capitalize all the other pronouns.

   | Always capitalize the **first-person singular pronoun**.

2. It's probably not because **I** am more special than <u>you</u>, but it does make <u>me</u> wonder.

   | Don't capitalize any <u>other pronouns</u> unless another capitalization rule applies.

Capitalization

When writing in Spanish, you do not capitalize days and months, but you do capitalize most holidays. In English, you capitalize days, months, and holidays. Nationalities, languages, and most religions, including the name for those who practice a religion, must also be capitalized in English.

1. **Problem:**

   Father's Day is on the third **sunday** in <u>june</u>.

   | **Days of the week** and <u>months</u> must be capitalized in English.

   Solution:

   Father's Day is on the third **Sunday** in <u>June</u>.

   | In Spain, Father's Day is in March, by the way.

2. **Problem:**

   My dad is a canadian muslim who speaks french.

   Solution:

   My dad is a Canadian Muslim who speaks French.

   | He's *really* hard to buy for.

9. Abbreviations

Abbreviations are shortened versions of words—like "Dr." for "Doctor" or "km" for "kilometers." They were invented back when everything was handwritten so that copyists didn't have to write out full words, which wasted precious ink, paper, and years of their lives. In this age of computers, the ink, paper, and years of our lives are less precious, so we should now use the full word instead of its abbreviation most of the time. However, many abbreviations are still used regularly in formal writing.

A. Abbreviations with Names

It is acceptable to abbreviate the titles of people that come before or after their names and to abbreviate first and middle names.

1. <u>Rev.</u> *Brown* and <u>Mrs.</u> *Brown* both see <u>Dr.</u> *Smith* in <u>St.</u> *Paul* for their elbow problems.

   > When you abbreviate <u>titles</u> before a *name*, be sure to add a **period** to the abbreviation.

2. <u>Dr.</u> *Smith* is a doctor of philosophy in linguistics, as is *Joe Jerry Smith*, <u>Jr.</u>, <u>Ph.D.</u>, his eldest son.

   > When you abbreviate <u>titles</u> that follow a *name*, separate them from the name with commas and add a **period**. Some guides prefer no periods with abbreviations for degrees like "PhD." That's fine. Just be consistent.

3. *Joe Jerry* Smith, Jr., usually goes by <u>J. J.</u> Smith to avoid embarrassment.

   > You can abbreviate a first and middle *name* by using the <u>initial letter</u> of each *name*, followed by a **period** and a space.

B. Acronyms

Acronyms take the first letter of multiple words to create a quick abbreviation. Do not use periods or spaces in abbreviations that consist of all capital letters, with only a few exceptions.

1. She tried to teach me the difference between <u>HTML</u>, <u>XML</u>, and <u>PHP</u>.

   > Do not use periods or spaces with the <u>acronyms</u> for well-known terms.

2. We really should have bought stock in <u>IBM</u>, <u>CBS</u>, and <u>GM</u>.

   > Do not use periods or spaces with <u>acronyms</u> for corporations.

3. The <u>FBI</u> and <u>CIA</u> are recruiting agents at <u>PSU</u> and <u>MIT</u>.

   > Don't use periods or spaces with the <u>acronyms</u> for schools or familiar institutions.

4. Some idiot put a <u>CD</u> in the <u>DVD</u> player, and this time, it wasn't me.

> Don't use periods or spaces with <u>abbreviations</u> for very familiar objects.

5. <u>FDR</u> and <u>JFK</u> were born in the <u>USA</u>.

> Don't add periods or spaces to <u>acronyms</u> for famous people or countries.

6. <u>U. S.</u> relations with Cuba seem to be warming up.

> Here's your exception. With the abbreviation of "United States," use **periods** after both <u>initials</u> but without a space in between.

C. Technical and Scientific Terms

In most cases, use technical and scientific abbreviations only when writing technical and scientific papers. Otherwise, spell out the full word.

1. The frog weighed 15 <u>kg</u> and was 25.7 <u>in.</u> tall.

> Do not use **periods** with most <u>abbreviations</u> of measurements. However, put a **period** after "in" to avoid confusion with the preposition "in."

2. The frog traveled at 30.4 <u>mph</u>.

> Do not use periods with <u>abbreviations</u> for commonly used terms like "mpg," "rbi," and so on.

3. The frog died at 2:30 <u>a. m.</u> from exhaustion.

> Use **periods** but not spaces for <u>abbreviations</u> of words used with numbers like "a.m." (*ante meridiem* — before noon), "B.C.E." (before common era), and so on.

4. We dissected the frog, examined the muscles, ran tests, <u>etc.</u>

> Use **periods** but not spaces with abbreviations for <u>common Latin terms</u>, such as "etc." (*et cetera* — and so on), "e.g." (*exempli gratia* — for example), and "i.e." (*id est* — that is).

In formal writing, do not abbreviate normal words such as "through" (thru), days of the week, months of the year, words at the beginning of a sentence, states' names, people's names, (such as "Jas." for "James"), or academic courses (such as "econ" for "economics").

Don't use abbreviations that your reader may not understand, either. If you must use an unfamiliar abbreviation, write out the full name the first time you use the term and then give the abbreviation in parentheses. After that, you can use the abbreviation.

Never use texting abbreviations such as "LOL," "IMHO," or "LMAO." That's just embarrassing.

10. Italics

Italics are letters set in a typeface that slants to the right—*like this*. They add emphasis to words or phrases, set off the titles of long works or of vehicles, and indicate non-English words or sounds used in English. If you are writing by hand or are using a typewriter because you enjoy living in 1983, <u>underline</u> words you would otherwise *italicize*.

A. Emphasis

With informal writing, italics create a sound effect. They show readers when to pronounce a word more loudly, as in, "You're not my best friend anymore—you're my *worst* friend." With formal writing, however, italics should only be used occasionally to highlight important words when it is necessary to make the meaning clear.

1. The doctor did not say that her elbow *would* recover but that it *might* recover.

   The *italics* add extra emphasis to highlight an important distinction.

2. We wondered why they saw a doctor of *linguistics* for tendinitis of the elbow.

   The *italics* add extra emphasis to draw attention to an important term that might otherwise be missed.

B. Titles of Larger Created Works

Italicize the titles of created works that are complete in themselves. This includes books, anthologies, periodicals, television shows, websites, and albums. For the titles of shorter works, see the Quotation Marks section earlier in this chapter.

1. *To Kill a Mockingbird* is a great movie but an even better book.

   Italicize the *titles* of books and movies.

2. You can download *Geogebra* software for free from *geogebra.org*.

   Italicize the *titles* of software and websites.

3. "Let It Be" is probably the worst song on *Let It Be*.

   Set off the *titles* of albums with italics. And while you're at it, set off the <u>titles of shorter works</u> within an album with quotation marks.

C. Names of Vehicles

Italicize the names of any specific vehicles that have been given names.

1. We were riding on *The City of New Orleans*, one of the most famous trains ever.

   | Italicize the *name* of a specific train or ship.

2. *Greased Lighting* is the name of my <u>Ford Focus</u>.

   | Italicize the *names* of specific cars but not the general <u>brand names</u> of vehicles.

D. Non-English Words and Sounds

Italicize non-English words and sounds that appear in your sentences.

1. *Radix lecti* sounds so much classier than its English translation: couch potato.

   | Italicize *Latin terms*.

2. A rose by any other name is still a member of the *rosoideae* plant family.

   | The *genus and species of plants* are usually italicized.

3. Because she had grown up in Germany, my sisters and I called our grand-mother *grossmutter*.

   | Italicize *non-English words*.

4. When she dropped me, my head hit the sidewalk with an ominous *thunk*.

   | Italicize *words that reproduce sounds*. It's hard to imagine when this would show up in a formal paper.

11. Hyphens (-)

Hyphens connect two or more words to create a compound word that combines the meanings of both into a single unit. Hyphens also allow you to divide a word in half at the end of a written line so that you can put the second half at the start of the next line.

A. Compound Adjectives

Use hyphens to combine two or more words into a single adjective before a noun.

1. I drove my Nissan Leaf the wrong way down a <u>one-way</u> *street*.

   > The **hyphen** combines separate words to create a <u>compound adjective</u> that describes the *noun*.

2. My <u>fourth-grade</u> *teacher* saw me.

   > Here's another example of a <u>compound adjective</u> that describes a *noun*.

3. This <u>fifteen-year-old</u> *bourbon* is fifteen years old.

   > Use **hyphens** to create a <u>compound adjective</u> when the adjective comes before the *noun*. However, if the same words come after the *noun*, they remain separate and unhyphenated.

B. Compound Nouns and Numbers

Use hyphens to combine two or more nouns or numbers into a single term or to combine a noun with certain prefixes.

1. The opening of your essay was a real <u>attention-grabber</u>.

   > The **hyphen** combines separate words to create a <u>compound noun</u>.

2. I felt like a <u>three-year-old</u> watching cartoons.

   > You aren't limited to combining only two nouns. Here we combine three.

3. I'm <u>thirty-six</u> now, so that was a nostalgic feeling.

   > Use **hyphens** to write <u>numbers</u> from twenty-one to ninety-nine.

4. The feeling stayed with me for <u>three-quarters</u> of an hour.

   > Use a **hyphen** to write out <u>fractions</u>.

5. Even at this age, I lack <u>self-*control*</u> when it comes to a good essay opening.

   > Many <u>prefixes</u> connect to *nouns* with a **hyphen** to create a compound noun. "Self-," "all-," and "ex-" usually require a hyphen. Other prefixes like "semi" rarely do. It's a good idea to check the spelling of compound nouns with a dictionary.

C. Line Breaks

If necessary, use a hyphen to divide words at the end of a line.

1. The road to Silverton was full of pot-
    holes that made driving dangerous.

    > Make the break only between <u>syllables</u>. Use the **hyphen** to show that the
    > word continues on the next line.

2. In the back seat, my screaming <u>third-</u>
    <u>grader</u> begged me to slow down.

    > If there's already a **hyphen** in a word, use it to divide the word into <u>parts</u>.

12. Common Problems

A. Excessive Ending Punctuation

With informal writing, it's not uncommon to register shock with more than one
exclamation point:

> You aren't wearing any pants!!!!

Similarly, you can register grave curiosity with more than one question mark:

> What are you thinking????

This excessive use of ending punctuation creates a sound effect. It shows readers
how emphatically to shout these statements or ask these questions. While this type
of excess is fine with informal writing, it's a problem with formal writing because
it distracts readers from the purpose of sentences, which is to present ideas clearly.

A second type of excess is overusing single exclamation points within a
paragraph:

> Credibility is Rick's problem! He's proven himself to be unreliable! He tells
> tall tales about Bigfoot stealing his wife! He has a wild imagination, and he
> lets it get away from him! Rick needs to take responsibility for his actions,
> or no one will ever believe him again!

In formal writing, there may be rare occasions when you appropriately register shock or surprise with an exclamation point, but they really are rare. When you
add an exclamation point after many sentences, the punctuation ceases to denote
shock or surprise.

How to Fix Excessive Ending Punctuation

Use just one period after almost all statements. Use just one question mark after any question. And if, from time to time, the idea of a sentence is so startling or outrageous that you cannot contain yourself and simply must shout, you may use a single exclamation point.

1. **Problem:**

   Why are people so violent???

   > That's a good question, but the excessive question marks make the sentence informal and whiny.

   Solution:

   Why are people so violent?

   > That's better. Now we can focus on the question.

   Another acceptable way to convey emphasis is to use italics. This is better because italics provide a more precise emphasis. An exclamation point emphasizes the entire idea. Italics emphasize the part of that idea that is most startling or surprising.

2. **Problem:**

   We have to change now!!!!!

   > That's true, but all those exclamation points make it seem like you're screaming. That distracts from your point, and it isn't professional.

   Solution:

   We have to change *now*.

   > Now the idea stands on its own for consideration. Italicizing the *key word* makes it clear that you wish to emphasize the urgency of the moment.

B. Apostrophe Abuse

In spoken English, most single nouns become plural nouns by adding the sound "s" to the end of them. Similarly, when matched with third-person subjects, most verbs add the sound "s" to the end of the verb. In written English, however, it's not enough to just add the *sound* "s." You also have to spell that "s" sound correctly so that the word you use has the correct meaning.

With all verbs and almost all plural nouns, you can't add an apostrophe and "s" to the end of the word to create that sound. If you do use an apostrophe and "s," you will confuse your readers.

How to Fix Apostrophe Abuse

This is pretty straightforward. Spell nouns and verbs correctly.

Plural Nouns

To form most plural nouns, add a single "s" directly to the end of the noun. If the noun already ends in "s" or something that sounds like "s," such as "sh" or "ch," add "es" to the end of the noun.

1. **Problem:**

   I rarely misuse my **apostrophe's**.

   > When you add an apostrophe and "s" to the end of a noun, it converts that noun into a **possessive adjective**. Because there's no noun following that adjective, readers think, "You rarely misuse your apostrophe's *what?*"

   Solution:

   I rarely misuse my **apostrophes**.

   > By adding a single "s" to the noun, it becomes a **plural noun**. Now the sentence makes sense, but it's also ironic now because you're not misusing your apostrophes anymore.

2. **Problem:**

   The environmental science **class's** went to the landfill.

   > The apostrophe and "s" have again turned a singular noun into a **possessive adjective**. The environmental science class's *what* went on a field trip? The class's mascot? The class's professor?

   Solution:

   The environmental science **classes** went to the landfill.

   > Oh, more than one class went on the field trip. Now we understand. By adding an "es" to the singular noun, it becomes a **plural noun** and makes sense in this sentence.

3. **Problem:**

My **friend's** help me with math.

> Your friend's *what* helps you with math?

Solution:

My **friends** help me with math.

> By adding a single "s" to the noun, it becomes a **plural noun**. Now we know that you have more than one friend and that these people help you with math.

4. **Problem:**

The **fly's** are terrible this summer.

> The fly's *what* is terrible?

Solution:

The **flies** are terrible this summer.

> If the singular noun ends in a consonant followed by a "y," replace the "y" with "ies" to form a **plural noun**.

Third-Person Verbs

To form verbs that go with third-person singular subjects such as "she," "LeAnna," and "the alligator," you add a single "s" directly to the verb. If the verb already ends in "s" or something that sounds like "s," add "es" directly to the end of the verb.

1. **Problem:**

The dog **run's** after the garbage truck.

> When you add an apostrophe and "s" to the end of a **verb**, the word sounds right but doesn't make any sense. Is this a contraction? The dog run *is* after the garbage truck? Is it a possessive adjective?

Solution:

The dog **runs** after the garbage truck.

> By adding a single "s" to the **verb**, the sentence now makes sense. It's a dumb dog, and it's running after a garbage truck.

2. **Problem:**

Weekly World News **publish's** some questionable articles.

> Because this **verb** can't also be a noun like "run," this spelling makes no sense at all.

Solution:

World Weekly News **publishes** some questionable articles.

┃ By adding a single "es" directly to the **verb**, the sentence makes sense.

3. **Problem:**

The bird **fly's** into the window.

┃ This apostrophe and "s" at the end of a **verb** makes the verb look like a
┃ contraction. The bird fly — whatever that is — is into the window? That
┃ *sort of* makes sense, but it's not what you mean.

Solution:

The bird **flies** into the window.

┃ Birds are not the brightest of animals. Anyway, if the **verb** ends in a conso-
┃ nant followed by a "y" — like with the word "fly" — replace the "y" with
┃ "ies" to form a third-person verb.

C. Punctuation for Sound Effects

The goal of informal writing is to write how you speak so that your readers will be able to "hear your voice."

To create the right sound effects, then, you use commas to create, short, pauses.

You can use periods to create. Longer. Pauses.

Ellipses will create the sound of a voice trailing off . . .

These tricks help to make your writing sound like talking, and that "voice" creates a personal connection between you and your readers. With informal writing, that kind of connection is a key to success.

With formal writing, however, the sound of your voice doesn't matter. The ideas in your brain are what matter. If you use ellipses to create a sound effect, you will confuse the meaning of your sentence because ellipses are only meant to do one thing — show readers where words have been omitted from a direct quotation. If you use commas whenever you hear a pause as you read aloud, you will confuse the meaning of your sentences because sometimes you're pausing to catch your breath rather than to show where parts of a sentence begin and end.

In short, using punctuation for sound effects will make your formal paper less effective because it will make your ideas harder to understand.

How to Fix Punctuation for Sound Effects

First, although it may be painful at first, you have to stop trying to create sound effects with your punctuation. That's not part of formal writing. None of your professors will find it charming. Just stop.

Second, study and then follow the actual rules of commas, colons, ellipses, and other punctuation marks. People learn how to do this every day. There's no reason you can't be one of those people.

D. Errors with Titles

Most writers don't have any trouble capitalizing the title of a created work because they know it's a proper noun — the official name of the book, play, painting, TV show, movie, magazine, or poem. The problem comes from trying to decide whether to set it off with italics or enclose it with quotation marks or leave it alone.

1. I really like *Let it Be*, but I hate **"Let It Be."**

   | I really like the *album*, but I hate the **song**.

2. I really like **"Let it Be,"** but I hate *Let It Be*.

   | I really like the **song**, but I hate the *album*.

If you don't format the title correctly, you give readers the wrong idea about the created work. That's a problem.

How to Fix Errors with Titles

The way to make sure you format titles correctly is to keep this in mind at all times:

- For the titles of larger works, use *italics*.
- For the titles of smaller works, use "quotation marks."

Now all you need to know is what "larger" and "smaller" means. It's not usually a matter of length. Larger works are usually works that contain many stand-alone parts:

- A book contains many chapters
- A magazine or newspaper contains many articles
- A poetry anthology contains many poems
- A TV series contains many episodes
- A movie contains many scenes
- A full-length play contains scenes and acts

Smaller works are usually part of some larger works:

- A chapter is a part of a book
- An article is a part of a magazine or newspaper
- A poem is a part of a poetry anthology

Use italics for the titles of larger works. Use quotation marks for the titles of smaller works.

1. My favorite song on *Let It Be* is **"Let It Be."**

   The **smaller work** is a song that appears on the *larger work*, an album of the same name.

2. Did you read **"Still I Rise"** by Maya Angelou in *The Complete Poetry*?

   The **smaller work** is a poem that appears in the *larger work*, a book of poetry.

3. Many high school classes study *The Odyssey*.

   This *larger work* is also poem, but it's a book-length poem made up of many stanzas, so we treat it like we would a chapter book, a play, or any other larger and more complex work.

4. The main character in *Hamlet* is Hamlet.

   "Hamlet" is the name of a person in the *larger work*, which is a play about that person. His name is capitalized as a proper noun, but it's not formatted with italics or quotation marks because in this example, it refers to the person.

5. I love *David*.

   The italics indicate that you love Michelangelo's sculpture, which is considered a *larger work*, and not the David who makes you coffee every morning.

6. **"Room for Debate"** is my new favorite *New York Times* feature.

   Articles, columns, and website pages are all considered **smaller works**, even if they are very long. The newspapers, magazines, and websites that publish these articles are all considered *larger works*, even if they are fairly short.

Word Choice

The words you choose help you to present your ideas professionally and clearly. Whenever you're writing in a formal situation—at school, work, court, and so on—your audience expects you to choose words that are appropriate and precise:

- **Appropriate:** Choose words that are fitting for a formal audience such as a professor, boss, or judge. Your words should be respectful, objective, and in no way distracting from the ideas you present.

- **Precise:** Your words should also mean exactly what you think so that your readers clearly understand your ideas.

Some student writers suppose that choosing the right word means they need to sound like a boring, long-winded textbook. They use lengthy words and elaborate phrases because they think that makes them sound intelligent. But in formal writing, the most intelligent thing you can do is to present ideas appropriately and precisely so that your readers will better understand them.

In this chapter, we'll explore how to choose words that are appropriate and precise. Then we'll look at some common word choice problems and how to fix them. Finally, we'll end with a list of some of the most commonly confused words.

1. Appropriate Words

Whether you are writing a research paper for a professor, a report for your boss, or a letter to a traffic court judge, your words should be appropriate for the situation in three important ways:

- Your words should be the correct words for what you mean.
- Your words should be objective toward the topic at hand.
- Your words should be more formal in style.

A. Correct Words

Every word in a formal paper should be correctly spelled, and it should mean what you think it means. In practice, this means that you should not guess about spelling or meaning. You shouldn't trust your spell-checker, either, because your spell-checker is also guessing.

Spelling matters. In formal writing, misspellings distract from the idea you are trying to explain. Misspellings also make you look lazy, at best, in the eyes of a careful reader. That may be unfair, but that's life. If you're not sure about the spelling of a word, look it up in a dictionary.

Spell-checkers are unreliable. If you're typing and see that your spell-checker has found a misspelling, don't let it choose the correct spelling for you. The spell-checker is only looking at the letters in your misspelled word and guessing at what you probably mean. That's why it often offers you several words to choose from. You should choose the word that means exactly what you are thinking.

Consider these spell-checker options for the misspelled word "opinun" (opinion) in this sentence: "A thoughtful opinun is worth sharing."

Suggested Replacement	Actual Meaning	Used in the Sentence
opining	verb, expressing an opinion	A thoughtful expressing an opinion is worth sharing.
opium	noun, a narcotic drug	A thoughtful narcotic drug is worth sharing.
opinion	noun, a reasoned judgment	A thoughtful reasoned judgment is worth sharing.
opine	verb, to express an opinion	A thoughtful to express an opinion is worth sharing.

If you trust your spell-checker's first or fourth guess, the sentence is confusing. If you trust the spell-checker's second guess, the sentence becomes a joke that your readers will tell others over dinner. If you trust your spell-checker's third guess, you get the correct word for this idea.

So don't trust your spell-checker. Look up your options, and choose the correct one.

Consider the following examples:

1. The pirate <u>bares</u> his chest.

   > Here, the pirate <u>uncovers</u> his upper torso. Careful there, pirate. Keep your shirt on.

2. The pirate <u>bears</u> his chest.

   > In this sentence, he <u>carries</u> his treasure chest, which is a thing pirates do. Carry on, pirate.

3. Charlotte <u>defiantly</u> disagrees with the author.

   > Here, Charlotte disagrees <u>with bold disobedience</u>, which seems a little much.

4. Charlotte <u>definitely</u> disagrees with the author.

   > Now she disagrees <u>without doubt</u>, which is still bold but more appropriate to the situation.

If you're not sure which word you need, show enough respect for your audience and their opinion of you to look the options up in a dictionary and choose the correct one. Many common errors are listed and explained at the end of this chapter, so check that out, too.

Correct Word Form

In English, words that mean the same basic thing have different spellings when used as nouns, verbs, adjectives, and adverbs. This isn't always the case in other languages.

Noun	*Verb*	*Adjective*	*Adverb*
Engagement: We announced our engagement.	Engage: I will now engage him in a game of chess.	Engaging, engaged: He is an engaging person and a good chess player.	Engagingly: He smiles at me engagingly.
Sadness: It is with great sadness that I write this letter to you.	Sadden: It saddens me to tell you that your money is running out.	Sad: You will be sad if you don't find a better job soon.	Sadly: He shook his head sadly as he read the letter.
Interest: My daughter has a passionate interest in cats.	Interest: She asked if she could interest me in getting a kitten.	Interesting: I said that it could be interesting to get a new cat.	Interestingly: Our adult cats, however, were interestingly unhappy with the idea.
Analysis: The reviewer's analysis suggested that movies that year often encouraged the drinking of sodas.	Analyze: She set out to analyze whether movies were "soda-pop" friendly.	Analytical: This analytical approach considered not only soda-drinking in movies but also dialogue that favored soda-drinking.	Analytically: Looked at analytically, movies are encouraging us to drink soda, she concluded.

Look at your sentence pattern to see how the word is being used. Then use a dictionary to make sure you use the right form for that part of speech. It will take some trial and error. Success depends on learning new words, reading, and listening. Be patient. And pay attention to how native English speakers use the different forms.

B. Objective Attitude

How you discuss your subject should be appropriate for the formal writing situation. This means reserving judgment about a topic while you present information and evidence.

Your word choice should consider not only the literal meaning of words, also called denotations, but also the emotive and figurative meanings, which are also called connotations. This is where reserving judgment comes in. Words may have positive or negative connotations, depending on the cultural, historical, and personal attitudes attached to the words. Having an objective attitude means choosing words that do not have overly positive or negative connotations.

Consider the difference between the words "cheap" and "affordable." At a literal level, both words mean that an item or service is inexpensive. However, "cheap" comes with negative connotations that suggest that the item or service is of poor quality. "Affordable," on the other hand, suggests that it's of sound quality and reasonably priced.

Look at the attitudes expressed by the connotations of words in the following examples. We'll move from positive to negative connotations to show how easy it is to express personal judgments with word choice.

1. This **cozy** and **affordable** <u>rental home</u> is located in the heart of a **vibrant urban area**.

   | These **adjectives** all suggest positive qualities about the <u>nouns</u>, which are also positive terms that suggest comfort and safety.

2. Many <u>individuals</u> have been **unfairly displaced** in this city.

   | There's no positive way to describe living without a home, but this **phrase** suggests that the individuals themselves are not to blame.

Negative connotations express negative attitudes toward the subject:

3. This **cheap**, **tiny** <u>hole-in-the-wall</u> is for rent in the **chaotic** <u>inner city</u>.

   | These **adjectives** carry negative associations, first in describing an apartment and then the location of that apartment. The <u>nouns</u> are both negative, too. The second has come to suggest neglect and poverty.

4. This city is full of <u>bums</u>.

   | This <u>noun</u> suggests the individuals are lazy and a public nuisance, putting the blame for homelessness squarely on the people experiencing it.

Neutral connotations express an objective attitude toward the subject. This is the right attitude to bring to formal writing because it allows readers to make up their own minds about how to view a subject.

Consider these examples that have a more objective attitude:

5. This **450-square-foot studio** <u>apartment</u> is now available <u>downtown</u>.

> These **adjectives** provide direct information about the size and style of the <u>noun</u> without adding any positive or negative judgments. The <u>nouns</u> are also informational and neutral.

6. There are 1,850 <u>individuals who are experiencing homelessness</u> in Marion and Polk Counties.

> In the same way, this <u>noun phrase</u> provides descriptive information about the subject without pointing blame toward or away from them.

Formal writing almost always presents a judgment of yours to your readers — that's what a thesis is, after all. However, that judgment should be supported with objective information and reasons based on objective information, not with judgmental words.

C. Formal Writing Style

You should also choose words that are appropriate for your relationship with a formal audience. Just as you would not talk to an ancient and somewhat angry grandmother with the same style of words that you use with your closest friends or your three-year-old cousin, you should carefully match the style of words you use to the audience you're addressing. With a formal audience, that means using a more formal or professional style.

Consider the levels of formality in the following examples, first from a cover letter to a future employer and then from a short essay.

1. **You know**, this project manager **gig** is **basically** perfect *cuz* I **totally** have a handle on that <u>stuff</u>.

> This example features **conversational words** that we use when talking but that add no actual information. Some words are <u>informal nouns</u> that don't define their meaning except in the broadest sense. And one word is a *phonetic spelling* of spoken language, which is just embarrassing in a cover letter.

2. **Well**, <u>I think</u> we all have to fight for freedom *nowadays*.

> **Verbal pauses** are useful as transitions in conversation, but they don't explain how sentences are related in the way that regular transitions do. <u>Self-references</u> are common in conversation but draw attention away from the subject in written works. *Colloquialisms* bring a folksy sound to a sentence, but that also draws attention away from the information they provide.

You can see that an informal style sounds a lot like conversation. At first glance, that might appeal to you because it's personal and friendly. While that's true of this style, it's also true that a conversational style tends to be more focused on making that personal connection than actually presenting useful information. That makes it inappropriate for formal writing where the purpose is to efficiently present ideas.

Here are two examples of a semiformal style:

3. **Thanks** for meeting with me to discuss the project manager position. I now feel more <u>in the loop</u> about the company's needs and look forward to applying for this position.

> **Conversational phrasing** within an otherwise formal style can make that formal style a little more personal. Similarly, <u>idioms</u> can bring a little liveliness to an otherwise professional style.

4. Freedom of speech allows **me** to communicate **my** opinions and ideas without fear of government retaliation or censorship. Therefore, **I'm** well within **my** rights to express grievances with the establishment.

> Sometimes **self-references** are relevant to the subject. The subject of personal rights, for example, includes the rights of the author. Warranted **self-references** and <u>contractions</u> may occasionally appear in a formal paper, but they still make the style more personal and less formal.

In some professional situations—such as an email to a colleague, a letter to your senator, or a blog entry on a company website—semiformal language is appropriate. In general, however, the personal element of semiformal style undercuts the professionalism that's expected in most formal writing situations.

Finally, here are two examples of a more formal style:

5. A good project manager fulfills all obligations in a timely, well-organized fashion. <u>My</u> objectives for this project, therefore, are to **assess past records**, **compile data on our demographic**, and **correspond with team leaders**. In this way, the team will be able to develop a more efficient business model for this company.

> This is a much less personal style. Aside from a single <u>personal pronoun</u>, the author focuses on the ideas at hand, providing **specific information** about what he or she will do in this role.

6. Freedom of expression is one of the cornerstones of democratic systems. For this reason, **the American Civil Liberties Union of Oregon** <u>is correct</u> in its aggressive protection of **the free speech rights** of **exotic dancers at Cheetah's**.

> This style of language also focuses specifically on the subject at hand. It provides **specific information** about the topic, and even though the core idea is an opinion, that <u>opinion</u> is stated as a direct assertion without using the "I think" phrasing that brings attention back to the author.

WORD CHOICE
Appropriate Words

Using clear, formal writing is appropriate when applying for a job. It's also important to focus on the issues at hand, like why you would do a good job, rather than on your personality. This is even more important in the formal writing required with college papers. With college papers, you've already gotten the job — to explain one idea clearly — and a more formal style is the appropriate way to share that idea with your readers.

2. Precise Words

Precision means choosing the words that mean exactly what you think.

General words like "good" and "effective" do tell readers what you think, but they are ambiguous. They can be understood in more than one way — and sometimes in dozens of ways. Is it good in the sense of moral goodness according to a particular religious code? Is it good in the sense of financial profitability? Is it good in the sense of personal well-being? With general terms, the lack of precision prevents readers from being able to correctly interpret your ideas.

General words are attractive because they're so easy to think of and use. They are all we need in conversation, too, where even a grunt will do ("That burrito was just *ugh*, you know?"). But the formal writing situation expects more from us. It expects us to take the time to choose precise terms so that our readers can spend less time working to understand us.

When you review what you've written and come across a general term that can be understood in more than one way, invest some time in replacing that general term with a more precise alternative that only allows one understanding. In that way, your readers will know exactly what you mean.

1. My sister **met with serious misfortune** today.

   > Did she **stub her toe**? Did she **lose her job**? Did she **get shot**? How serious is this misfortune?

2. I missed class because **I wasn't feeling well.**

   > Were you **throwing up**, **feverish**, or **tired and hungover**? All of these would be examples of not feeling well but vary significantly in their severity.

3. The concert was **awesome**. I was <u>very</u> tired the next day, but it was worth it.

   > **Empty superlatives** substitute scale for precision, making the term even more general than it needs to be. Similarly, <u>intensifiers</u> amplify a general word instead of making it more precise. We have a word for "very tired" — "exhausted." Use it. And while you're at it, offer a more precise term that tells us more clearly what you mean by "awesome."

When you're writing about real-world events, ask yourself if the words will create a clear visual image in the reader's mind. If not, then change them until they do.

4. The <u>red</u> **car** drove quickly past the house.

> This general **noun** could mean any kind of car. The only precision is the <u>adjective</u>, red. When I think of a "red car," I picture a mid '80s Corvette. My friend George pictures a Pontiac Vibe for some reason. Tell us which car you saw, so we can picture that instead.

5. The <u>red</u> Pontiac Vibe drove quickly past the house.

> I don't mean to be picky here, but there are many different shades of this general <u>adjective</u>: cherry red, blood red, ruby red, scarlet, and crimson to name a few. Tell us which shade of red you're talking about, and that's what we'll picture.

6. The cherry red Pontiac Vibe **drove** <u>quickly</u> past the house.

> This general **verb** and <u>adverb</u> tell us a little about the nature of the car's passage past the house, but not much. How quick is "quickly"?

7. The cherry red Pontiac Vibe raced past the **aqua and orange ranch house** at seventy-four miles per hour.

> Nice work. Now you have given your readers a more precise picture of this moment. We can see the car itself better. We understand that it was traveling over the speed limit. You've also presented "the house" in more detail, so we can see what it looks like and understand that it needs a paint job in the worst way.

The more precise your words are, the more effectively they will show readers exactly what you think. Because a clear presentation of ideas is the primary goal of formal writing, precision becomes one of your best tools for achieving that goal.

3. Common Problems

A. Slanted Language

Slanted language chooses words with strong negative or positive connotations. Those connotations are embedded opinions about a topic, opinions that have not been presented clearly or defended with evidence. When you use slanted language, you fail to maintain an objective attitude toward a topic.

With formal writing, this is a problem because readers demand objectivity from formal writers. If readers see from slanted language that the writer is not considering or presenting information objectively, they will not take the writer seriously. Even if the ideas are based on the thoughtful consideration of valid evidence, slanted language can invalidate the paper. A careful reader will see slanted language for what it usually is — bias on the part of the author — and take the argument less seriously or with skepticism.

How to Fix Slanted Language

To fix slanted language in your own writing, you have to look at the words you have chosen and check to see if they have positive, negative, or neutral connotations. You want neutral connotations. If the word seems appropriate but has positive or negative connotations, it is only appropriate for your paper if your paper supports that opinion with actual evidence and reasons.

1. **Problem:**

   The pit bull has a **proud** history of **valiant victories** over other breeds.

   > Although many of the words in this sentence help to maintain an objective attitude toward the topics, the **slanted words** and their positive connotations suggest to readers that this author has a bias in favor of pit bulls. The slanted language becomes a reason to take the writer less seriously.

   Solution:

   Pit bulls have a history of success in fighting with other breeds.

   > Removing the slanted terms makes this sentence more neutral. The careful reader is ready for more information now and is not automatically skeptical of the writer.

2. **Problem:**

   The **vicious** pit bull has a **dark** history of **bloody conquests** over other dogs.

   > This writer comes at the topic from a different attitude, but the result is the same for the careful reader. The **slanted words** make the writer less credible.

Solution:

Pit bulls have a history of success in fighting with other breeds.

> Check it out. Whether the slanted language is positive or negative, the fix is the same — an objective attitude. Let the evidence, not the slanted language, do all the hard work of presenting your ideas.

3. **Problem:**

The **zealots** supporting this **costly** bill **foolishly imagine** that it will provide jobs and environmental benefits, but they are **crazy** to think so.

> The **slanted words** ridicule the bill and its proponents instead of focusing on the information that would allow readers to come to their own conclusions. Ridiculing anyone with **slanted words** means that those people will resist your ideas because you did not respect them as thinkers.

Solution:

Supporters of this bill assert that it will provide jobs and environmental benefits, but evidence suggests that this may not be the actual result.

> By using neutral language, the sentence now focuses on the central point that supporters make about the bill. Now it's time to look at the facts of the bill, and because you haven't alienated people who disagree with you, you might actually have a chance of changing their minds.

But slanted language is so much more colorful. Yes, it is. However, you're not writing to entertain with formal papers. You're writing to share ideas and information. Your success depends primarily on presenting ideas and information clearly, and that requires an objective, neutral, and respectful attitude.

If you can present ideas clearly and be entertaining, then good for you. You'll make a wonderful graduate student. But even then, you have to use something other than slanted language to entertain your readers.

B. Exclusionary Language

Exclusionary language is any word or phrase that excludes, devalues, or judges a person or group of people, often on the basis of gender identity, race, color, age, or religion.

Exclusionary language is a problem for several reasons. First, it causes harm to those it excludes. There is direct harm in the form of the hurt feelings or frustration your words cause. There is also indirect harm from the harmful ideas and value judgments about others that your words perpetuate within your community—and within *you*.

This is also a practical problem for your formal writing because excluding others reduces the effectiveness of your paper. It's likely to anger or irritate those you happen to exclude, and it might do the same with readers who may not themselves be excluded but who also don't approve of excluding others. It also undercuts your credibility as a writer. That makes it much harder for readers to take you or your ideas seriously.

How to Fix Exclusionary Language

Fixing exclusionary language begins by you choosing to be careful about the words you choose to describe people and situations. Exclusionary attitudes have a way of sneaking into our thinking and then our language, but when we choose to care about how we phrase ideas, we expose those attitudes for what they are and can avoid the phrasing that perpetuates them.

Is this "political correctness"? Yes. Is that a bad thing? Not when it exposes and contends against attitudes that harm others.

Here then are some practical problems and solutions that are related to exclusionary language.

Problem 1: The Generic He

1. **Problem:**

    If <u>a student</u> signs up for this writing class without having the prerequisite skills, **he** will have to work twice as hard.

    > Using the **masculine pronoun** to refer to a gender-neutral <u>antecedent</u> excludes everyone who does not identify as male.

Solution 1:

If a student signs up for this writing class without having the prerequisite skills, **he** or **she** will have to work twice as hard.

> English doesn't have an official gender-neutral singular third-person pronoun, so when the gender-neutral antecedent is singular, your best option is to include both the masculine and feminine **third-person pronouns**.

Solution 2:

If students sign up for this writing class without having the prerequisite skills, **they** will have to work twice as hard.

> A more graceful solution is to use a plural antecedent and a **plural third-person pronoun**. "They" is becoming more acceptable to readers as a singular, gender-neutral pronoun, but rephrasing sentences to use it as a plural pronoun is acceptable to all readers.

2. **Problem:**

If a student signs up for this writing class without having the prerequisite skills, **he** will have to work twice as hard.

> It's back!

Not-a-Solution 1:

If a student signs up for this writing class without having the prerequisite skills, **he/she** will have to work twice as hard.

> You see this in some of the forms you have to fill out, but it's a dated and clumsy way to address the problem. Slashes also belong to informal writing. Use one of the solutions above.

Not-a-Solution 2:

If a student signs up for this writing class without having the prerequisite skills, **s/he** will have to work twice as hard.

> Even worse. Out of curiosity, how would you read that out loud? Never mind. Just use one of the solutions above.

Not-a-Solution 3:

If a student signs up for this writing class without having the prerequisite skills, **they** will have to work twice as hard.

> We predict that the formal writers of the future will use "they" as both a singular and plural pronoun (like "you" is now), but that usage is not yet universally accepted. So for this edition of the handbook, don't use this **plural pronoun** with a singular antecedent. Instead, use one of the solutions above.

Problem 2: The Generic Man

Like the first problem, it's also been common to use "man" in place of "person."

1. **Problem:**

   That's one small step for a man, one giant leap for **mankind**.

   > Neil Armstrong's famous words as he first set foot on the moon includes an **exclusionary word** that ignores or devalues half the population. Come on, Neil. You're better than that.

   Solution:

   That's one small step for <u>a man</u>, one giant leap for **humanity**.

   > This **inclusive word** is more accurate. The <u>reference to himself</u> is okay because it is also accurate.

2. **Problem:**

   Who's going to **man** the lemonade stand?

   > The same **exclusionary word** can also be used as a verb.

   Solution:

   Who's going to **run** the lemonade stand?

   > That's better.

3. **Problem:**

   Jane is the **chairman** of the committee.

   > Many words use "man" in this general sense of "person." When they do, the whole word becomes an **exclusionary term**.

   Solution:

   Jane is the **chair** of the committee.

   > The **inclusive term** means the same thing and saves you having to type three letters. Today, there are many common gender-neutral terms for traditional "man" terms—fire fighter, mail carrier, police officer, salesperson, and so on.

Problem 3: Irrelevant Gender Distinctions

Many gender-based nouns or titles are also exclusionary because they make an irrelevant distinction between men or women doing the same thing, which usually suggests a difference in the value of work done by women.

1. **Problem:**

   Jane is also a promising **actress** at our community theater.

WORD CHOICE
Exclusionary Language

Solution:

Jane is also a promising **actor** at our community theater.

> The **inclusive term** used to refer to men only, but now it means anyone who acts, regardless of their gender identity.

2. **Problem:**

My uncle is a **male nurse**.

> Does a male nurse do anything different because of his maleness?

Solution:

My uncle is a **nurse**.

> I didn't think so.

Problem 4: Stereotypes

Stereotypes are broad and usually oversimplified judgments about individuals that are based on the general groups they belong to, such as profession, religion, gender identity, age, race, color, and so on. When these ideas affect our word choices, the words become exclusionary.

1. **Problem:**

Doctors don't get to spend enough time with their **wives** and **children**.

> This sentence contains the **exclusionary words** that assume that all doctors must be married, have children, and probably be male. It excludes those who don't fit that stereotype.

Solution:

Doctors don't get to spend enough time with their **families**.

> By using a more **inclusive term**, the idea no longer excludes doctors with husbands.

2. **Problem:**

Salvatore is **confined** to a wheelchair.

> This **exclusionary term** assumes that people who use wheelchairs are trapped in them and defined by them. However, a disability is simply one part of who a person is.

Solution:

Salvatore **uses** a wheelchair.

> This **word** is factual.

C. Wordy Sentences

Wordy sentences use more words than necessary to present their ideas. They may become wordy through repetition or by using long phrases when a more precise word or two could do the same work.

This is a problem because it makes your writing less effective. Readers have to work harder to figure out your ideas when those ideas are not stated clearly. They may also become confused by the wordiness and never quite understand your idea.

How to Fix Wordy Sentences

The key to fixing a wordy sentence is to closely examine the meaning of each word or phrase. If the word or phrase adds no new meaning to the sentence, it is unnecessary. Out it goes.

1. **Problem:**

   Technology is something <u>we</u> **as humans** all use.

   > This **wordy phrase** repeats an idea inherent in an <u>earlier word</u>. If "we" means the author and readers, then let's hope both are human. Because it adds no additional information, out it goes.

   Solution 1:

   Technology is something <u>we</u> **all** use.

   > It could be argued **this word** is also implied by the <u>earlier word</u>, but it adds the additional information that the "we" includes everyone, no exceptions. It can stay.

   Solution 2:

   Everyone uses technology.

   > Wordy sentences can also be trimmed by rearranging words. By making "everyone" the subject and "use" the verb, we cut this sentence down to just three words without losing the main idea. This is close to a record.

2. **Problem:**

   In my opinion, **I think that** college should be free of charge to college students.

   > These **wordy phrases** mean the same thing, so we know that one can go. However, readers can see that it's an opinion without you having to point that out, so both can go.

   Still a problem:

   College should be free **of charge to college students**.

   > These **wordy phrases** don't add any additional meaning to the sentence, so

out they go. "Of charge" is already part of "free." And because only college students are paying (or not) for college, we already understand that this applies to them.

Solution:

College should be free.

| Here's the same idea in just four words. It's a much more effective sentence.

3. **Problem:**

   It is clear that excessive verbiage associated with communication can contribute in great part to the institutional failure of participating parties to transmit information across various media platforms.

   | Yikes. Sometimes a sentence is so flatulent with **wordy phrases** that you need to retrieve the idea and start over with new words.

Solution:

Wordy sentences impede communication.

| Here's the same idea in four words. Nice work.

D. Clichés

Clichés are phrases and metaphors that were once memorable and original ways of expressing an idea, but through overuse, they have become automatic and boring.

Clichés are a problem for two reasons. First, they probably don't capture your idea clearly. If you write that the college's failed anti-smoking policy is now "dead as a doornail," we get the idea that it won't survive, but what's a doornail? And why are doornails so illustrative of death? The cliché has a nice ring to it, perhaps, but it's not precise or vivid.

The second problem is that clichés are usually inefficient. "Dead as a doornail" takes four words to say "dead." The cliché has ceased to bring vividness to the meaning of the sentence. It now only brings wordiness.

How to Fix Clichés

In a nutshell, don't use them.

Instead, choose words that mean exactly what you think. If you can do so in a unique and colorful way, that's great. Go for it. Someday your originality will become a cliché for later generations to avoid. Otherwise, just focus on presenting your idea precisely and avoiding clichés.

1. **Problem:**

   I encourage you to think **outside the box** for this project.

   | It's doubly painful to use an uncreative **cliché** to describe creativity.

Solution:

I encourage you to think **creatively** for this project.

> This is the same idea in a single **word** instead of three.

2. **Problem:**

Matthew slept **like a baby** after his long night of rampage.

> This **cliché** is supposed to mean untroubled sleep, but anyone who's spent much time with babies knows that there's nothing untroubled about sleep that's interrupted every two hours to exchange food for dirty diapers. This **cliché** is both wordy and inaccurate.

Solution:

Matthew slept **peacefully** after his long night of rampage.

> That's better.

3. **Problem:**

His clothes look **like they were thrown on with a pitchfork**.

> This **cliché** was a classic three hundred years ago when pitchforks were a thing. Who knows what this even means now?

Solution:

His clothes look **like they had been slept in**.

> This phrasing actually means something to readers who are unfamiliar with pitchforks.

4. **Problem:**

By replacing clichés with your own original illustrations, you can **kill two birds with one stone**: presenting your ideas more clearly and engaging readers with new creativity.

> This **cliché** means to accomplish two outcomes with one action, and it's been so overused that we don't even notice the violence anymore.

Solution 1:

By replacing clichés with your own original illustrations, you can **achieve two goals at once**: presenting your ideas more clearly and engaging readers with new creativity.

> Replacing the cliché with a **clear statement of the idea** makes the sentence more direct and effective.

Solution 2:

By replacing clichés with your own original illustrations, you can **feed two birds with one biscuit**: presenting your ideas more clearly and engaging readers with new creativity.

> Replacing the cliché with a **new image** gives readers both the concept and a new mental image. These two effects make the sentence more interesting and vivid. Someday this could be a great cliché that future generations will have to remove from their papers.

E. Unnecessary Self-Reference

In formal writing, the focus should remain on your ideas and evidence, not on you the writer. This is why you have been told in the past that you should never use "I" in a formal paper. That's not wholly true, but it's at least pointing you in the right direction. If you are part of the evidence in your paper, then you can refer to yourself because your experience is a necessary part of the paper. However, any other self-references are unnecessary.

Unnecessary self-reference is a problem for two reasons. First, it draws attention away from your ideas and evidence. Second, it's a chatty, informal style that quickly becomes annoying for serious, careful readers, such as writing professors.

How to Fix Unnecessary Self-Reference

Eliminate statements where you announce what your writing is doing, reflect on the writing process, or refer back to your own writing. No one needs to watch home movies of your mental process. Instead, state your point simply, clearly, and succinctly.

1. **Problem:**

   In this paper, I will talk about photosynthesis, and **I will hopefully explain** the key steps involved, including light-dependent reactions and the Calvin cycle.

   > These **self-references** have nothing to do with the ideas at hand. It's the author talking about his or her own experience, and because the author is presumably not a green plant, that experience has nothing to do with photosynthesis.

   Solution:

   Photosynthesis involves several key steps, including light-dependent reactions and the Calvin cycle.

   > Now the point is clear. We know what to expect.

2. **Problem:**

When we first got the assignment sheet, I wasn't sure what to write about. Then I thought about my grandma. **I want to talk about her and** her life **and how she** influenced **me.**

> Whoa. Most of the words here describe the writer's process. That has nothing to do with poor old Grandma.

Solution:

My grandma has had a colorful life, and she has also had a huge influence on my life.

> Now the focus is on the grandma's life story and her influence on the writer—not the writing process or the writer's uncertainty. In this paper, the writer's experience is part of the evidence, so it's okay to refer to him- or herself as the recipient of Grandma's influence, but any other self-references should still be cut.

3. **Problem:**

I think that Hamlet's greatest problem is his inability to let go of his dead father.

> You don't need to preface an idea by stating that it's your idea. That's an **unnecessary self-reference** because we can tell from the sentence that it's an idea, and we can tell that it is your idea because you wrote the paper, right?

Solution:

Hamlet's greatest problem is his inability to let go of his dead father.

> You might want to add "I think" to soften a bold assertion. Don't. Be as bold as your evidence allows you to be. You don't need to soften that.

4. **Problem:**

I feel that Hamlet's greatest problem is his inability to let go of his dead father.

> You *feel* it? Really?

Solution:

Hamlet's greatest problem is his inability to let go of his dead father.

> Keep your feelings out of this, too. Focus on your ideas.

WORD CHOICE
Unnecessary Self-Reference

F. Jargon

Jargon is wording that is only familiar to people within a specific field where that wording is typically used. Specialized scientific, medical, and engineering fields are often prone to jargon, but no field is immune.

Jargon isn't a problem when it is appropriate for the writing situation. If you are only writing to experts in a field, then it makes sense to use the more precise, technical terms that those experts understand. The problem is when part or all of your readers are not experts. In that case, jargon can become incomprehensible and make the paper highly ineffective.

How to Fix Jargon

When you are not writing exclusively to experts, you can fix jargon in one of two ways. The first option is to replace specialized terms with more universally understood terms. If jargon is unavoidable—as it is in a writing handbook, for example—then your second option is to help the non-experts by introducing the specialized terms and offering a brief definition that will make the terms meaningful for all your readers.

1. **Problem:**

   I couldn't send an email because I wasn't **getting a ping** to my **LAN.**

   > Someone who understands computers may appreciate the **jargon** here, but to others, the meaning isn't clear.

   Solution:

   I couldn't send an email because I **couldn't connect to the Internet.**

   > Most people understand this **general term** that means the same thing.

2. **Problem:**

   Applicants will be provided time to do their *due diligence* after submitting their **LOI.**

   > *Industry-specific terms* and **acronyms** are common jargon terms.

   Solution:

   Applicants will be provided time to do their *necessary research* after submitting their **letter of intent** (<u>LOI</u>).

   > Even in technical writing, it's a good idea to introduce the **full term**, followed by its <u>acronym</u>, the first time you use it. You can replace industry-specific jargon with *general terms* when they mean the same thing.

3. Problem:

Within our **logframe**, the <u>behavior-change activities</u> fall under <u>intermediate result two</u>, but the health outcomes are all tied to <u>intermediate result one</u>.

> Some jargon words may be **shortened versions of a larger term**. Other jargon phrases may be <u>truncated versions of longer phrases</u>. This is efficient when the entire audience is familiar with the terms, but otherwise it's a barrier to understanding.

Solution:

Within our **logical framework**, the **activities likely to change behaviors** fall under **the second intermediate result category**, but the health outcomes are all tied to **the first intermediate result category**.

> Jargon is efficient, so there's a trade-off when you replace it with the **full terms**. The writing requires more words. However, if that's what your readers need, then there's no getting around that trade-off.

4. Problem:

I'm dragging a mid-well top to sell my lead, going with a happy fish dying on the pass.

> Don't even try to decode the **jargon** used in the restaurant industry.

Solution:

A medium well-done top sirloin steak is the only item unfinished on an order, and it's running longer than it should be. Meanwhile, the happy-hour fish that goes with it is getting cold in the serving window.

> If you say so.

4. Commonly Confused Words

The English language is full of words that sound or look similar to each other but have vastly different meanings. However, that doesn't give you an excuse to misuse them. Every time you choose a word that sounds or looks similar to the word you actually need, you end up looking less intelligent than you are, and that makes your formal paper less effective.

The key to avoiding this error is to learn from your mistakes. Your readers will tell you when you make one of these mistakes because they're often funny mistakes. When that happens, make a note and then do a little checking to make sure you have the meanings figured out.

Becoming more aware of common mistakes like using "accept" when you need "except" will also help you to slow down and check the meanings when you need to choose one of those words. Grammar or spell-checking software won't catch this sort of error, so this is on you — you and your dictionary.

Accept / Except

The thrift store will **accept** all children's items <u>except</u> car seats.

> **Accept** is a verb that means "to welcome or admit." <u>Except</u> is a preposition that means "not including."

Advise / Advice

I **advise** you to take your mother's <u>advice</u>.

> **Advise** is a verb that means "to recommend." <u>Advice</u> is a noun that is a recommendation.

Affect / Effect

Adding chlorine will negatively **affect** the experiment. The <u>effect</u> will be a catastrophic decline in the frog population.

> **Affect** is a verb that means "to have an impact on something." <u>Effect</u> is the noun for that impact.

Already / All ready

We <u>already</u> were **all ready** in case the hurricane reached land.

> **All ready** is a phrase that means "fully prepared." <u>Already</u> is an adverb that means "done previously."

Capital / Capitol

The **capitol** building in the <u>capital</u> city was paid for with <u>capital</u> raised from a bond measure.

> **Capitol** is a noun or adjective that refers to a building where lawmakers meet. <u>Capital</u> is a different noun that refers to the city where that building is located or other things such as monetary resources.

Conscious / Conscience / Couscous

Jenny was **conscious** of how much her <u>conscience</u> bothered her when she lied about how much *couscous* she ate.

> **Conscious** is an adjective that means "aware or awake," but the noun <u>conscience</u> mean "an inner sense of right and wrong." *Couscous* is a delicious North African pasta that's often mistaken as a grain. It's also a frequent spell-check solution to misspelled versions of the other two words.

Every day / Everyday

Every day in our modern lives we take advantage of <u>everyday</u> innovations.

> **Every day** is a phrase that means "each day," while <u>everyday</u> is an adjective that describes a noun as being commonplace or ordinary.

It's / Its

It's too bad that Shannon's favorite necklace lost <u>its</u> clasp.

> **It's** is always and only a contraction of "it is" or "it has." <u>Its</u> is always the possessive adjective form of the pronoun "it." If you're not sure which word to use, read the sentence with "it is" in place of the word. If that makes sense, use **it's**. If it doesn't, use <u>its</u>.

Lose / Loose

Did you **lose** some of your <u>loose</u> change?

> **Lose** is a verb that means "to give up or misplace something." <u>Loose</u> is an adjective that means that something is not gathered or doesn't fit very well.

Principal / Principle

The **principal** embodies all the <u>principles</u> of good education.

> **Principal** is a noun that means "the main thing" or "the head of a school." It can also refer to the main amount of money being raised or borrowed. <u>Principle</u> is a different noun that means "a rule or standard."

Quite / Quiet / Quit

It is **quite** <u>quiet</u> in here, so I won't *quit* writing yet.

> **Quite** is an adverb that means "truly" or "to a large degree." <u>Quiet</u> is an adjective that means "not loud." *Quit* is a verb that means "to stop."

Than / Then

If you have more money **than** I have, we can go to the movies and <u>then</u> have waffles and chicken.

> **Than** is usually a conjunction that's used to compare two things. <u>Then</u> is usually an adverb that refers to a point in time.

They're / Their / There

They're parking <u>their</u> car over *there*.

> **They're** is the contraction for "they are." <u>Their</u> is the possessive adverb for the pronoun "they." And *there* is most often an adverb that explains where you are doing something.

Thorough / Through / Threw / Thru

In a show of **thorough** domination <u>through</u> eight innings, Colby **threw** strike after strike.

> **Thorough** is an adjective that means "complete." <u>Through</u> is most commonly a preposition with many meanings, including "from the beginning to the end." *Threw* is the past tense form of a verb that refers to throwing or tossing something. "Thru" is an informal abbreviation of "through" that shows up almost exclusively in the term "drive-thru." Don't use it in formal writing.

To / Two / Too

If you liked the first **two** *Dumb and Dumber* movies, you should come <u>to</u> the third one, *too*. It's *too* funny for words.

> **Two** is always a number that means "one more than one." <u>To</u> is a preposition that shows direction or movement. *Too* is an adverb that either means "also" or "excessively."

Where / Were / We're

We're going to the same place <u>where</u> they *were* last night.

> **We're** is the contraction for "we are." <u>Where</u> is most often an adverb or conjunction that refers to a place. *Were* is the past-tense form of the verb "to be."

Whether / Weather / Wether

Whether we are able to attend the concert will depend on the <u>weather</u>, not the *wether*.

> **Whether** is a conjunction that usually introduces a choice. <u>Weather</u> is a noun that means that it's raining—again—and should not be confused with *wether*, which is a castrated sheep or goat.

Who's / Whose

Who's going to <u>whose</u> house tonight?

> **Who's** is the contraction for "who is" or "who has." <u>Whose</u> is the possessive adjective form of the pronoun "who." If you're not sure about which version to use, read the sentence with "who is" in place of the word. If that makes sense, use who's. If it doesn't, use <u>whose</u>.

Your / You're

You're not going to put <u>your</u> phone in the refrigerator, are you?

> **You're** is the contraction for "you are." <u>Your</u> is the possessive adjective form of the pronoun "you." A refrigerator is a bad place for a phone.

False Friends

False friends are words from two languages that look alike but have different histories and meanings. Spanish and English have many false friends. Here are just a few to be aware of.

English	Spanish
actual	actual ("current")
compromise	compromiso ("commitment")
constipated	contipado ("to have a cold")
costume	costumbre ("custom")
embarrassed	embarazada ("pregnant")
eventually	eventualmente ("occasionally")
excited	excitado ("aroused")
exit	éxito ("success")
media	media ("stocking")
phrase	frase ("sentence")
success	suceso ("event")

PART TWO
Research Basics

Research

Research is the process of finding information to help you figure things out. This is important because knowing more about a topic helps you arrive at better conclusions.

In your day-to-day life, even the simplest decision—like choosing which shoes to wear—usually involves a little research. You look out the window or check the weather forecast before deciding on rain boots or sneakers or flip-flops. If your roommate asks you to pick a movie to watch, you check online to see what's available, read a few reviews, watch a movie trailer or two, and then choose the least apocalyptic of the bunch.

In your college classes, the goal of research is also to find information that will help you figure things out. If you're assigned a paper in your history class that requires you to analyze the effects of the American Civil War on the educational systems in Confederate states, you'll need to gather information about those educational systems before and after the war so that you can understand what changed and whether it was the war or something else that led to those changes.

Whether at home or in college, then, the research process follows the same basic process:

1. Ask a good question.

2. Gather and assess information.

3. Form a conclusion.

In this chapter, we'll take a brief look at this three-step process and then introduce you to the basics of formal documentation that you'll use to show readers which ideas comes from you and which come from other sources.

1. The Research Process

A. Ask a Good Question

Research always starts with a question, and it's a good question if you don't already have the answer figured out from the start.

Sometimes, when information is lacking, these can be questions of fact: What really happened? What's really happening? With college writing, you more often want questions of meaning: Why did that happen? How was it possible? What causes that? These types of questions require both sufficient evidence and thoughtful interpretation of that evidence.

Sometimes research questions start pretty simply. For example, you might ask your college biology professor, "Do cows really have four stomachs?" The answer might have a lot of scientific information about biology and cud-chewing, but the first part of the answer will immediately teach you something new: A cow has one stomach, but it has four compartments. Answering that simple question now allows you to ask better questions about why and how.

If you already have a strong suspicion about the answer to a question, it's important that you don't then use the research process to back up that idea. That's not gathering information to help you figure something out. That's defending yourself against better alternatives to your current way of thinking. Instead, you can ask yourself how good that current idea is and then gather information to test your current thinking and improve upon it.

You will find many engaging questions waiting for you within any topic, by the way, even the seemingly boring ones that you're assigned in some classes. No matter what's assigned, do some light exploration of the topic by reading a little about it or talking to your professor until you uncover some little issue or controversy that makes you curious. You will always find something like that because there's never enough information for us to be sure about everything.

Another method is to narrow your focus to some small part of a larger topic so that you can get into more detailed information. Once you get into the details, your imagination has something to work with, and that's more enjoyable than trying to make sense of broad ideas and summarized information.

So start asking questions. Look for one that doesn't have an obvious answer and that interests you in some way. Once you find that starting point, the rest of the process will go much smoother.

B. Gather and Assess Information

Gathering information begins with your research question. You identify the keywords in that question and use them to search for information. The second step is then to assess that information so that you don't use unreliable information to make up your mind.

Identify Key Terms

To find information on the Internet, you need to search for it with keywords. That's what you use when you need to find a good place to eat. You tell your phone: "Thai food. Inexpensive. Downtown Salem." Your phone then searches the Internet for websites that contain those keywords so that you can gather information from those sites and make up your mind about where to eat.

That's also what you do when you research more complex questions using more reliable sources of information in your college library. You identify the keywords in your research question and then use those words, usually the nouns, to start searching for information in library catalogs and databases.

Consider this pretty good question, for example:

> What impact has the reintroduction of wolves had on ranching operations in the western United States?

That question gives us the following key terms:

- wolves
- reintroduction of wolves
- impact of wolves on ranching
- western United States

That's enough to get you started. As you begin to search for information about this question, you can then experiment with the terms to see which ones seem to pull in the most valuable evidence. Perhaps wildlife managers use "restoration" rather than "reintroduction." If so, then go with that.

Find Your Information through the Library

When you turn to the Internet for general information, you'll find some good university, organization, and government websites that provide free access to valuable information. However, these sites are rare exceptions and not always easy to track down. So while the Internet is great for helping you find affordable Thai food, it has much less help to offer when it comes to answering college research questions.

For college writing, you need to go to your college library. College libraries pay large sums of money for access to scholarly research and high-quality publications that are not available for free on the Internet. These publications get into the deep details of information about topics — the sort of details that professional scholars need to answer their questions. This information is carefully edited and tested by other professionals, too, so it's much more reliable than the average website, which anyone can create with about three clicks of a mouse.

You might be able to use Google or Google Scholar to learn that there's an academic journal called *Journal of Wildlife Management* and that it published an article on wolf restoration in Idaho and Oregon. But without the library access, you'd have to pay $19.95 for access to that article — and that's before you even know how useful it will be with your research question. Pay for two or three of these articles, and we're starting to talk about real money.

If you struggle to access a specific article or journal for free, your library also comes with librarians, and librarians are experts at finding information. They're also efficient at helping you improve your search terms so that it will be easier to find more and better information on your own. And finally, they are much nicer than their reputation suggests. Rather than shushing you, they will jump at the chance to help you and smooth out any bumps you might have in your research process.

Types of Publications

Not all of the information housed in your college library is appropriate for research-based writing. Scholarly publications are written by scholars and intended for scholarly audiences. The quality of this information is exactly what you want for research-based writing. Popular publications are meant to inform and amuse general audiences. These popular publications are usually written by professional writers rather than scholars, so they do not usually provide the quality of information you need for research-based writing. Because of these differences, you have to be the judge of what to read and what to take seriously.

When articles are moved from physical publications into an online library database, it becomes harder to tell the difference between scholarly publications, which contain pages upon pages of text and very few ads, and popular publications, which feature lots of ads and photographs and much less text. However, there are still many ways to tell the difference between the two in an online library database.

Scholarly Publications	Popular Publications
The authors use the specialized vocabulary of experts.	The authors use common, everyday language.
The authors' names and professional credentials are given.	The authors' names are either not given or given without any professional credentials.
The article often begins with a short summary, which is called an abstract.	The article may begin with a few lines of text that act as a "teaser" to get you to read more, but these do not provide a full summary of the article. Popular articles don't have abstracts.
Authors report on their research. They often include descriptions of the methodology used and statistical analysis of the results.	Authors often write about current events or popular interests like cat ownership, gardening, or rock and roll. They rarely use charts except as visual aids.
The authors expect the topic to be interesting—not the writing.	The authors use colorful language to keep you interested in the topic.
The articles tend to be long and thorough.	The articles tend to be short and superficial.
The authors use formal documentation to show where information comes from. This means in-text citations and full listings of cited works at the end of the article.	The authors may or may not mention where the information comes from. If it is mentioned, it's done informally within the article only. There is no list of cited works at the end of the article.

Many publications blur the distinctions above. That's why it's important to evaluate the quality of the sources before you allow them to influence your thinking.

Evaluate the Quality of Your Sources

A Google search for "reintroduction of wolves in the western United States" returns almost four hundred thousand potential sources of information. You would never be able to read that many articles, of course, but that's okay because very few of those sites offer reliable information. A library search offers more reliable sources, but it typically does little to distinguish between the timeliness or depth of evidence in one source or another. This means again, you have to be the judge about what to read and what to take seriously.

When evaluating the quality of your sources, it's important to keep four key criteria in mind: currency, reliability, authority, and point of view.

- **Currency:** Depending on the information you are looking at, when the information was created tells you about its usefulness for your paper. If you're looking into the history of wolf reintroduction, older information may be necessary to demonstrate a trend over time. But an article from 1970 complaining about the lack of compensation for Oregon ranchers whose cows have been slaughtered by wolves is outdated. It may be written by an authority in the field and have reliable information, but those ranchers receive compensation now, so the currency dramatically limits the source's usefulness.

- **Reliability:** To test a source's reliability, you need to examine the way the author is presenting the ideas. Does the author logically connect the paper's claims to properly-cited evidence? Does the author address and treat fairly any counterarguments to the paper's claims? Does the author provide a list of sources? Authors of reliable work will have done these things—just like you have—because reliability is important.

- **Authority:** Smart people are not equally qualified to speak on all topics. This means you'll have to do a little research on your research to understand the author's qualifications to provide the information you find in the source. You can often tell a lot about people's credentials based on what jobs they've had, accomplishments they've achieved, or education they've received. Your research should extend to the publisher as well. By running the piece, the publisher provides its endorsement of the material, and publishers have reputations just like individuals.

- **Point of view:** If you notice slanted language or suspect claims in a source, you may need to stop and research it for evidence of a bias. Does the author or publisher have anything to gain or lose based on the findings of the source? Recognizing and questioning your own biases is one of the cornerstones of academic work. Hold your sources to the same standard if you're going to use them in a formal research paper.

Take Notes

It doesn't matter who you are. Your memory isn't good enough on its own. As you gather information, you must keep track of what you find from each source.

Keep a separate note for each source you consider, even if you don't plan to use the information. At a minimum, jot down the author's name, the title of the work, where you found it (including a page number, if any), and, in your own words, the main point. With simple notes like this, you won't need to reread sources to track down an important idea or piece of information. That headache is a good one to avoid.

C. Form a Conclusion

You've asked a good question. You've carefully gathered reliable information that will help you figure out an answer to that question. Now it's time for you to form your own conclusion, the best answer that you can figure out from the information you've gathered.

This above all is a matter of honesty. Only conclude what your evidence allows. You may be tempted to conclude more than that. You may want to be bold and emphatic because you care so much about a topic, or to tear down the ideas of others because you dislike them so much, or just to show off a little. But formal writing requires objectivity, and that means taking your evidence for what it is and working within those boundaries.

If your evidence suggests that something *might be* valid, explain why something *might be* valid. Then back that position up with the evidence that led you there. Be fair and objective. What matters in formal writing is not the boldness of the idea but the honesty.

2. Documentation

Proper documentation involves two intertwined processes: in-text citations and end-of-paper citations.

Together, they form a system for showing readers of formal writing which words, ideas, and information in your paper come from outside sources. This is how formal writers give credit to one another.

Failure to document your sources accurately is called plagiarism, one of the high crimes of college writing. People tend to think of plagiarism as intentionally stealing the ideas of others. That's certainly one kind of plagiarism, but most plagiarism in student writing comes from sloppy or uninformed forms of documentation. Sources aren't given proper credit because the writers either haven't taken the appropriate care or simply don't understand how to document them properly. So pay attention to what follows. Your professor will hold you responsible for understanding it.

A. In-Text Documentation

In-text documentation uses small pieces of information in the body of your paper to show readers that an idea belongs to someone else. MLA style requires the author's last name and a page number if page numbers are available. APA style requires the author's last name, the date of publication, and page numbers when available. Chicago style uses a superscript number that points to further information in a footnote. In each case, in-text documentation points readers to specific works listed in more detail in your end-of-paper documentation.

You must include in-text documentation whenever you incorporate outside ideas in any of three different ways:

- direct quotation
- summary
- paraphrase

Plagiarism

Many cultures value the authority of the group over that of an individual. Consequently, people from these cultures tend to attribute ideas more generally with phrases that show consensus like "many people agree" or "some people say." In the world of formal writing, however, it is always necessary to give credit to the individuals who have produced the ideas or research that you are using in your paper.

1. **Problem:**

   Many people agree that Cinderella accepts this abuse passively by smiling and singing and making friends with the birds and rodents to whom she has been relegated.

   > Many people may agree with the idea in this sentence, but Mosher and Cox are the individuals who thought of the idea. This **attribution** does not give them credit for their work.

   Solution:

   As **Mosher and Cox** claim, "Cinderella accepts this abuse passively by smiling and singing and making friends with the birds and rodents to whom she has been relegated" **(89)**.

   > This **citation** uses MLA guidelines to give credit to the individuals who came up the idea you are using in your paper. The quotation marks also show that these are their exact words, not yours.

Source Framing

No matter how you choose to present the work of others, it's vital that you know how to ethically integrate it into your own writing. There will always be at least two and sometimes three required components to properly give credit to your sources:

Introduction	Borrowed Material	Parenthetical Citation or Footnote Number
The introduction might consist of an introductory statement or a signal phrase that identifies the author and uses a well-chosen verb like "claims," "refutes," "recommends," or "acknowledges" to show that the author is the owner of this idea. Pick your verb with care. They don't all mean the same thing.	Whether you choose to present a quotation, summary, or paraphrase, be careful not to add or remove words that change the meaning or otherwise misrepresent the original author's idea. You're giving them credit for their idea, so don't change anything about it.	If the introduction didn't identify all of the information required by the documentation style, it will show up in a parenthetical citation if you are using MLA or APA. With Chicago, a footnote number will follow the borrowed material no matter what you wrote in the introduction.

Let's take a look at how this works, starting with direction quotations.

Direct Quotation

Direct quotation is taking the exact words of an outside source and including them in your paper. This is the most straightforward way to document an idea from an outside source. You repeat the exact words of your source, using quotation marks to show where those words begin and end. In the case of a long quotation, use block formatting instead of quotation marks to show where those words begin and end.

Within the direct quotation itself, omit unnecessary words by using an ellipsis. You can also use brackets to indicate words or letters that have been added to a quotation to improve readability or follow the rules of grammar.

To show how this works, we'll use a passage entitled "On Getting Out of Bed" from Marcus Aurelius' *Meditations* for the examples that follow:

> In the morning, when you rise unwillingly, let this thought be present—I am rising to do the work of a human being. Why then am I dissatisfied if I am going to do the things for which I exist and for which I was brought into the world? Or

have I been made for this, to lie in bed and keep myself warm?

"But this is so pleasant!"

Do you exist then to take your pleasure, and not at all for action or hard work? Do you not see how all other things in the world are—all trees and plants, sparrows and ants, spiders and bees? They are all working together to put in order their various parts of the universe. And are you unwilling to do the work of a human being? Do you hold back from doing the work appropriate for your nature?

"But one must rest, too!"

Rest is necessary, but nature has set boundaries for this, too. She has set boundaries both for eating and drinking, yet you go beyond those boundaries, beyond what is sufficient. However, in your actions, this is not so. You stop short of what you can do. Thus you do not love yourself, for if you did, you would love your human nature and its will.

Others—as many as take pleasure in their trade and profession—will exhaust themselves for that work. But you value your own nature less than the carpenter values his craft, less than the dancer values his dancing, less than the greedy man values his money, less than the vain man values his applause. These people, when they have a strong attraction to a thing, choose to go without food or sleep for the sake of the things they care about. Do actions taken for the common good of human society appear more vile to you or less worthy of your respect and labor?

Now let's consider some ways to include parts Aurelius' writing in a college paper, starting with direct quotation.

1. **In "On Getting Out of Bed," Marcus Aurelius puts a series of pointed questions to the reader:** "Do you exist then to take your pleasure, and not at all for action or hard work? Do you not see how all other things in the world are—all trees and plants, sparrows and ants, spiders and bees? They are all working together to put in order their various parts of the universe. And are you unwilling to do the work of a human being? Do you hold back from doing the work appropriate for your nature?" (10).

   > The **introduction** to this direct quotation cites the author and title as it states the purpose of the quotation that follows. It ends with a parenthetical citation that includes the page number in the publication where the quotation appears. It's important to directly quote the author here because the point of the quotation is to share the specific questions from the original text.

2. **In discussing the nature of work in "On Getting Out of Bed," Marcus Aurelius claims,** "Others . . . will exhaust themselves for that work . . . . These people, when they have a strong attraction to a thing, choose to go without food or sleep for the sake of the things they care about" (11).

> This **introduction** uses a signal phrase to identify the title and author. Within the quotation, the <u>first ellipsis</u> shows that a word or phrase has been omitted from the sentence. The <u>second ellipsis</u>, which follows a period, shows that a sentence or more has been omitted.

While this method is the easiest way to bring ideas and information into your paper, it should also be the one you use the least often. The only time to directly quote a source is when the actual words that the source uses to present an idea are as important as the idea itself. The paper should primarily be your explanation of your own idea, so the main way to incorporate outside information should be through summary and paraphrase of that information.

Summary

Summary is taking a set of detailed information and compressing it into a shorter statement that describes what that information means or adds up to. Instead of listing all of the free-ranging wolves in Idaho, for example, you could summarize that there are currently 872 free-ranging wolves in Idaho. Summary strips the original passage down to its meaning, allowing readers to stay focused on your ideas.

To summarize outside ideas or information, begin with a reference to the original work. Describe the author's main ideas in fewer sentences than the original used and without commenting on the content or changing the author's meaning by overemphasizing one idea over another. In each case, an in-text citation must follow the last sentence of the summary. When possible, provide a page number or page range to direct readers to the part of the text you summarize.

3. **In "On Getting Out of Bed," Marcus Aurelius** weighs the pleasures of life against the importance of work, reconciling a love of self with a love for the greater needs of humanity <u>(10–11)</u>.

> This **introduction** to this summary notes the original author and title. The summary itself is much smaller than the original material, as you would expect. It doesn't include any of your ideas about the work, either. It just states the author's ideas as clearly as possible. Finally, the summary ends with another <u>parenthetical citation</u> that provides the page numbers where these ideas are explained.

You might think you don't need a citation when you summarize. After all, you put the idea in your own words—and you agree with the idea. Why credit the author for something you wrote and you believe? The answer is that coming up with the idea and gathering the evidence deserves credit. After all, just because you understand how your toilet works, it doesn't mean you deserve credit for indoor plumbing. Always cite the original work — always.

Paraphrase

Paraphrasing is putting another person's ideas into your own words while using different words and different word order. Paraphrasing is appropriate when you want to incorporate an idea someone else expressed but need to simplify a complex sentence structure or technical terms for your reader. The goal of paraphrasing is to make the idea more understandable to your specific audience, which is probably different from the audience of the original source.

You must always give credit to the original source who came up with the ideas you paraphrase. Just as with summary, putting someone else's ideas into your own words does not make those ideas your own. An in-text citation must follow the last sentence of the paraphrase. When possible, provide a page number or page range to direct readers to the part of the text you paraphrased.

4. **In "On Getting Out of Bed," Marcus Aurelius describes** the difficulty of waking up in the morning, exploring the tension between *the satisfaction inherent to work and the satisfaction of personal comfort* (10).

   > The paraphrase begins with an **introduction** that notes the author and title while also compressing the original quotation. In this case, the author of the paper has *rephrased the rhetorical questions into statements*. In addition, the paraphrase uses simpler terms, exchanging Aurelius' "rise unwillingly" for "difficulty of waking up." The paraphrase ends with the page number in a parenthetical citation that follows the MLA style.

5. **In "On Getting Out of Bed," Marcus Aurelius describes** *the difficulty of waking up in the morning, exploring the tension between the satisfaction inherent to work and the satisfaction of personal comfort.*[1]

   > This example is the same as the prior one except it is in the Chicago documentation style. The **introduction** and *borrowed material* are identical but instead of a trailing parenthetical citation that expresses the page number, it is followed by a footnote number. Readers who want to know what page that paraphrase appears on will have to consult the footnote.

When you paraphrase, you should address both the ideas and the evidence the author employs, but your wording of those ideas shouldn't mirror the phrasing or sentence structure of the original. Simple word rearranging is called patchwriting, a common problem that we'll look at later in this chapter. You can occasionally include unique or specialized language taken from the original source in your paraphrase, but that information should still appear within quotation marks.

Common Knowledge

Ideas that fall under common knowledge are the only ideas, other than your own, that you don't need to cite with in-text documentation. But what is common knowledge? Once upon a time, finding an idea cited in five credible sources was considered a reliable test for common knowledge. These days, knowledge spreads so quickly on the Internet that this rule is less useful. Instead, it's important to understand what common knowledge means instead of simply being able to detect it.

Common knowledge is what we call ideas that are no longer up for debate. Society settled the argument and moved on. We didn't know, in the first few minutes after his assassination, who shot President John F. Kennedy. In the hours that followed, authorities had a pretty good idea that it was Lee Harvey Oswald. Ultimately, he didn't stand trial where society could "prove" his guilt or innocence, due to his own assassination by Jack Ruby. As a result, a commission led by Supreme Court Chief Justice Earl Warren had to settle the matter with a thorough investigation that led to a ruling that Oswald, in fact, committed the crime. History now remembers Oswald as the shooter. Until new evidence—not to be confused with new *theories*—comes forward to reopen the argument, Oswald's guilt is considered common knowledge.

When an idea or piece of information is considered common knowledge, it does not need to be cited, even if the knowledge is something you didn't personally know until you came across it. Common knowledge is about society's knowledge, not your own. These are simultaneously the results of our society's creative inquiry and the building blocks that make future inquiry possible. They'll similarly be the building blocks of your own ideas and will be a major part of the logic you use to prove your thesis.

B. End-of-Paper Documentation

End-of-paper documentation provides all of the publication information that readers will need to track down the exact source that you used in your paper. This allows readers of your writing to test your ideas by examining your support. It also allows them to build upon your ideas and further their own understanding. This is how cultures develop knowledge over time, and documentation makes this task much easier.

The documentation at the end of the paper varies among different types of documentation styles, but it almost always includes these key pieces of information:

- author
- title
- publisher
- how you accessed it

It would be distracting to put all this information into the body of the paper, especially if you cite the same work multiple times. To avoid that, the relatively brief in-text citations alert readers that you are using material from an outside source and then point readers toward a single, complete listing at the end of the paper.

This is similar to the way hypertext functions on a web page. Highlighted hypertext words show readers that highlighted ideas or information can be found in more detail on another web page. When you click on the link, the computer instantaneously reads the publication information necessary to bring the reader to the website where the original idea is located. In much the same way, the in-text citation shows readers where to look at the end of your paper for information about finding the full source that you are using.

3. Common Problems

A. Poor Note-Taking

Poor note-taking means failing to keep track of each piece of information and where it comes from as you gather it. In the moment, your brain can remember clearly where each piece of information comes from because it just happened. Over time, memories fade and quietly disappear.

This is a problem because formal writing requires accurate and precise handling of information. If you don't have accurate and precise notes, your paper won't deliver accurate and precise information. Your brain will try to help out with its fading memories, but that will only make things worse by bringing broad summaries and vague references to "studies" or "reports" without any in-text citations of where that information came from. Conscientious students may simply leave out the evidence they can no longer cite, but that's not a big improvement. Their papers will contain little outside evidence, which makes the papers look like guesswork rather than the product of credible, objective evidence and critical thinking.

Poor note-taking is also a problem because the lack of accurate notes often results in incorrect or absent documentation. Without accurate documentation, readers will not be able to track down your resources and use them to build upon your work.

How to Fix Poor Note-Taking

Use a note-taking method—any note-taking method—that allows you to connect useful ideas and information to the sources they come from. It can be a spreadsheet. It can be notes on your phone. One of the easiest and best systems is still the little index cards that your grandparents used when they read books. The key, though, is to just do *something*. The results will be dramatic:

1. **Problem:**

   Sexual harassment is a big problem in lots of places. Women say they get in trouble when they report problems. **The head of Fox News got fired** for sexual harassment because it is illegal (<u>"Sexual Harassment"</u>).

   > You read over a couple of sources on your topic but wrote nothing down. Now your paper is due in a few hours, so you try to pull together what you remember, but you have very little to go on. You find <u>an article from a government website</u> that describes sexual harassment and stick it in. But you lack specific examples, specific points, or citations to back up your thinking. Your ideas are disorganized, and **you're getting facts wrong**. Things are not looking good.

   Solution:

   Even though it is illegal ("Sexual Harassment"), recent news accounts make it clear that sexual harassment remains a big issue in the workplace. In 2016, it became clear that the problem was rampant at Fox News. Former news anchor Gretchen Carlson sued Fox News Chairman Roger Ailes for sexual harassment (Koblin). Within a month, an internal investigation at Fox News found at least six other women attesting to Ailes harassing them, and he resigned (Rutenberg et al., "Internal Inquiry"). Days after his resignation, floods of reports of similar behavior by men across the Fox News network came out in a *New York Times* investigation (Rutenberg et al., "At Fox"). The most common reason that the eighteen women interviewed cited for not reporting harassment was "embarrassment and fear of retribution."

   > You must have taken good notes this time. Nice work. You have specific sources and concrete examples to help you make specific points and prove a claim. Careful note-taking not only helps you remember where you got your information, it can help you see why the information is particularly interesting and help you realize other research you might need to do. In this case, it was surprising that such a prominent organization had this happening all the time and that people were not reporting it. Specific points and the examples that illustrate them are your tickets to success with a researched argument like this.

B. Missing Citations

Missing citations are any in-text and end-of-paper citations that you fail to include alongside the outside ideas and information. Any quotation, summary, or paraphrase from an outside source that is not common knowledge must be cited. It doesn't matter if you put it into your own words—any quotation, summary, or paraphrase from an outside source that is not common knowledge must be cited.

Omitting citations is a problem because it's dishonest, which is bad for your soul. It's also plagiarism, which is bad for your academic career. It's also unprofessional to not give credit where credit is due. That's just bad manners.

How to Fix Missing Citations

The way to fix uncited information is to correctly cite it in the body of the paper and with an end-of-paper citation for that same source. Taking good notes will help with this.

1. **Problem:**

   The famous Japanese family film *My Neighbor Totoro* quickly reveals that it is different from American family movies. A dad and two little girls move into a house in the country and go about their lives among the people and spirits of their new neighborhood. That's essentially it. American films seem to focus on adventure, conflict, and danger. This movie depends on situation instead of a plot and suggests that the wonder of life and the resources of imagination supply all the adventure you need.

   > You've clearly seen the movie and have an observation about what it's like. You found a great source that helps you expand on your idea, but you aren't introducing the idea in this paragraph at all. This makes it look like you are pretending to be the one who came up with these thoughts, which in fact come from Roger Ebert. Not only that, it looks like you wrote that final sentence when Ebert actually wrote it.

   Solution:

   The famous Japanese family film *My Neighbor Totoro* quickly reveals that it is different from American family movies. A dad and two little girls move into a house in the country and go about their lives among the people and spirits of their new neighborhood. That's essentially it. <u>In his review of the movie, Roger Ebert notes that</u> **American films seem to focus on adventure, conflict, and danger**, but not this film: "This movie depends on situation instead of a plot and suggests that the wonder of life and the resources of imagination supply all the adventure you need."

Now we can see what you wrote and thought and then what your source wrote and thought. When you started writing about Ebert's ideas, you cited him with an <u>introductory signal phrase</u> and then, after you **paraphrased** part of his ideas, you put quotation marks around his actual words. Because this is an online source without page numbers, you didn't need to include a parenthetical citation after the quoted material.

C. Relying on Citation Generators

Citation generators are not perfect. They often mangle the information as it changes between documentation styles. They are also out of date at times, meaning they format your citation in a style that is no longer in use. If you want people to take your ideas seriously, you have to be able to demonstrate that you have taken the time and careful attention to present them appropriately. Citation generators are unreliable shortcuts to achieve that goal, so relying on them is a problem.

How to Fix Unreliable Citations

Your professors can tell when you use citation generators. If you aren't willing to write out the citation yourself, the only true solution is to double-check every element for accuracy, so it matches the rules of your documentation style.

1. **Problem:**

Mahoney, Phillip. "GRAY IS THE NEW BLACK: RACE CLASS AND ZOMBIES." *Generation Zombie: Essays on the Living Dead in Modern Culture*, edited by Stephanie Boluk and Wylie Lenz, McFarland, 2011, pp. 55–72.

Library databases and citation builders will often generate titles in all caps. This is wrong. Even if the original author wrote the title in all caps, which seems unlikely, you still must present the title consistent with your documentation style and none of them require all caps.

Solution:

Mahoney, Phillip. "Gray Is the New Black: Race, Class, and Zombies." *Generation Zombie: Essays on the Living Dead in Modern Culture*, edited by Stephanie Boluk and Wylie Lenz, McFarland, 2011, pp. 55–72.

This reference is in MLA style. Notice that you capitalize "is" in the title above, even though it's a short word. That's because it is a verb, and you capitalize verbs in MLA titles. "The" is lower case because it is an article. "And" is lowercase because it is a coordinating conjunction.

Because this is a smaller work within a larger one, the same capitalization rules apply to the title of the work where this article appears. "On" and "in" are lowercase because they are prepositions. See the "Title" section of the MLA, APA, or Chicago chapters for full details on the specific rules.

2. Problem:

Mahoney, Phillip. Gray Is the New Black: Race, Class, and Zombies. Generation Zombie: Essays on the Living Dead in Modern Culture, edited by Stephanie Boluk and Wylie Lenz, McFarland, 2011, pp. 55–72.

This citation has two titles. One is for the article name and the other is for the name of the edited collection that published the article. The capitalization is correct for MLA style, but the citation generator failed to apply the proper formatting.

Solution:

Mahoney, Phillip. "Gray Is the New Black: Race, Class, and Zombies." *Generation Zombie: Essays on the Living Dead in Modern Culture*, edited by Stephanie Boluk and Wylie Lenz, McFarland, 2011, pp. 55–72.

The title of the larger work is now italicized, and the title of the smaller work within that larger work is written within quotation marks. This is the only way anyone will take a paper about zombies seriously, by the way.

3. Problem:

Racy, A. J. (2016, Spring/Summer). Domesticating otherness: The snake charmer in American popular culture. *Ethnomusicology, 60*(2), 197–232. Retrieved from http://proxy.chemeketa.edu:2048/login?url=http://go.galegroup.com/ps/i.do?p=GPS&sw=w&u=oregon_chemeke&v=2.1&it=r&id=GALE%-7CA454437482&asid=1c1e86fdafb0bec720de65365c78f30

Proxy URLs are often built by your citation generator to supply information for the location element. Some only work if you are logged in to your school's database. Others only work the one time no matter what. If your reader has the patience to type in that URL, they won't connect to your source, and that's a problem. The point of a reference, after all, is to help the reader find the source you used. Proxy URLs don't help with that.

Solution:

Racy, A. J. (2016, Spring/Summer). Domesticating otherness: The snake charmer in American popular culture. *Ethnomusicology, 60*(2), 197–232. Retrieved from **www.jstor.org/stable/10.5406/ethnomusicology.60.2.0197**

This citation follows APA style. This **stable URL** will work for any scholar with access to this specific database. One popular form of stable URL is the DOI or digital object identifier. When available, they are the most reliable location to cite.

4. **Problem:**

Racy, A. J. (2016, Spring/Summer). "Domesticating otherness: The snake charmer in American popular culture." *Ethnomusicology*, 60(2), 197–232. Retrieved from www.jstor.org/stable/10.5406/ethnomusicology.60.2.0197

> You would think this would be correct. However, in APA end-of-text references, you omit the quotation marks for article names. The title of the larger work should still be italicized, which is a journal, and so should the journal's volume number.

Solution:

Racy, A. J. (2016, Spring/Summer). Domesticating otherness: The snake charmer in American popular culture. *Ethnomusicology*, *60*(2), 197–232. Retrieved from www.jstor.org/stable/10.5406/ethnomusicology.60.2.0197

> Always check your documntation style's specific rules.

D. Unquoted Quotations

Whenever you use the exact words from an outside source, you must put those words inside quotation marks and cite the author in the text of the paper. If you use those words without correctly identifying them or citing them, you're taking two things that don't belong to you—the other author's idea and the other author's exact words.

This is a problem because it's dishonest, because it's plagiarism, and because it's unprofessional.

How to Fix Unquoted Quotations

To fix this error, you have two options. First, if the words themselves are essential, you can show that you are quoting by placing quotation marks around the exact words you are using and then citing your source. In most cases, however, it's the ideas or information that matter more than the phrasing. When that's the case, your best option is to summarize the information or paraphrase the idea and then cite that correctly.

1. **Problem:**

Clutter is a problem in many people's households. The **best criterion for choosing what to keep and what to discard is whether it will make you happy, whether it will bring you joy**.

> You started with your own idea, but you then used **someone else's idea and words** without identifying the author or putting the words into a quotation. The words in the second sentence are from a best-selling book, *The Life-Changing Magic of Tidying Up* by Marie Kondo.

Solution 1:

Clutter is a problem in many people's households: "The best criterion for choosing what to keep and what to discard is whether it will make you happy, whether it will bring you joy" **(Kondo 42)**.

> The words are the same as before, but now you've noted the quotation and cited the **author** and **page number** with a parenthetical citation. The art of the research paper is using your sources honestly and displaying your own creativity and critical thinking in applying them.

Solution 2:

Clutter is a problem in many people's households. **In her best-selling book,** *The Life-Changing Magic of Tidying Up,* **Marie Kondo** has a solution for this problem that is radical—get rid of everything you don't love. She writes, "The best criterion for choosing what to keep and what to discard is whether it will make you happy, whether it will bring you joy" (42).

> This solution also credits the author but uses the **introductory signal phrase** to introduce her, helping the reader understand why Kondo is someone to listen to on this matter. The parenthetical citation at the end adds the page number of the quotation.

2. **Problem:**

However, the obsession with clearing up clutter can also lead to self-righteousness about clean spaces. **People suggest that learning to keep your surroundings in order and take responsibility for your messes is important to becoming a competent, socially mature adult. But there is no correlation between keeping a neat room and leading a functional, goal-oriented life**.

> You have a further point to make, that messiness isn't necessarily a bad thing, and you've found someone to help you make that point, but you use **her ideas** without giving her credit.

Solution:

However, this cultural obsession with clearing up clutter can also lead to self-righteousness about clean spaces. One tidy mother explored this issue in an essay in the *New York Times* because her daughter was a messy, creative girl, and she tried to figure out why this drove her crazy: "People suggest that learning to keep your surroundings in order and take responsibility for your messes is important to becoming a competent, socially mature adult" (Batalion). After much research, Batalion concludes that "there is no correlation between keeping a neat room and leading a functional, goal-oriented life."

Now you are giving credit where credit is due, and your paragraph is more interesting. Giving credit to a source does not make you look like you can't come up with ideas by yourself. It shows that you are playing in the world of ideas and giving credit to the other players you found to be on your team.

E. Patchwriting

Patchwriting is paraphrasing someone in a way that too closely mirrors the punctuation, vocabulary, and sentence structure of the original author. Rather than providing a precise restatement of the original idea, patchwriting uses most of the original wording, only swapping out a few words—the patches.

This isn't as big of a crime as unquoted quotations, which take 100 percent of the original author's words without given credit, but taking 80 or 90 percent of the original author's words without giving credit is still a Class C misdemeanor.

How to Fix Patchwriting

There are many ways to change the grammar and sentence structure of paraphrased material while maintaining the original meaning. Start by putting the core idea into your own, unique words. Then set aside the original and just explain that idea more clearly.

The real challenge is feeling confident enough in your own writing to do that without leaning so heavily on your outside sources. It's reasonable for you to feel shy about your abilities when you are new to this style of writing, but you have to get over that, and the only way to get over that is with practice. So suck it up. Do your own work. Pretty soon you'll feel good about it, too.

Even if you don't feel confident, the surest way to avoid patchwriting is to condense the original passage into a smaller summary of thought. If the passage is a paragraph long, make it a sentence. If it is two paragraphs, make it one paragraph. And then give credit where credit is due.

1. **Problem:**

   Obama: "Barack and I were raised with so many of the same **values: that you work hard for what you want in life; that your word is your bond and you do what you say** you're going to do; **that you treat people with** dignity and respect, even if you don't know them, and even if you don't agree with them."

   Trump: "From a young age, my parents impressed on me the <u>values that you work hard for what you want in life, that your word is your bond and you do what you say</u> and keep your promise, <u>that you treat people with respect</u>."

   Notice how close the sentence patterns and word clusters in Melania Trump's 2016 speech are to Michelle Obama's speech from 2008. This is patchwriting.

Solution:

<u>As Michelle Obama has said of her own upbringing,</u> from a young age, my parents impressed on me a strong work ethic, a sense of personal responsibility, and respect for others.

> These are the same common sentiments Trump was trying to express, but now they are clearly different from Obama's phrasing. The solution uses some alternate phrases ("work ethic" instead of "work hard for what you want") and condenses some similar ideas (like combining the ideas of keeping your word and following through on promises into "personal responsibility"). As a result, this version is not only distinctive from the original, it's also more concise. Still, it's best to <u>cite the source</u> to avoid any embarrassing claims of plagiarism.

F. Quote Bombs

A photo bomb is when a person jumps into a photo where he or she doesn't belong. Similarly, a quote bomb is when a quotation occurs in a paragraph where it doesn't belong. The quotation (or summary or paraphrase) is typically related to the topic in some way but doesn't support the central idea of the paragraph.

Seeing a stranger making a funny face at the camera in your precious family photos is distracting. Similarly, a quote bomb will distract from the specific idea the paragraph is attempting to express.

How to Fix Quote Bombs

It's hard to fix a photo bomb, but in writing, it's fairly easy to fix a quote bomb. The delete key leaves behind no trace of what came before. With copy and paste, you might even be able to relocate that quotation to somewhere more appropriate.

1. **Problem:**

    Running marathons requires hard work and a lifelong dedication. **"At times, Rio must have felt impossibly far away to Linden, but she maintained her confidence even at the beginning of what turned out to be a year away from racing"** <u>(Heald 37).</u> But with the right mindset, runners can overcome any obstacle and achieve their goals.

    > This **quotation**, from a 2016 *Runner's World* article by Oregon writer Michael Heald, is <u>cited</u>, which is nice, but why is it here? Who is "Linden" and what is "Rio," and what do either have to do with the hard work and right mindset of running marathons? No quote is an island. Either this quote doesn't belong here, or we need a better introduction to connect it to this passage.

Solution 1:

Running marathons requires hard work and a lifelong dedication. But with the right mindset, runners can overcome any obstacle and achieve their goals.

> Because this paragraph is simply making general statements, the Heald quotation is unnecessary. It's a nice enough quotation, but it's not directly tied to our purpose here, so we can cut it altogether. Problem solved.

Solution 2:

Running marathons requires hard work and a lifelong dedication, even through hard times like training delays and injuries. **This was the case for Olympic marathon runner Desiree Linden, who suffered an injury while training for the Rio Olympics.** In a profile of Linden in *Runner's World*, <u>Michael Heald</u> explains that "at times, Rio must have felt impossibly far away to Linden, but she maintained her confidence even at the beginning of what turned out to be a year away from racing" <u>(37)</u>. With this kind of determined mindset, runners like Linden can overcome any obstacle and achieve their goals.

> But perhaps our purpose is less general and more complex. Perhaps we're writing about the kinds of obstacles a runner might need to overcome with determination, and we need an example of that. The Heald quotation provides that, so we can use it if we connect it more directly to the idea at hand. In this version, we have not only provided **context** for the Heald quotation, we have also enriched the passage by adding more information regarding our own topic. Finally, as required by law, we've <u>cited</u> our source.

G. Incorrectly Using and Citing Images

When incorporating visual sources like charts, photographs, or tables into your writing, you must credit the author just like you would with a written source. This includes visual sources you manipulated or edited. After all, summaries and paraphrases are edited versions of original texts, and you give credit to the original author for those. Right? Right. The same thinking applies here.

In addition, you must properly label each of the images you include in your writing. This is true for each separate image but also for parts of the image that need to be identified in order for the image to make sense. Your reader can easily understand and keep track of your images like this.

1. Problem: chart with no legend or caption.

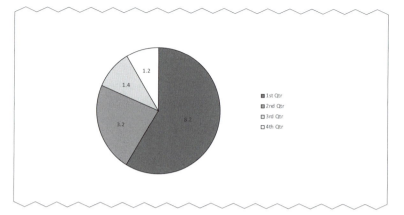

Look at this pie graph. It looks great, but what's it doing here? It's just plopped into your writing with no signals about what the graph is, what kind of data it represents, or where the data came from. That's a problem. Without a label or caption, this hunk of information is meaningless. Also, if you aren't responsible for the data this chart presents, you need to give credit to the person or people who are. Even if you created the chart yourself – and it really is a beautiful chart – you need to give the appropriate credit.

Solution 1: APA

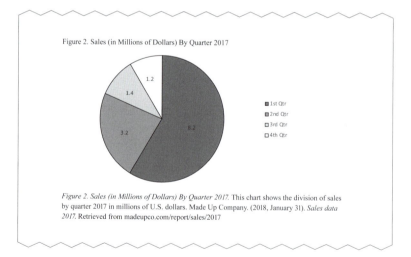

Figure 2. Sales (in Millions of Dollars) By Quarter 2017

Figure 2. Sales (in Millions of Dollars) By Quarter 2017. This chart shows the division of sales by quarter 2017 in millions of U.S. dollars. Made Up Company. (2018, January 31). *Sales data 2017.* Retrieved from madeupco.com/report/sales/2017

At the top of the chart, add a legend with the word "Figure" followed by its number and a period. Then, provide a brief description of the chart, capitalizing all major words. Follow the chart with a caption. It will begin with the label from the legend, italicized. Then, write a brief but sufficiently descriptive title. Finally, add any acknowledgments about the specific elements of your chart that come from other sources. Be sure to include all the information required by APA.

Solution 2: MLA

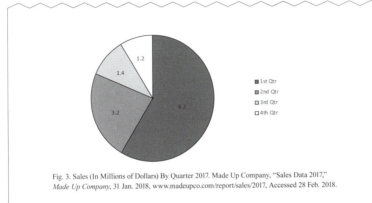

Fig. 3. Sales (In Millions of Dollars) By Quarter 2017. Made Up Company, "Sales Data 2017," *Made Up Company*, 31 Jan. 2018, www.madeupco.com/report/sales/2017, Accessed 28 Feb. 2018.

At the bottom of the chart, add a caption with the abbreviation "Fig." followed by its number and a period. Then, provide a brief description of the chart, capitalizing all major words. Finally, add any acknowledgments about the specific elements of your chart that come from other sources. Be sure to include all the information required by MLA. In this citation, use commas as you would for a typical citation, but substitute commas anywhere a period would be used to separate information. Maintain the capitalization as if it were a period. End your citation with a period.

2. **Problem: photo with no legend or caption**

> You found this image through a Google Image Search. You even cropped it and made it black and white, but unless you took the photo yourself, you have to give credit to the person who did. There's no label or caption on this one, either, so you'll need to add those, too.

Solution 1: APA

Figure 5. St. John's Bridge, Portland, Oregon

Figure 5. *St. Johns Bridge, Portland, Oregon.* Bridge showing suspension bridge architecture. Peterson Law Offices. (2015, April 27). *St. Johns Bridge.* Retrieved from flickr.com/photos/petersonlawoffices/32671542674/

> Notice that in APA, photos work the same as the pie chart. The same holds true for all figures: charts, graphs, maps, drawings, and photographs. Tables will work a little differently.

Solution 2: MLA

Fig. 6. View of St. Johns Bridge in Portland, Oregon, from Peterson Law Firm, *St. Johns Bridge*; Flickr, 27 Apr. 2015, flickr.com/photos/petersonlawoffices/32671542674/, Accessed 28 Feb. 2018.

In MLA, you need to add the abbreviation 'Fig.' and its number. After this, include a brief description of the image's contents, then the word "from," followed by a complete MLA citation. One difference between the citation in the caption and a Works Cited citation is that the caption doesn't invert the artist's first and last names. As with a chart, periods become commas to separate information, and you maintain the capitalization rules as if it were a period.

3. **Problem: table with no legend or caption**

Women	19–30 years old	2.5 cups
	31–50 years old	2.5 cups
	51+ years old	2 cups
Men	19–30 years old	3 cups
	31–50 years old	3 cups
	51+ years old	2.5 cups

No labels, again. You should see a pattern by now. Always label your images. The missing title and label is particularly confusing on this one, too. Cups of what? Whether you made the table from someone else's data or you are using a table someone else made, you still must give credit to the source.

Solution 1: APA

Table 2

Daily Recommend Vegetable Intake for Women and Men

Sex	Age	Amount
Women	19–30 years old	2.5 cups
	31–50 years old	2.5 cups
	51+ years old	2 cups
Men	19–30 years old	3 cups
	31–50 years old	3 cups
	51+ years old	2.5 cups

Note. From United States Department of Agriculture. (2018, January 3). *Choose My Plate.* Retrieved from www.choosemyplate.gov/vegetables

At the top of the table, add a legend with the word "Table" followed by its number. Then, on a new line, provide a brief description of the chart, capitalizing all major words. If you need to provide additional information about the table, add it below the table, beginning with the italicized word "*Note,*" followed by a period. Then provide any acknowledgments about the specific elements of your chart that come from other sources. Be sure to include all the information required by APA.

Solution 2: MLA

Table 2

Daily Recommend Vegetable Intake for Women and Men

Sex	Age	Amount
Women	19–30 years old	2.5 cups
	31–50 years old	2.5 cups
	51+ years old	2 cups
Men	19–30 years old	3 cups
	31–50 years old	3 cups
	51+ years old	2.5 cups

Source: United States Department of Agriculture, Choose My Plate, 3 Jan. 2018, www.choosemyplate.gov/vegetables, Accessed 28 Feb. 2018.

At the top of the table, add a legend with the word "Table" followed by its number. On the next line, provide a brief description of the chart, capitalizing all major words. Follow the table with a caption. It will begin with the word "Source" followed by a colon. Then provide a full MLA citation, substituting commas for periods. Maintain the capitalization as if it were a period. End your citation with a period.

MLA Style

The Modern Language Association (MLA) is a professional organization that supports disciplines in the humanities, including literature, art, music, philosophy, religion, and foreign languages. MLA style is a set of agreed-upon guidelines for scholars in these disciplines to follow when writing for classes or for publication. When we follow these guidelines, our readers can easily gather important reference information like who wrote something and on what pages, while remaining focused on the ideas in the writing.

Most of the MLA disciplines study visual or printed texts from throughout history, and MLA style reflects that focus. In the body of papers, MLA cites the author and page number from the text rather than the author and date of publication. That's because knowledge is considered timeless in the humanities. Therefore, when you talk about the ideas you cite in MLA, you use present-tense verbs. To the MLA scholar, the lioness forever "pounces" upon Chronos on page 69 of Jennifer Egan's *A Visit from the Goon Squad.* Furthermore, a scholar's interpretation of that pounce is as valid now as it would have been five years ago or as it will be five, ten, or even fifty years from now.

MLA style consists of three main categories—in-text citations, a list of work(s) cited, and paper formatting. In the body of the paper, you will cite outside sources with MLA-style in-text citations. At the end of your paper, you will add an MLA-style bibliography called a Works Cited page. The paper as a whole uses MLA-style formatting to set margins, line spacing, page numbering, and so on.

Think of MLA style as a filter. When your ideas pass through this filter, your paper will conform to MLA guidelines and emerge looking like every other MLA manuscript. The two things different about your paper will be the two most important ingredients—the idea you present and how you explain it to your readers.

1. In-Text Citations

In-text citations show readers that an idea belongs to someone other than the writer of the paper and usually show where that idea can be found within a source. They do so by providing readers with the last name of the source's author and, if available, the page number where the information or ideas came from.

The two places where you cite your sources in the text are in the introduction of that information and in a trailing parenthetical citation. The introduction might consist of an introductory statement or a signal phrase, and depending on the size of any direct quotations, some punctuation will also be involved.

It's typical to name the author of the work in this introduction, but you can also cite the author and page number in the introduction, or you can cite both in the parenthetical citation. The thing you can't do is cite the information more than once. If you put this information in the introduction, don't put the same information in the parenthetical citation.

A. Author in the Introduction

If you cite the author in your introduction, you do not also need to put the same information in the parenthetical citation.

1. **<u>Shamah</u> argues that it's not just one specific or even one type of out-of-school activity that matters:** "Out-of-school activities of all kinds appear to support the development of a sense of purpose" (56)**.**

   > The author's <u>last name</u> in the **introduction** tells us who the quoted idea belongs to. The number inside the parenthetical citation tells us which page of the journal this idea appears on. Notice that the **period** goes after the citation and not inside the quotation marks, even if the original quoted material used a period there.

2. **In his review of** *Mouse Guard: Winter 1152* **for** *PopMatters*, <u>Walter Biggins</u> **writes**, "Because a talking animal wearing human clothes is a ridiculous concept to begin with, most funny-animal comics tend toward exaggeration**.**"

> When there's no page number, as with online articles, you only need to report the author's <u>name</u>. If you do that in the **introduction**, you won't have a parenthetical citation. Notice that now the **period** is tucked inside the closing quotation marks.

3. Biggins writes that "most funny-animal comics tend toward exaggeration." <u>He</u> **goes on to demonstrate how this exaggeration can disarm readers.**

> The **second sentence** is another idea from Biggins that deserves citation, but you don't have to mention his name in the parenthetical because the <u>pronoun</u> "he" stands in for his name. As long as the pronoun is clear, it can stand in for the author's name when giving credit in in-text citations.

4. **As** <u>Shamah</u> **has shown**, there's a clear relationship between out-of-school activities and a student's sense of purpose (56).

> The same patterns apply to paraphrased material. If you name the <u>author</u> in an **introduction**, don't put that information in the parenthetical citation.

B. Author Absent from the Introduction

If you don't cite the author in an introduction, the last name must then be mentioned in the parenthetical citation.

1. It's not just one specific or even one type of out-of-school activity that matters: "Out-of-school activities of all kinds appear to support the development of a sense of purpose" (**Shamah** <u>56</u>).

> The **last name** and page number go inside the <u>parenthetical citation</u>. This information can be in the introduction or <u>parenthetical citation</u> but not both.

2. Most comic artists understand and maximize the conventions of their form: "Because a talking animal wearing human clothes is a ridiculous concept to begin with, most funny-animal comics tend toward exaggeration" (**Biggins**).

> When there's no page number to cite and the author is not named in the introduction, the author's **last name** is the only information in the <u>parenthetical citation</u>.

3. At least one expert claims that there's a clear relationship between out-of-school activities and a student's sense of purpose (**Shamah** <u>56</u>).

> And it's the same deal with citations of paraphrases or summaries. If you don't name the **author** in an introduction, then put the **last name** in the <u>parenthetical citation</u>.

C. More than One Work by an Author

If you use more than one work by a single author, the author's last name will no longer point to just one work on the Works Cited page. To distinguish which work you're citing, you must add the title to the parenthetical citation. Use the full title if it's a single noun phrase or shorter, and use an abbreviated title if it's longer than that.

1. In support of this position, **Shamah** asserts that out-of-school activities "appear to support the development of a sense of purpose" (<u>"Supporting" 56</u>).

   > The author's **last name** is in the introduction, so only the shortened title and page number appear in the <u>parenthetical citation</u>. Because this is a short work, the title is marked with quotation marks, but because the full title is kind of long, we only use a key word to identify it.

2. It's not just one specific or even one type of out-of-school activity that matters: "Out-of-school activities of all kinds appear to support the development of a sense of purpose" (**Shamah, "Supporting"** 56).

   > If you don't name the author in the introduction, the author's last name, a shortened title of the work, and a page number all go inside the <u>parenthetical citation</u>. Note that in this case, you need to separate the **name** and **title of the article** with a **comma**.

3. Most comic artists understand and maximize the conventions of their form: "Because a talking animal wearing human clothes is a ridiculous concept to begin with, most funny-animal comics tend toward exaggeration" (Biggins**, "Coffee Table Mice"**).

   > Because this is a short **title**, we put **the full title** inside the parentheses. The **comma** remains between the author and **title** even though there are no page numbers for this online work.

4. At least one expert claims that there's a clear relationship between out-of-school activities and a student's sense of purpose (Shamah, "Supporting" 56).

   Shamah claims that there's a clear relationship between out-of-school activities and a student's sense of purpose (<u>"Supporting" 56</u>).

   > And it works the same way with <u>citations</u> of paraphrases or summaries.

D. Authors with the Same Last Name

When you use works written by different authors who happen to have the same last name, use the first initial of the author to make it clear which of the works you're referring to on your works cited page.

1. <u>D</u>. **Shamah** claims that there's a clear relationship between out-of-school activities and a student's sense of purpose (56).

   It's not just one specific or even one type of out-of-school activity that matters: "Out-of-school activities of all kinds appear to support the development of a sense of purpose" (<u>D</u>. **Shamah** 56).

   > Whether it's in the introduction or the parenthetical citation, include the <u>first initial</u> with the **last name**. Of course, that only works if the other author with the same last name has a different first initial.

2. At least one expert claims that there's a clear relationship between out-of-school activities and a student's sense of purpose (<u>Devora</u> **Shamah** 56).

   > If the first initial is also shared with a different author in your Works Cited page, write out the author's entire <u>first name</u> and **last name**.

E. Two or More Authors

For citing multiple authors, follow the same basic rules that you use with one author. List the authors as they are listed in the original citation — not alphabetically. The first author listed is considered the primary author.

1. Growing up in a small town affords some important benefits to kids. <u>According to</u> **Shamah** <u>and</u> **MacTavish**, "The smallness and safety of rural communities promotes the development of place-based knowledge among the youth" (1).

   > The <u>introduction</u> maintains the original order of the authors' **names**.

2. Growing up in a small town affords some important benefits to kids: "The smallness and safety of rural communities promotes the development of place-based knowledge among the youth" (**Shamah** *and* **MacTavish** 1).

   > Note that the **last names** are separated with the *coordinating conjunction* "and" when there are two authors.

3. Things are not always as they seem: "On the surface of things, the place seems to be about as far from the history of race in America as one could get" (**Baldwin** et al. 250).

Baldwin et al. write that this city appears to be "about as far from the history of race in America as one could get" (250).

> With three or more authors, use the first author's name that is listed in the source. Follow the **name** with "et al.," a Latin phrase that means "and others."

4. George Orwell, never a healthy man, wrote his masterpiece *Nineteen Eighty-Four* in the last years of his short life while struggling with tuberculosis. Scholars suggest that the dark mood of the book is in part a reflection of the strain he was under while grappling with this terrible illness that ultimately led to his death (Symons xix; McCrum).

> When the same idea is conveyed by two different works, separate the two citations with a **semicolon** within a single set of parentheses. The lower case Roman numeral in the citation refers to an introductory page in the book. No page numbers are listed for the McCrum source because it's online.

F. Organization or Agency as Author

When the ideas you cite are found within official materials coming from an organization or government agency and are not attributed to a specific author, cite the organization or government agency as the author.

1. According to the **U.S. Census Bureau**, "The official poverty rate in 2006 was 12.3 percent, down from 12.6 percent in 2005."

The **U.S. Census Bureau** reported that the official poverty rate dropped by 0.3 percent between 2005 and 2006.

> The **name** of the government agency is cited in the introductory signal phrase just like an individual author would be cited.

2. The official poverty rate dropped by 0.3 percent between 2005 and 2006 (**U.S., Census Bureau**).

The economic recovery was starting to show results: "The official poverty rate in 2006 was 12.3 percent, down from 12.6 percent in 2005" (**U.S., Census Bureau**).

> When an organization or agency is not named in the introduction, put that **name** in the parenthetical citation. If this were a print source, the page number would follow the **name**. If the organization has multiple administrative units separated by commas, give all the names in the parenthetical citation.

G. Unknown Author

If you don't know the author of your source, and it isn't an organization or government agency, use the title of the work (if it's short) or a key word from the title (if it's not short) in your citation.

1. The original source material deserves a close examination. Grendel is described as a "brutish demon who lived in darkness" (***Beowulf*** 4).

   Grendel is described in ***Beowulf*** as a "brutish demon who lived in darkness" (4).

   > The author of the epic poem *Beowulf* is unknown, so we use the **title** of the work where the author would typically go in either the introduction or the parenthetical citation. Because this is a long work, the title is italicized.

2. Ten years ago, the City of Portland set in motion an ambitious plan to end homelessness in this city, but today there are even more homeless men, women, and children living in Portland (**"Crisis"**).

   As reported in "Crisis in Portland's Homeless Population," there are more homeless men, women, and children living in Portland than there were ten years ago—in spite of the city's ten-year plan to end homelessness.

   > Many newspaper articles are published without a named author. In these cases, use a **key word** from the title in place of the full title in the parenthetical citation. In an introduction, however, it's easier to understand if you use the full title of the article. Because this is a shorter work within a larger publication, the title is enclosed by quotation marks.

3. The instruction in the Bible to "Rejoice always, pray continually," is similar to instruction on meditation found in other sacred texts (*New International Version*, **1 Thess.** 5:16–17).

   > To cite a sacred text, put the book, chapter, and verse in a parenthetical citation. Abbreviate the **book name**, but don't italicize it like you would other books. The first time you cite a verse, make sure to include which translation of the sacred text you used. The *name of the translation* is italicized. Leave the translation out of future citations of the same text.

H. Indirect Citation

Within her article, Dr. Shamah cites an idea from a book by William Damon. If you want to cite the same idea from Damon that Dr. Shamah cites in her article, what do you do? You go to the library, of course, and get Damon's book. That's what you do. If it has one idea worth incorporating into your paper, it might have more and better ideas for you to consider.

However, if you don't have time to get that book or your library can't access it, you can use an indirect citation. Give credit in the introduction to the person who came up with the idea, and use the parenthetical citation to show readers that this came from within one of the works on your works cited page.

1. **Damon** <u>claims that</u> "finding one's place in the world is a developmental process that spans the life course" (qtd. in *Shamah* 45).

   > The **indirectly cited author** appears in the <u>introductory signal phrase</u> while *the author whose work you actually read* appears within the citation. Note that you must include the phrase "qtd. in" — quoted in — before the author's name in the citation.

2. <u>At least one expert claims that</u> "finding one's place in the world is a developmental process that spans the life course" (**Damon,** qtd. in *Shamah* 45).

   > If the **indirectly cited author** is not mentioned in the <u>introduction</u>, then both the **indirectly cited author** and the *author whose work you read* both go in the parenthetical citation. Note where the **comma** goes, too.

I. Block Quotations

Use block quotations for those rare occasions when you must quote more than three lines of poetry, more than four lines of prose, or dialogue between characters. You still need to introduce the quote in your own words, but the quotation is separated from your text by more space than you're used to.

1. Roy K. Humble argues for the use of note cards**:**

> If you're using note cards, you simply unleash their awesome, low-tech power. You lay the note cards on the dinette table and move them around. I know that doesn't sound like much, but trust me—it's awesome and powerful. Note cards allow you to visually arrange the evidence into its natural patterns**.** (97)

Despite the logic of the argument he presents, many students refuse to try the technique.

> Block quotations use formatting instead of quotation marks to show that this is a direct quotation. Typically, you should introduce a block quotation with a statement and a **colon**. Indent a block quote one half inch from the left margin. Unlike other in-text citations, the parenthetical citation sits just outside the **ending punctuation** of the block quotation. If the paragraph continues after the block quote, do not indent the sentence that follows the block quote. That shows readers that this enormous quotation is supporting information within a longer paragraph.

2. There are good reasons to use note cards while researching**:**

> If you're using note cards, you simply unleash their awesome, low-tech power. You lay the note cards on the dinette table and move them around. I know that doesn't sound like much, but trust me—it's awesome and powerful. Note cards allow you to visually arrange the evidence into its natural patterns**.** (**Humble** 97)

Despite the logic of this argument, however, many students refuse to try the technique.

> If you don't name the **author** in the introduction, then name the **author** in the parenthetical citation. But you know that by now.

2. List of Works Cited

The MLA list of works cited is a complete list of the works that are used—cited—in your paper. This list presents two important pieces of information:

- how the work was used in your paper
- how readers can find the work

With MLA style, you can document the same work in several different ways. This allows you to show how you use it in your paper. For example, if your writing addresses the differences in the translations of Pablo Neruda's poetry, you would list the translator in the author's place within the citation. If you're writing about the meaning of Pablo Neruda's poetry, you would list Neruda in the author's place.

The complete publication information also allows your readers to find any work that you used and study it themselves. MLA divides that publication information into three mandatory sections and one optional section, presented in this order:

A. Author

B. Title

C. Container (publication)

D. Other information

Because an MLA works cited citation is divided into its key elements, you build it by gathering and presenting the information that fits into each element. MLA style then guides you in how to format the variations that occur within each.

A. Author

The author is the person or people or organization responsible for creating the source. This is the first piece of information you must find to build your citation.

With books, the author's name is usually on the spine. Magazines, newspapers, and journals typically put the author's name near the title of the article. However, the name may also appear at the end of short articles. If the source is a corporate or governmental publication and a specific author is not given, the organization itself is usually the author.

One Author

1. **McCloud, Scott.** *The Sculptor*. First Second Books, 2015.

   | List the author's **last name** first, followed by a **comma** and then the author's first name. End the author section with a **period**.

2. **Williams, John Sibley.** *Controlled Hallucinations*. FutureCycle Press, 2013.

   | Include the middle name or middle initial if it is listed in the original text.

3. **Churchill, Winston.** *Triumph and Tragedy*. Houghton Mifflin, 1953.

   | That's *Sir* Winston Churchill to you and me, but in a citation, don't include titles like "Sir," "PhD," "M.S.W.," "King," "Saint," or "Dr."

Two Authors

1. **Ede, Lisa, and Andrea A. Lunsford.** *Writing Together: Collaboration in Theory and Practice*. Bedford/St. Martin's, 2012.

   | Use a **comma** and the **conjunction** "and" between the authors' names. Note that the second author's name is written with the first name followed by the last name. Always list the authors in the order they appear in the text, not alphabetically, because libraries list authors this way, and readers who want to find the work may not be able to if you don't list them the same way.

Three or More Authors

1. **Murray, Robin M., et al.** *The Epidemiology of Schizophrenia*. Cambridge UP, 2002.

   | When there are three or more authors for a text, list the first author listed in the source. Follow the name with a **comma** and "et al.," a Latin phrase that means "and others."

Organizational or Governmental Author

Business and professional documents are often considered a work product and property of the company rather than that of the poor, nameless authors who work for that organization. In that case, list the organization as the author.

1. **United States, Census Bureau.** *Strength in Numbers: Your Guide to 2010 Census Redistricting Data from the U.S. Census Bureau*. U.S. Dept. of Commerce, Economics and Statistics Administration, U.S. Census Bureau, 2010.

   | When citing a source by a government agency as the author, begin with the name of the government followed by a **comma** and then the name of the agency.

2. ***Insure Your Next Trip with Travel Guard.*** Travel Guard, 2016.

   | When a corporate author is both the author and the publisher, omit the author and go straight to the title.

Screen Name

Many online authors write under a screen name. You don't have to go searching for the author's secret (true) identity. You can use the screen name.

1. **chewingofthecud.** "What Currents or Movements Are Currently Happening in Literature?" *Reddit*, 2014, www.reddit.com/r/literature/comments/20by05/ what_currents_or_movements_are_currently.

> Simply list the screen name in the author's place. You can also see in this example the importance of choosing a good screen name.

No Author

If no author is listed for the text, skip the author's place and begin the citation with the information for the next element — the title of the source. Do not use the word "Anonymous" in place of the author.

1. **The Qur'an.** Oxford World's Classics Edition, edited by M. A. S. Abdel Haleem, Oxford UP, 2005.

> If there's no author listed for the text, as is common in ancient texts, skip the author's place and begin the citation with the information for the next element — the title.

2. "**Facetious.**" *Vocabulary.com*, 2016, www.vocabulary.com/dictionary/facetious.

> Do not cite the editor of a reference work unless the specific entry is signed by an author. Most won't be. Instead, begin with the title, which in this case is the word you looked up.

Other Contributors

Sometimes the person or organization most important to your use of a work is someone other than an author. Some terms you are likely to use in your documentation are "performer," "director," "editor(s)," and "translator."

1. **Bevington, David, and David Scott Kastan, <u>editors</u>.** *Macbeth*. By William Shakespeare, Bantam, 2005.

> A discussion of *Macbeth* where the emphasis isn't on the play itself but rather the specific edited collection in which it appears — such as this work's essay about Shakespeare film adaptations included after the main text — would require listing the <u>editors</u> in the author's place in the citation.

2. **Low, Amanda Kissin, <u>producer</u>, and Bob O'Brien, <u>writer</u> and <u>reporter</u>.** *The Hoboken Sound*. Metromedia Telecenter, 1985. www.youtube.com/watch?v=clNuALHa_6E.

> Only list the most important contributors in the author's place and note their roles in the work by following their names with **a comma** and <u>a description of their contribution</u>.

B. Title

The second key section in an MLA citation is the title of the work. MLA style requires you to format the title to distinguish between larger and smaller works. MLA also requires you to capitalize the first word, the last word, and all nouns, pronouns, verbs, adjectives, adverbs, and subordinating conjunctions in the title. Note that when you have compound words joined with a hyphen, both words are capitalized. What you won't capitalize are articles, prepositions, coordinating conjunctions, or the "to" of an infinitive (as in "to walk" or "to run") whenever any of these types of words fall in the middle of the title.

Look for the title of the source near the author's name, usually at the beginning of the work.

Larger Works

MLA uses formatting to quickly indicate whether the title of the source is a larger, self-contained work or a smaller work within a larger one. Larger works include books, anthologies, magazines, newspapers, websites, book-length poems, movies, and so on. Italicize the titles of these larger works.

1. Georges, Nicole J. *Calling Dr. Laura.* Houghton Mifflin Harcourt, 2013.

    This is a full-length book, so the title is italicized. Put a **period** at the end of this section.

2. *The Walking Dead.* Created by Frank Darabont, performance by Andrew Lincoln, American Movie Classics, 2010–2016.

    This television series is a larger work that contains episodes within it. Because it has no single author, we leave the author section blank.

3. Bartow, Rick. *After the Fall III.* Paint on clay, 1975, Portland Art Museum, Portland, OR.

    MLA considers works of art to be larger works, even if they aren't physically large.

4. Roemmele, Jacqueline A., and Donna Batdorff. *Surviving the "Flesh-Eating Bacteria": Understanding, Preventing, Treating, and Living with the Effects of Necrotizing Fasciitis.* Avery, 2001.

    Put a **colon** between the main title and a subtitle. With larger works, both remain italicized. If the title contains words within quotation marks, those words are also italicized.

5. Bishop, Kyle W. *American Zombie Gothic: The Rise and Fall (and Rise) of* The Walking Dead *in Popular Culture.* McFarland, 2010.

    In this unusual example, however, there is a **television series title;** within the book title that must be *de*-italicized to distinguish it from the rest of the book's title. If a part of the larger work's title would normally be italicized, then you must de-italicize it within the italics of the rest of the title.

Smaller Works (within a Larger Work)

Mark titles with quotation marks when the work is nested within a larger work. For example, for articles within newspapers, journals, or reference books, the article titles go inside quotation marks. You'll also use quotation marks for short stories and essays in an anthology, short poems within a collection, episodes within a television series, songs within an album, pages within a website, and so on.

1. Toobin, Jeffrey. **"Our Broken Constitution."** *The New Yorker*, 9 Dec. 2013, pp. 64–73.

   A magazine article is a shorter work that's nested inside a larger publication, so it's marked by **quotation marks** rather than italics. Notice that the **period** after this part of the citation slips inside those **quotation marks**.

2. Mahoney, Phillip. **"Gray Is the New Black: Race, Class, and Zombies."** *Generation Zombie: Essays on the Living Dead in Modern Culture*, edited by Stephanie Boluk and Wylie Lenz, McFarland, 2011, pp. 55–72.

   The Mahoney article appears within a larger collection of essays, so its title also appears within quotation marks.

3. Tuchman, Barbara. **"Ch. 19: Retreat."** *The Guns of August*, Macmillan, 1962, pp. 341–372.

   Chapters or other sections within a book are considered shorter works, even if they are quite long. This one isn't so bad, but some chapters really go on forever.

4. Mayo Clinic Staff. **"Gallstones-Definition."** *Mayo Clinic*, Mayo Foundation for Medical Education and Research, 25 July 2013, www.mayoclinic.org/diseases-conditions/gallstones/basics/definition/con-20020461.

   Web pages are shorter works within websites.

5. Miller, Elise. **"The 'Maw of Western Culture': James Baldwin and the Anxieties of Influence."** *African American Review*, vol. 38, no. 4, Winter 2004, pp. 625–636.

   When quotation marks appear within the title of a shorter work, the inner quotation marks are **single quotation marks**. With shorter works, you also put a **colon** between the main title and any subtitle.

6. Kenny, Glenn. **"A Perfect Day."** **Review of** *A Perfect Day*, **directed by Fernando Leon de Aranoa.** *Rogerebert.com*, Ebert Digital, 15 Jan. 2016, www.rogerebert.com/reviews/a-perfect-day-2016.

   When the work is a review of another work, add **a note** that includes "Review of" and the name of the work being reviewed. Follow that with a **comma** and then the person or people responsible for the work.

C. Container (Publication)

The third and most complex section of an MLA citation is the one that captures publication information about the source. The MLA calls this section a container, but you can also think of it as the publication, which is usually the case.

The container will include information about some or all of the following subcategories of information, separated by a comma, and always in this order:

1. Title of publication

2. Other contributors

3. Version

4. Number

5. Publisher

6. Publication date

7. Location

Not every source has information for each of the subsections in this list—in fact, most don't. For example, a book by a single author probably won't have "other contributors" to recognize. A periodical does not typically come in "versions" but in volumes and issues, two variations that fit in the "number" subsection. When a work does not contain information for one of the subsections, move on to the next subsection. Once you're done, place a period at the end of this section to show readers that your publication information is complete.

We'll show you how this works with different types of works.

1. Title of Publication

For larger works, the title of the work and the title of the publication are the same thing, so that title goes in section for the title of the work.

1. Boluk, Stephanie, and Wylie Lenz, editors. *Generation Zombie: Essays on the Living Dead in Modern Culture*. McFarland, 2011.

    Because the citation focuses on the book as a whole, there's nothing to put in the title of publication slot. That's okay. Move along.

2. Mahoney, Phillip. "Gray Is the New Black: Race, Class, and Zombies." ***Generation Zombie: Essays on the Living Dead in Modern Culture,*** edited by Stephanie Boluk and Wylie Lenz, McFarland, 2011, pp. 55–72.

    However, in this second example, the citation focuses on the Mahoney article within the larger work. Now the article title goes in the title-of-work section, and the title of the larger work goes in this publication section. Add a **comma** after the title of the larger work.

3. Rockmore, Ellen Bresler. "How Texas Teaches History." *The New York Times,* 12 Oct. 2015, www.nytimes.com/2015/10/22/opinion/how-texas-teaches-history.html.

> With articles in periodicals, the title of the publication is typically the name of the journal, magazine, or newspaper.

4. Mayo Clinic Staff. "Gallstones-Definition." *Mayo Clinic,* Mayo Foundation for Medical Education and Research, 25 July 2013, www.mayoclinic.org/diseases-conditions/gallstones/basics/definition/con-20020461.

> When the focus of the source is on one page of a website, the name of the website goes into the title-of-publication place.

5. "Agrippina (Agrippina the Younger)." *Encyclopedia of World Crime,* edited by Jay Robert Nash, CrimeBooks, Inc., 1989, pp. 39–40.

> With reference works, the title of publication is the title of the book or website.

6. Silence. "War Drums." *The Deafening Sound of Absolutely Nothing,* Profane Existence, 2016.

> When citing a song, the song title goes in the first title section and the name of the album or collection goes in this slot as the title of the publication.

2. Other Contributors

Other contributors are people who play important roles in creating the publication but are secondary to the named author of the work. These contributors are identified by their role in the publication with terms such as "directed by" or by a title such as "editor," followed by a comma.

You'll find the names of other contributors on title pages or other places where credit is given to collaborators, like the credits of a film or the liner notes of an album. Only bring in the additional contributors whose work is directly applicable to the topic of your writing.

1. Shakespeare, William. *Macbeth.* **Edited by David Bevington and David Scott Kastan,** Bantam, 2005.

> Name the <u>role</u> of the other contributor(s) first. Then list the contributors by first name and then last name. End with a comma to show that while this slot is over, the publication container continues. In this example, listing the editors helps your reader tell which version of *Macbeth* you used, since editors sometimes change minor words and punctuation in Shakespeare's plays.

2. LaTour, Jason. "Greater Power Part Four." *Spider-Gwen,* **<u>penciled and inked by</u> Robbi Rodriguez, <u>colored by</u> Rico Renzi,** no. 4, Marvel, 2015.

> With works that involve multiple contributors, list each and his or her <u>role</u>, separating each with a **comma**. Combine <u>roles</u> when they are performed by the same person.

3. Version

Works often have multiple versions or editions that are identified by numbers that tell you how many times the publication has been revised — 2nd edition, for example — or names that tell you the nature of the revision — like "unabridged" or "expanded."

When they exist, version numbers or names can usually be found next to the title of the publication.

1. Rottenberg, Annette T., and Donna Haisty Winchell. *The Structure of Argument*. **8th ed.,** Bedford/St. Martin's, 2015.

   Use numbers rather than full words with numbered editions. Do not use superscript endings.

2. *The Bible*. **New International Version,** Zondervan, 1984.

   Write out any named editions in full.

4. Number

Books that are too long to be published in a single volume are often split into multiple volumes, and each is given its own volume number. In addition, periodicals that are published on an ongoing basis — as is the case with most scholarly journals — are assigned volume, issue, or volume *and* issue numbers to distinguish one publication of the periodical from another.

The number is typically found near the title of the publication. However, it may be found within the publication on a page with more information about the publication, contributors, and so on.

1. Conan Doyle, Arthur. *Sherlock Holmes: The Complete Novels and Stories*. **Vol. 1,** Bantam Classics, 1986.

   "Vol." is an abbreviation for "volume" and should precede the volume number. Use the numeral rather than the word. Note that the first letter of "Vol." is capitalized only when it appears after a **period** in the citation.

2. Coates, Ta-Nehisi. "The Case for Reparations." *The Atlantic,* **vol. 313, no. 5,** June 2014, pp. 54-71.

   If a periodical has both volume number and issue number, mention the volume number first, followed by the issue number. "No." is an abbreviation for "number" and should come before the issue number. Note that "vol." and "no." are lowercase because they each follow a **comma**.

3. Sheffield, Rob. "Getting to Know Colbert." *Rolling Stone,* **no. 1295,** p. 30.

   If there's no volume number, mention the issue number only.

5. Publisher

The publisher is the company or person who actually produced a book, government report, film, website, or other works. Film and television series generally involve multiple publishers. In that case, cite the publisher that is primarily responsible for the work. Periodicals do not usually have a publisher, in which case you can skip this section.

With works of art, the medium is considered the publisher. Just as a print publisher helps to bring a book into existence, so too do the acrylic paints, clay, or metal play a role in bringing the artistic vision into being. It's a stretch, we know. Just work with us, okay?

With a book, you can find the name of the publisher on the title page or on a page near the front of the book that provides more information about the publication and its copyright. On pamphlets, look on the back or the innermost leaf of the folded paper. On brochures, look at the front or back covers. A website will usually list the publisher at the bottom of the page in the footer or on its version of the "About" page.

1. McCloud, Scott. *The Sculptor*. **First Second Books,** 2015.

   For books, list the name of the publishing company. In previous versions of MLA, you also listed the city in which the publisher is or was located. That information is now optional and is only included when it avoids confusion.

2. Engber, Daniel. "The Neurologist Who Hacked His Brain—And Almost Lost His Mind." *Wired*, **Condé Nast,** 26 Jan. 2016, www.wired.com/2016/01/phil-kennedy-mind-control-computer.

   Condé Nast publishes many magazines and websites, including *Wired*. When the publisher of a periodical or online magazine is listed, you can include that information here. If the publisher or publication shares the same name as the website, however, do not include the name.

3. "Frank Lisciandro." *The Writing Life*, produced by Stephen Long, **McMinnville Community Media,** 21 Mar. 2016.

   With television broadcasts, films, and albums, the publisher is the company or organization that paid for the creation of the work.

4. Siler, Buzz. *Lena (D)*. **Acrylic and oil on canvas,** 2011, Siler Gallery, Portland, OR.

   In a work of art, insert the name of the medium itself in the place of the publisher.

6. Publication Date

The publication date is the specific date the work was published. A book is published once and therefore only features the year. A periodical is published regularly throughout the year, so its publication date identifies which part of the year it was published in. A monthly magazine notes the month and year. A daily newspaper lists the day, month, and year.

The location of the publication date varies from publication to publication. In a book, the date should be on the title page or copyright page. The date of articles that appear in periodicals will often appear next to the byline and title of the source. This applies to online articles as well, but if a date is missing, you can also search the bottom of the web page for a publication year to stand in for something more precise. Finally, use the last modified date rather than the original publication date when possible due to the ever-changing nature of web content.

1. Federoff, Nina, and John Block. "Mosquito vs. Mosquito." *The New York Times*, **6 Apr. 2016,** p. A23.

   The most common format is day and month followed by the year because so many works come out on a specific day. Note that the month is abbreviated.

2. Barone, Richard. "The Power of Song: Recording Pete Seeger." *Tape Op*, no. 113, **May–June 2016**.

   Bimonthly publications will often use a month range followed by a **year**. Only the names of May, June, and July are written out in full. The rest use three-letter abbreviations. Use an en dash (–, usually option-hyphen or alt-hyphen) to separate a range of dates.

You may use the abbreviation "n.d." for no date, but do not use it lightly. It is rare that a publication date is truly not included in a print source. In web sources, the date can be difficult to find, but it almost always exists in the web page's HTML code. Most web browsers will allow you to search the HTML code, but that may take some work. Ask for help.

7. Location

The location varies by the type of work. For shorter works within anthologies or periodicals, the location is usually a page number or a range of pages. Film and music locations might be physical discs or their digital equivalent. The location for a work of art is often the place where the piece is on exhibit. For online sources, the location is a web address (URL) or DOI. Because of the possibilities here, your main task is to be as precise as possible.

1. Behar, Evelyn, et al. "Concreteness of Positive, Negative, and Neutral Repetitive Thinking about the Future." *Behavior Therapy*, vol. 43, no. 2, 1998, **pp. 300–312**.

   For more than one continuous page, put "pp." before the page range. Use an en dash (–, usually option-hyphen or alt-hyphen) to separate a range of pages.

2. "OSU Women Try to Keep a Storied Season Going." *The Oregonian*, 2 Apr. 2016, **p. A1**.

   If a work appears on only one page, put just the letter "p" and a period before the page numbers. Some page numbers, especially in print newspapers, include **letters** before the number to show in which section the page is located.

3. Erlanger, Steven, et al. "Airing of Hidden Wealth Stirs Inquiries and Rage: Iceland Premier Steps Down as Release of Files Reverberates around World." *The New York Times*, 6 Apr. 2016, **pp. A1+**.

   For a multipage work that appears on nonconsecutive pages, list the first page number and a plus sign.

4. Bartow, Rick. *After the Fall III*. Paint on clay, 1975, **Portland Art Museum, Portland, OR**.

   For items that appear in physical locations, name the place where the work is housed and sufficient distinguishing details like city, state, or country.

5. Grosvenor, Emily. "The Dude Abides in Salem." *Desperately Seeking Salem*, 8 Aug. 2010, **desperatelyseekingsalem.wordpress.com/2010/08/08/the-dude-abides-in-salem/**.

   For online works, include a **URL** if it will reliably and consistently allow a reader to navigate to the cited page. Avoid using one-time URLs generated for a specific browsing session. They get way too long. Do not include the "http://" part, either, with MLA style.

6. Aagaard, Jesper. "Media Multitasking, Attention, and Distraction: A Critical Discussion." *Phenomenology and the Cognitive Sciences*, vol. 14, no. 4, Dec. 2015, p. 885, **doi:10.1007/s11097-014- 9375-x**.

   DOIs (digital object identifiers) are more reliable than URLs and should be used when available. You will usually find the DOI for an electronic article listed on the article's first page or the database landing page for the article.

D. Other Information

In addition to the first three mandatory sections of a works cited citation, MLA style also provides a fourth section to include additional information that will usually show readers more detail about where the source is located or clear up possible confusion.

Second Container (Publication)

This section allows you to provide readers with information about a second publisher when a publication is republished in another book or online or in a library database.

Library databases are a good example of a second publication container. They republish millions of articles that were first published in newspapers, academic journals, and reference works. Streaming services like Spotify and Netflix also provide access to music and film, respectively. Google Books provides access to books online.

The second publication container is usually easy to spot because this is probably where you found the work. In fact, sometimes the harder task is to find out who the first publisher is. If you aren't looking at the actual work itself—you aren't holding a printed book or article in your hands, for example—then what you have is probably something that has been republished for easier access.

1. Kerr, William R., et al. "Entrepreneurship as Experimentation." *The Journal of Economic Perspectives*, vol. 28, no. 3, 2014, pp. 25–48. **JSTOR**, www.jstor.org/stable/23800574. Accessed 10 Feb. 2016.

   This article was accessed via an academic database. The *URL* works as a second location for the source in this container. Note that the name of the **second publisher** is italicized.

2. Twain, Mark. *Life on the Mississippi.* Harper, 1917. ***Google Books***, **books.google.com/books?id=h99O07cNtEMC**.

   With many books now available online, it's helpful to show readers who has republished them and where they're located.

3. Mould, Bob. "Dreaming, I Am." *Workbook.* Virgin Records America, 1989. *Spotify,* **play.spotify.com/track/2SmknAMU59qMW6LwpPw3cL.**

   Here, the *name* of streaming music service is the second container, and the URL is the location.

Date of Access

Information on a website can change at any time. Date of access documents the precise day and time the person citing the source accessed it.

> Adams, Sarah. "Be Cool to the Pizza Dude." *This I Believe,* hosted by Jay Allison, This I Believe, 29 Dec. 2015, cdn.audiometric.io/9487820912.mp3. **Accessed 29 Feb. 2016**.

> At the end of the citation, write "Accessed" and then the date of access. Use the same day, month, year format used in the publication section.

This information only relates to sources accessed online. MLA considers this information optional, so defer to your professor as to whether or not you should include it in your citation.

City of Publication

The city of publication is the name of the place where the publisher is located. It is traditionally located just before the name of the publisher, which is where it goes in the citation as well. This information matters increasingly less to modern scholars and is not required in the newest edition of the *MLA Handbook*. It should only be included when your professor requires it.

1. Ede, Lisa, and Andrea A. Lunsford. *Writing Together: Collaboration in Theory and Practice.* **Boston,** Bedford/St. Martin's, 2012.

> If you choose to include it, the city of publication precedes the publisher and is separated from the publisher by a **comma**.

2. Humble, Roy K. *The Humble Argument.* **Dallas, OR,** Problem Child, 2010.

> Only include the state if failing to do so would cause confusion. Here, the state distinguishes the modest town of Dallas in Oregon from the less modest city in Texas.

E. Putting It All Together

The table below shows you how to put the pieces of information about a work into the right order for the citation. You start with the author and just keep working your way down the list. Once you've identified which information goes where, you compile it into an entry on your Works Cited page.

Information	Example 1	Example 2	Example 3
A. Author.		Kerr, William R., et al.	Russell, Mark.
B. Title.	"Facetious."	"Entrepreneurship as Experimentation."	*Prez.*
C. Container (Publication)			
1. Title of publication,	*Vocabulary.com,*	*The Journal of Economic Perspectives,*	
2. Other contributors,			Illustrated by Ben Caldwell,
3. Version,			
4. Number,		vol. 28, no. 3,	no. 5,
5. Publisher,			DC,
6. Publication date,		2014,	Oct. 2014.
7. Location.	www.vocabulary.com/dictionary/facetious.	pp. 25–48.	
D. Other Information			
Second container, location.		*JSTOR,* www.jstor.org/stable/23800574.	
Date of access.		Accessed 10 Feb. 2016.	

These are the citations that you then put on your Works Cited page:

"Facetious." *Vocabulary.com,* www.vocabulary.com/dictionary/facetious.

Kerr, William R., et al. "Entrepreneurship as Experimentation." *The Journal of Economic Perspectives,* vol. 28, no. 3, 2014, pp. 25–48. *JSTOR,* www.jstor.org/stable/23800574. Accessed 10 Feb. 2016.

Russell, Mark. *Prez.* Illustrated by Ben Caldwell, no. 5, DC, Oct. 2014.

F. Works Cited Examples

As you see from the past section, MLA style divides citation information into four main sections:

A. Author

B. Title

C. Container (usually a publisher)

D. Other (often including second container)

In each of the examples that follow, we'll show you a complete and formatted sample citation, followed by a breakdown of each section in the citation from the above list.

Even though these are common examples, you still have to adapt them to fit the information about the works you're using. You may have to tinker with the author section or the container section to accurately capture the information about a given work.

But that's a good thing. It means that you can build each citation to match the work instead of having to somehow tailor the information about a work to match a template that doesn't really fit.

Books

One Author

Georges, Nicole J. *Calling Dr. Laura*. Houghton Mifflin Harcourt, 2013.

> Author: Georges, Nicole J.
> Title: *Calling Dr. Laura*.
> Container: Houghton Mifflin Harcourt, 2013.
> Other: —

Edition Other Than the First

Rottenberg, Annette T., and Donna Haisty Winchell. *The Structure of Argument*. 8th ed., Bedford/St. Martin's, 2015.

> Author: Rottenberg, Annette T., and Donna Haisty Winchell.
> Title: *The Structure of Argument*.
> Container: 8th ed., Bedford/St. Martin's, 2015.
> Other: —

MLA

Edited Collection

Boluk, Stephanie, and Wylie Lenz, editors. *Generation Zombie: Essays on the Living Dead in Modern Culture.* McFarland, 2011.

> Author: Boluk, Stephanie, and Wylie Lenz, editors.
> Title: *Generation Zombie: Essays on the Living Dead in Modern Culture.*
> Container: McFarland, 2011.
> Other: —

Online Book

Twain, Mark. *Life on the Mississippi.* Harper, 1917. *Google Books*, books.google.com/books?id=h99O07cNtEMC.

> Author: Twain, Mark.
> Title: *Life on the Mississippi.*
> Container: Harper, 1917.
> Other: *Google Books*, books.google.com/books?id=h99O07cNtEMC.

Sacred Text

New International Version. Zondervan, 1984.

> Author: —
> Title: *New International Version.*
> Container: Zondervan, 1984.
> Other: —

Comic Book

LaTour, Jason. "Greater Power Part Four." *Spider-Gwen,* penciled and inked by Robbi Rodriguez, colored by Rico Renzi, no. 4, Marvel, 2015.

> Author: LaTour, Jason.
> Title: "Greater Power Part Four."
> Container: *Spider-Gwen*, penciled and inked by Robbi Rodriguez, colored by Robbi Rodriguez, colored by Rico Renzi, no. 4, Marvel, 2015.
> Other: —

Parts of a Book

Chapter of a Book

Tuchman, Barbara. "Ch. 19: Retreat." *The Guns of August*, Macmillan, 1962, pp. 341–372.

> Author: Tuchman, Barbara.
> Title: "Ch. 19: Retreat."
> Container: *The Guns of August*, Macmillan, 1962, pp. 341–372.
> Other: —

Work in an Anthology

Mahoney, Phillip. "Gray Is the New Black: Race, Class, and Zombies." *Generation Zombie: Essays on the Living Dead in Modern Culture*, edited by Stephanie Boluk and Wylie Lenz, McFarland, 2011, pp. 55–72.

> Author: Mahoney, Phillip.
> Title: "Gray is the New Black: Race, Class, and Zombies."
> Container: *Generation Zombie: Essays on the Living Dead in Modern Culture*, edited by Stephanie Boluk and Wylie Lenz, McFarland, 2011, pp. 55–72.
> Other: —

Article in a Reference Book (Print)

"Agrippina (Agrippina the Younger)." *Encyclopedia of World Crime*, edited by Jay Robert Nash, CrimeBooks, Inc., 1989, pp. 39–40.

> Author: —
> Title: "Agrippina (Agrippina the Younger)."
> Container: *Encyclopedia of World Crime*, edited by Jay Robert Nash, CrimeBooks, Inc., 1989, pp. 39–40.
> Other: —

Article in a Reference Book (Library Database)

"Iūlia Agrippīna, 'Agrippina the Younger'." *Oxford Dictionary of the Classical World*, edited by John Roberts, Oxford University Press, 2007. *Oxford Reference*. Accessed 30 July 2016.

> Author: —
> Title: "Iūlia Agrippīna, 'Agrippina the Younger'."
> Container: *Oxford Dictionary of the Classical World*, edited by John Roberts, Oxford University Press, 2007.
> Other: *Oxford Reference*. Accessed 30 July 2016.

Articles

Journal Article (Print)

Racy, A. J. "Domesticating Otherness: The Snake Charmer in American
Popular Culture." *Ethnomusicology*, vol. 60, no. 2, Spring/Summer 2016, pp.
197–232.

> Author: Racy, A. J.
> Title: "Domesticating Otherness: The Snake Charmer in American Popular
> Culture."
> Container: *Ethnomusicology*, vol. 60, no. 2, Spring/Summer 2016, pp. 197–232.
> Other: —

Journal Article (Library Database)

Racy, A. J. "Domesticating Otherness: The Snake Charmer in American
Popular Culture." *Ethnomusicology*, vol. 60, no. 2, Spring/Summer 2016, pp.
197–232. *JSTOR*, www.jstor.org/stable/10.5406/ethnomusicology.60.2.0197.

> Author: Racy, A. J.
> Title: "Domesticating Otherness: The Snake Charmer in American Popular
> Culture."
> Container: *Ethnomusicology*, vol. 60, no. 2, Spring/Summer 2016, pp. 197–232.
> Other: *JSTOR*, www.jstor.org/stable/10.5406/ethnomusicology.60.2.0197.

Magazine Article (Print)

Coates, Ta-Nehisi. "The Case for Reparations." *The Atlantic*, vol. 313, no. 5, June
2014, pp. 54–71.

> Author: Coates, Ta-Nehisi.
> Title: "The Case for Reparations."
> Container: *The Atlantic*, vol. 313, no. 5, June 2014, pp. 54–71.
> Other: —

Magazine Article (Website)

Engber, Daniel. "The Neurologist Who Hacked His Brain—And Almost Lost
His Mind." *Wired*, Condé Nast, 26 Jan. 2016, www.wired.com/2016/01/
phil-kennedy-mind-control-computer.

> Author: Engber, Daniel.
> Title: "The Neurologist Who Hacked His Brain—And Almost Lost His Mind."
> Container: *Wired*, Condé Nast, 26 Jan. 2016, www.wired.com/2016/01/
> phil-kennedy-mind-control-computer.
> Other: —

Magazine Article (Library Database)

Koster, John. "Hating the 'Hun' at Home: When America Went to War against the Kaiser, German-Americans Caught Hell." *American History*, vol. 51, no. 3, 2016, pp. 58+. *General OneFile*. Accessed 30 July 2016.

> Author: Koster, John.
> Title: "Hating the 'Hun' at Home: When America Went to War against the Kaiser, German-Americans Caught Hell."
> Container: *American History*, vol. 51, no. 3, 2016, pp. 58+.
> Other: *General OneFile*. Accessed 30 July 2016.

Newspaper Article (Print)

Erlanger, Steven, et al. "Airing of Hidden Wealth Stirs Inquiries and Rage: Iceland Premier Steps Down as Release of Files Reverberates around World." *The New York Times*, 6 Apr. 2016, pp. A1+.

> Author: Erlanger, Steven, et al.
> Title: "Airing of Hidden Wealth Stirs Inquiries and Rage: Iceland Premier Steps Down as Release of Files Reverberates Around World."
> Container: *The New York Times*, 6 Apr. 2016, pp. A1+.
> Other: —

Newspaper Article (Website)

Rockmore, Ellen Bresler. "How Texas Teaches History." *The New York Times*, 12 Oct. 2015, www.nytimes.com/2015/10/22/opinion/how-texas-teaches-history.html.

> Author: Rockmore, Ellen Bresler.
> Title: "How Texas Teaches History."
> Container: *The New York Times*, 12 Oct. 2015, www.nytimes.com/2015/10/22/opinion/how-texas-teaches-history.html.
> Other: —

Newspaper Article (Library Database)

Rector, Kevin. "Hope and Politics Collide at March." *The Baltimore Sun*, first edition, 25 Apr. 2016, pp. A1+. *LexisNexis Academic*. Accessed 30 May 2016.

> Author: Rector, Kevin.
> Title: "Hope and Politics Collide at March."
> Container: *The Baltimore Sun*, first edition, 25 Apr. 2016, pp. A1+.
> Other: *LexisNexis Academic*. Accessed 30 May 2016.

"Facetious." *Vocabulary.com*, 2016, www.vocabulary.com/dictionary/facetious.

> Author: —
> Title: "Facetious."
> Container: *Vocabulary.com*, 2016, www.vocabulary.com/dictionary/facetious.
> Other: —

Reference Article (Library Database)

"Iūlia Agrippīna, 'Agrippina the Younger'." *Oxford Dictionary of the Classical World*, edited by John Roberts, Oxford University Press, 2007. *Oxford Reference*. Accessed 30 July 2016.

> Author: —
> Title: "Iūlia Agrippīna, 'Agrippina the Younger'."
> Container: *Oxford Dictionary of the Classical World*, edited by John Roberts, Oxford University Press, 2007.
> Other: *Oxford Reference*. Accessed 30 July 2016.

Online Publications

Entire Website

Sports Illustrated. Time, 2016, www.si.com.

> Author: —
> Title: *Sports Illustrated*.
> Container: Time, 2016, www.si.com.
> Other: —

Web Page

Mayo Clinic Staff. "Gallstones-Definition." *Mayo Clinic*, Mayo Foundation for Medical Education and Research, 25 July 2013, www.mayoclinic.org/diseases-conditions/gallstones/basics/definition/con-20020461.

> Author: Mayo Clinic Staff.
> Title: "Gallstones-Definition."
> Container: *Mayo Clinic*, Mayo Foundation for Medical Education and Research, 25 July 2013, www.mayoclinic.org/diseases-conditions/gallstones/basics/definition/con-20020461.
> Other: —

Social Media

@LibrariansTNT. "Cassandrasaurs for Sure Roamed this Earth." *Twitter*, 6 Jan.
2016, 8:49 a.m., twitter.com/LibrariansTNT/status/684778779034517504.

Author: @LibrariansTNT.
Title: "Cassandrasaurs for Sure Roamed this Earth."
Container: *Twitter*, 6 Jan. 2016, 8:49 a.m., twitter.com/LibrariansTNT/status/
684778779034517504.
Other: —

Blog

Grosvenor, Emily. "The Dude Abides in Salem." *Desperately Seeking Salem*.
8 Aug. 2010, desperatelyseekingsalem.wordpress.com/2010/08/08/
the-dude-abides-in-salem/.

Author: Grosvenor, Emily.
Title: "The Dude Abides in Salem."
Container: *Desperately Seeking Salem*. 8 Aug. 2010, desperatelyseekingsalem.word-
press.com/2010/08/08/the-dude-abides-in-salem/.
Other: —

Online Video

ArtsAlive YamhillCo, director. "ArtsAlive: Stephanie Lenox." *YouTube*, 25 Mar.
2015, youtube.com/watch?v=xOQIKeERJTE.

Author: ArtsAlive YamhillCo, director.
Title: "ArtsAlive: Stephanie Lenox."
Container: *YouTube*, 25 Mar. 2015, youtube.com/watch?v=xOQIKeERJTE.
Other: —

Media and Performance

Film

The Princess Bride. Directed by Rob Reiner, Act III Communications, 1987.

Author: —
Title: *The Princess Bride*.
Container: Directed by Rob Reiner, Act III Communications, 1987.
Other: —

Television Show (Broadcast)

"Frank Lisciandro." *The Writing Life*, produced by Stephen Long, McMinnville
Community Media, 21 Mar. 2016.

Author: —
Title: "Frank Lisciandro."
Container: *The Writing Life*, produced by Stephen Long, McMinnville Community
Media, 21 Mar. 2016.
Other: —

"World on Fire." *Daredevil*, directed by Farren Blackburn, performances by
    Charlie Cox and Vincent D'Onofrio, ABC Studios, 10 Apr. 2015. *Netflix*.

> Author: —
> Title: "World on Fire."
> Container: *Daredevil*, directed by Farren Blackburn, performances by Charlie Cox
>   and Vincent D'Onofrio, ABC Studios, 10 Apr. 2015.
> Other: *Netflix*.

Audio (Album)

Mould, Bob. *Workbook*. Virgin Records America, 1989.

> Author: Mould, Bob.
> Title: *Workbook*.
> Container: Virgin Records America, 1989.
> Other: —

Audio (Digital)

Adams, Sarah. "Be Cool to the Pizza Dude." *This I Believe*, hosted by Jay Allison,
    29 Dec. 2015, cdn.audiometric.io/9487820912.mp3. Accessed 29 Feb. 2016.

> Author: Adams, Sarah.
> Title: "Be Cool to the Pizza Dude."
> Container: *This I Believe*, hosted by Jay Allison, This I Believe, 29 Dec. 2015, cdn.
>   audiometric.io/9487820912.mp3. Accessed 29 Feb. 2016.
> Other: —

Advertisement (Print)

BF Goodrich Co. "Put the Magazine Down and Go." *Automobile Magazine*, the
    Enthusiast Network, July 2016, p. 5.

> Author: BF Goodrich Co.
> Title: "Put the Magazine Down and Go."
> Container: *Automobile Magazine*, the Enthusiast Network, July 2016, p. 5.
> Other: —

Comic Strip

Barry, Lynda. "Issue." *Ernie Pook's Comeek, City Pages*, 23 Oct. 1985.

> Author: Barry, Lynda.
> Title: "Issue."
> Container: *Ernie Pook's Comeek, City Pages*, 23 Oct. 1985.
> Other: —

MLA

Bartow, Rick. *After the Fall III.* Paint on clay, 1975, Portland Art Museum, Portland, OR.

> Author: Bartow, Rick.
> Title: *After the Fall III.*
> Container: Paint on clay, 1975, Portland Art Museum, Portland, OR.
> Other: —

Performance

Pride and Prejudice. Created by Jane Austen, directed by David Sikking, Arts & Communications Magnet Academy (ACMA) Theatre Company, 14 Mar. 2015, ACMA Visual and Performing Arts Center, Beaverton, OR.

> Author: —
> Title: *Pride and Prejudice.*
> Container: Created by Jane Austen, directed by David Sikking, Arts & Communications Magnet Academy (ACMA) Theatre Company, 14 Mar. 2015, ACMA Visual and Performing Arts Center, Beaverton, OR.
> Other: —

Other Works

Pamphlet, Brochure, or Press Release

Insure Your Next Trip with Travel Guard. Travel Guard, 2016.

> Author: —
> Title: *Insure Your Next Trip with Travel Guard.*
> Container: Travel Guard, 2016.
> Other: —

Government Report

United States, Census Bureau. *Strength in Numbers: Your Guide to 2010 Census Redistricting Data from the U.S. Census Bureau.* U.S. Dept. of Commerce, Economics and Statistics Administration, U.S. Census Bureau, 2010.

> Author: United States, Census Bureau.
> Title: *Strength in Numbers: Your Guide to 2010 Census Redistricting Data from the U.S. Census Bureau.*
> Container: U.S. Dept. of Commerce, Economics and Statistics Administration, U.S. Census Bureau, 2010.
> Other: —

Unpublished Dissertation

Kennison, Kristen Renee. *Smoke Derived Taint in Grapes and Wine.* Dissertation, Curtin University, 2011.

> Author: Kennison, Kristen Renee.
> Title: *Smoke Derived Taint in Grapes and Wine.*
> Container: Dissertation, Curtin University, 2011.
> Other: —

Personal Interview

Snoek-Brown, Samuel. Interview with Tom Franklin. 21 Mar. 2000.

> Author: Snoek-Brown, Samuel.
> Title: Interview with Tom Franklin.
> Container: 21 Mar. 2000.
> Other: —

Email

Franklin, Tom. "Re: Visit to Texas." Received by Gertrude Mornhenweg, 3 Apr. 2003.

> Author: Franklin, Tom.
> Title: "Re: Visit to Texas."
> Container: Received by Gertrude Mornhenweg, 3 Apr. 2003.
> Other: —

3. Paper Format

MLA style also offers guidance about how to format your paper so that it looks like all the other MLA papers. This helps ensure that readers will stay focused on your ideas.

Here are the general guidelines to keep in mind:

1. Type your paper on a computer and print it on standard, white 8.5 × 11 inch paper. Set the margins of your document to one inch on all four sides.

2. Use a businesslike font that doesn't draw attention to itself and is easy to read. Times New Roman is a popular choice, and a 12-point size in this font is readable.

3. Double-space everything—no more, no less.

4. Leave only one space after periods or other punctuation marks—unless you're told otherwise by an elderly person who learned how to type on an actual typewriter. It was a different time.

5. Indent the first line of paragraphs one half-inch from the left margin. Use the tab key to do that. Pushing the space bar five times to create a half-inch indentation worked on a typewriter, but it doesn't work with computers. Like we said, these are different times.

6. Create a header in the upper right-hand corner of each page that is one half-inch from the top of the page and even with the right margin. This should include your last name and the page number. Use automatic page numbering for that. Trying to do that manually will cause needless suffering.

7. Never use boldface. Only use italics as required for the titles of larger works and some publications and, with sober moderation, for emphasis within the paper.

8. MLA style does not require a title page. Get right to work on the first page.

We'll show you how this works in the following pages by looking at some examples of actual pages. As we do, we'll add a few more guidelines that apply only in specific situations.

A. First Page

Jack Wiegand **A**

Prof. Roy K. Humble

WR122

29 February 2016

B

Proving the Negative

C   With the arrival of social media, society has seen a marked increase in armchair academia. Like the dilettantes of the Victorian era, today's hobbyist intellectuals spend their free time engaging in the gentleman's sport of debate, study, and showing off their brains, rather than their muscles. Also like the dilettantes of old, they treat it as strictly leisure, while eschewing rigorous academic commitment. While they might be able to regale their friends for hours about the brilliance of Voltaire, they've likely read his Wikipedia page, rather than *Candide,* or *Plato's Dream.* While they may be able to offer a criticism of a documentary about humanism, they would likely struggle to offer a worthwhile analysis of Thomas More's *Utopia.* Not that there's anything wrong with dilettantism. If anything, it does for society much more than reality television or competitive Frisbee.

C   It can, however, create a few issues. In every scholarly field, information tends to change slightly as it moves from the academic sphere to the public sphere. When simplifying ideas to make them accessible to the public, the foundational information — that can, in many cases, take years of study to understand — is necessarily lost. To borrow from *The Science of Discworld,* we tend to "bend the truths just sufficiently to make the basic principles of the operation clear to a layman while not actually being entirely wrong" (Pratchett et al. 14). What the authors go on to describe as "lies to children" may seem wholly benign (15), but they often lead to small misunderstandings which can accumulate to form vast misunderstandings.

Keep these points in mind when you format your paper:

A. In the upper left-hand corner of the first page of the paper, include your name, the name of your professor, the name of the course, and the date, each on its own line. Note the date format, too.

B. Center the title on the next double-spaced line. Don't add extra space.

C. Indent the first sentence of each paragraph one half-inch.

D. Add a running header at the top of the first and every page.

B. Middle Pages

D

Wiegand 4

moon, as it moved through its annual cycle, indicated that the moon was a sphere (StarChild Team).

E

Many people have used this example as an argument against scientific understanding, claiming that if we were wrong about something like that, we could be wrong about anything. In rebuttal, rationalists are fond of saying that while we may not be absolutely right about certain things, we are continuously becoming less wrong. As Richard Feynman put it, in a lecture given at the 1964 Galileo Symposium:

F

> A scientist is never certain. We all know that. We know that all our statements are approximate statements with different degrees of certainty; that when a statement is made, the question is not whether it is true or false but rather how likely it is to be true or false. . . . We must discuss each question within the uncertainties that are allowed. . . . We absolutely must leave room for doubt or there is no progress and there is no learning. (111–112)

People tend to think of correctness as a binary; one is simply correct or incorrect. To wit, we now know that the Earth is not round, or at least not perfectly so. Isaac Newton observed, correctly, that the Earth is an oblate spheroid rather than a perfect sphere (Choi). While both previously held positions are incorrect, surely it is *less* incorrect to describe the Earth as round rather than flat.

Just as positive evidence can be used to make more reasonable positive statements, so too can negative evidence — or, the *absence* of evidence — be used to make more reasonable negative statements. Unfortunately, this is another case of widespread misunderstanding. The popular belief, known as Rees' Maxim, is that absence of evidence is not evidence of absence. This misunderstanding is not only prevalent in the public sphere but has also found a foothold among

E. Double-space every line, and don't add any extra space anywhere. Ever.

F. For block quotations, it's best to use your word-processor's ruler tool to indent the entire paragraph one half-inch from the left margin. Leave the right margin alone. Don't try to do this with tabs or spaces. That's a fool's errand.

When you get to the end of your paper, insert a manual page break so that the Works Cited page will start at the top of its own page.

C. Works Cited Page

A Works Cited

Cham, Jorge. "PHD Comics: Proving a Negative." *Piled Higher and Deeper*, no. 1194, 3 July
C 2009. *Comic Rocket*, www.comic-rocket.com/read/piled-higher-and-deeper-phd/1194.

Choi, Charles Q. "Strange but True: Earth Is Not Round." *Scientific American*, Nature Publishing
D Group, 12 Apr. 2007, www.scientificamerican.com/article/earth-is-not-round/.

Craig, William Lane. "#115 Is God Imaginary?: Santa Claus, Tooth Fairies, and God." *Reasonable
Faith with William Lane Craig*, Reasonable Faith, 29 June 2009,
www.reasonablefaith.org/is-god-imaginary.

E "Facetious." *Vocabulary.com*, www.vocabulary.com/dictionary/facetious.

Feynman, Richard P. "What Is and What Should Be the Role of Scientific Culture in Modern
Society." *The Pleasure of Finding Things Out: The Best Short Works of Richard P.
Feynman*, Perseus, 1999, pp. 111–112.

Jillette, Penn. "There Is No God." *This I Believe*, National Public Radio, 21 Nov. 2005,
www.npr.org/2005/11/21/5015557/there-is-no-god.

Pratchett, Terry, et al. "Science and Magic." *The Science of Discworld*, Ebury Publishing, 1999,
pp.14–15.

F Rowling, J.K. *Harry Potter and the Deathly Hallows*. Arthur A. Levine Books, 2007.

---. *Harry Potter and the Half-Blood Prince*. Arthur A. Levine Books, 2005.

Sagan, Carl. *The Demon-Haunted World: Science as a Candle in the Dark.* Ballantine, 1997.

StarChild Team. "Who Figured out the Earth Is Round?" *StarChild: A Learning Center for Young
Astronomers,* NASA, Feb. 2013, starchild.gsfc.nasa.gov/docs/StarChild/questions/
question54.html.

MLA

MLA
Paper Format

The list of works cited includes all the works that you actually use in your paper. If you read and thought about a work but didn't end up using it, then it doesn't go on this list.

The list of works cited starts at the top of its own separate page. That's why you need to put a manual page break at the end of your paper. If you don't, then every time you add or subtract a line from the body of the paper, it will push the title of this page up or down.

Here's what you keep in mind while formatting this page:

A. The title is "Work Cited" if you just cite one work or "Works Cited" if you cite more than one work. See how that works? Both words are capitalized. Center the title.

B. The running header continues on this page, too.

C. Double-space everything here just like you did on all the other pages. Be vigilant.

D. The first line of each citation should begin at the left margin. Any subsequent lines are indented a half-inch. This is called a hanging indent. The only way to do this sensibly is with the ruler tool that comes with your writing software. Even that isn't easy, so search for video tutorials online. It will be worth your while to figure this out.

E. You alphabetize your sources by the first word or words in each citation. If the author isn't known, then you use the title for that work. Alphabetize any numbers as if they were spelled out. Finally, ignore any accents or special characters like "@" when alphabetizing. "É" is the same as "e" and @LibrariansTNT would be alphabetized under "L."

F. If you cite more than one source by the same author, you alphabetize by the next word in the citation—first word in the title that isn't an article like "a" or "the," in other words—and with those other works by the same author, you replace the author's name with three hyphens.

This is another place where taking good notes during the research process will save you time and heartache. You need to include all the information that MLA style demands. If you don't already have that information at your fingertips, you need to go back to the work and gather it after the fact, which you may or may not have time to do.

APA Style

The American Psychological Association (APA) is a professional organization that supports research and publication in the behavioral and social sciences, including psychology, sociology, social work, and related areas of human services. APA style is a set of agreed-upon guidelines for scholars in these disciplines to follow when writing for classes or for publication. When we follow these guidelines, our readers can easily gather important reference information—like who wrote something, when they wrote it, and on what page—while remaining focused on the ideas in the writing.

Most of the APA disciplines are still relatively new, and the knowledge within them continues to change rapidly. APA style reflects that focus. In the body of papers, APA uses past-tense verbs and cites the author, page number, and—uniquely—the date of publication. That's because *when* an idea is from says a lot about its reliability. Ken Kesey's 1962 novel *One Flew Over the Cuckoo's Nest* depicted a time when scholars believed electroshock therapy, lobotomies, and the institutionalization of the mentally ill were humane, therapeutic treatments. Our ideas have evolved much since then, and a social science source from the mid-twentieth century has a high potential to be as outdated as those ideas.

APA style consists of three main categories—in-text citations, lists of references, and paper formatting. In the body of the paper, you will cite outside sources with APA-style in-text citations. At the end of your paper, you will add an APA-style bibliography called a References page. The paper as a whole uses APA-style formatting to set margins, line spacing, page-numbering, and so on.

Think of APA style as a filter. When your ideas pass through this filter, your paper will conform to APA guidelines and emerge looking like every other APA manuscript. The two things different about your paper will be the two most important ingredients—the idea you present and how you explain it to your readers.

1. In-Text Citations

In-text citations show readers that an idea belongs to someone other than the author and usually show where that idea can be found within the original source. They do so by providing readers with the author's last name, the year of the publication, and, if available, the page number where the idea resides.

The two places where you cite your sources in the text are in the introduction of that information and in a trailing parenthetical citation. The introduction might consist of an introductory statement or a signal phrase, and depending on the size of any direct quotations, some punctuation will also be involved.

It's typical to name the author and year of the work in the introduction and the page number in the parenthetical citation, but you can cite the author, year, and page number in the introduction, or you can cite all in the parenthetical citation. The thing you can't do is cite the information more than once. If you put it in the introduction, don't put it in the parenthetical citation.

A. Author in the Introduction

If you cite the author in your introduction, you do not also need to put the same information in the parenthetical citation.

1. In "Supporting a Strong Sense of Purpose: Lessons from a Rural Community," Dr. Devora Shamah (2011) argued that "out-of-school activities of all kinds appear to support the development of a sense of purpose" (p. 56).

   The **introduction** tells us who the quoted idea belongs to and when the idea was presented. If you mention the author in the introduction, the publication date goes next to the author's name while "p." and the page number follows in a parenthetical citation at the conclusion of the quotation. Note that the **period** goes after the citation and not inside the quotation marks, even if the original quoted material used a period there.

2. **In his review of** *Mouse Guard: Winter 1152* **for** *PopMatters*, **Biggins** (2009) **claimed**, "Because a talking animal wearing human clothes is a ridiculous concept to begin with, most funny-animal comics tend toward exaggeration."

> When there is no page number, as with online articles, you only need to report the author's name and publication date. If you do that in the **introduction**, you won't have a parenthetical citation. Note the closing **period** is now tucked inside the closing quotation mark.

3. Biggins (2009) wrote that "most funny-animal comics tend toward exaggeration." **He went on to demonstrate how this exaggeration can disarm readers.**

> The **second sentence** is another idea from Biggins that deserves citation, but you don't have to mention his name in the parenthetical because the pronoun "he" stands in for his name. As long as the pronoun is clear, it can stand in for the author's name when giving credit in in-text citations.

4. **As Shamah (2011) showed**, there's a clear relationship between out-of-school activities and a student's sense of purpose (p. 56).

> The same patterns apply to paraphrased material. If you name the author and publication date in an **introduction**, don't put that information in the parenthetical citation.

B. Author Absent from the Introduction

If you don't cite the author in an introduction, the last name must then be mentioned in the parenthetical citation:

1. **It's not just one specific or even one type of out-of-school activity that matters:** "Out-of-school activities of all kinds appear to support the development of a sense of purpose" (Shamah, 2011, p. 56).

> If the author isn't identified in the **introduction**, the last name, publication date, and page number go inside the parenthetical citation.

2. **Most comic artists understand and maximize the conventions of their form:** "Because a talking animal wearing human clothes is a ridiculous concept to begin with, most funny-animal comics tend toward exaggeration" (Biggins, 2009).

> When there is no page number to cite and no mention of the author in the **introduction**, the author's last name and publication date will be the only information inside the parenthetical citation. Note the **comma** that separates the author's name from the publication date.

3. **At least one expert claimed that** there's a clear relationship between out-of-school activities and a student's sense of purpose (Shamah**,** 2011**,** p. 56).

> And it's the same deal with citations of paraphrases or summaries. If you don't name the author in an **introduction**, then put the author's last name, date of publication, and page number in the parenthetical citation.

C. More Than One Work by an Author

If you use more than one work by a single author, the two works remain distinct from each other if the date of publication is different or one contributing author in a coauthored work is different. If the authors and years are both the same, however, the standard in-text information will no longer point to a single work on the references list. You must add distinguishing information to the publication date in the in-text citation to properly identify which work you mean.

1. To support this position, *Shamah* (**2011**a) argued that "out-of-school activities of all kinds appear to support the development of a sense of purpose" (p. 56).

> If you are citing two sources by the same *author* from the same year, add the letter "a" to the **publication date** for the first such entry. Proceed alphabetically to distinguish any remaining sources that overlap in this way.

2. Shamah (**2011**a) claimed that there's a clear relationship between out-of-school activities and a student's sense of purpose (p. 56).

> The **date** and letter also appear with paraphrases and summaries.

D. Authors with the Same Last Name

When you use sources written by different authors who happen to have the same last name, include the initials of the author to make it clear which of the sources you are referencing.

1. It's not just one specific or even one type of out-of-school activity that matters: "Out-of-school activities of all kinds appear to support the development of a sense of purpose" (*D.* Shamah, 2011, p. 56).

> Whether it's in the introduction or the parenthetical citation, include the *first initial* with the last name. Of course, that only works if the other author with the same last name has a different first initial.

2. At least one expert has claimed that there's a clear relationship between out-of-school activities and a student's sense of purpose (*Devora* Shamah, 2011, p. 56).

> If the first initial is also shared with the other author in your references list, write out the entire *first name* and last name.

APA

In-Text Citations

E. Two Authors

For works by two authors, cite both authors and maintain the order listed in the original work.

1. **According to Shamah and MacTavish (2009)**, "The smallness and safety of rural communities promotes the development of place-based knowledge among the youth" (p. 1).

    > The **introductory signal phrase** maintains the order the authors were listed in the original publication. Note that the author names are separated with the word "and" when listed in the introduction.

2. Growing up in a small town affords some important benefits to kids: "The smallness and safety of rural communities promotes the development of place-based knowledge among the youth" (Shamah & MacTavish, 2009, p. 1).

    > When the author names appear in the parenthetical citation, they are separated by an **ampersand**.

3. George Orwell, never a healthy man, wrote his masterpiece *Nineteen Eighty-Four* in the last years of his young life while struggling with tuberculosis. Scholars suggest that the dark mood of the book is in part a reflection of the strain he was under, trying to complete the story while grappling with this terrible illness that ultimately led to his death (Symons, 1992, p. xix; McCrum, 2009).

    > When the same idea is conveyed by two different works, separate the two citations with a **semicolon** within the parenthetical citation. Note that one idea appears on page xix in the introduction to a book, and the other has no page number because it appears in an online article.

F. Three or More Authors

Academic articles frequently have three or more authors or contributors. The number of contributors determines how to cite these sources in your paper.

1. **Thomas, Walker, Verplanken,** and **Shaddick** (2016) argued that there is "substantial disagreement amongst people about how most appliances can be categorized" (p.10).

   > When citing sources authored by three to five people, list all the **names** the first time you refer to them in your paper.

2. **Thomas** et al. (2016) went on to claim their findings support "earlier research demonstrating that householders do not understand domestic energy consumption very well" (pp. 10–11).

   > After naming all of the authors the first time, shorten any subsequent references in your paper to the **lead author's name** followed by "et al.," a Latin phrase meaning "and others."

3. Schilling **et al.** (2016) observed that "very often childhood maltreatment is not the result of one single type of maltreatment" (p. 9).

   > For a work by six or more authors, list the lead author's name followed by "et. al." at each mention. Forget about listing them the first time. If they wanted to be listed, they should have worked on a smaller team.

4. The problem is often compounded: "Very often childhood maltreatment is not the result of one single type of maltreatment" (Schilling et al., 2016, p. 9).

   > Do the same "et al." thing when the information goes inside the parenthetical citation, too.

G. Organization or Agency as Author

When the ideas you cite are found within official materials coming from an organization or government agency but are not attributed to a specific author, cite the organization or government agency.

1. According to the **U.S. Department of Housing and Urban Development** (HUD) (2016), there was "a 17 percent decrease in veteran homelessness between January 2015 and January 2016."

   > Place the organization or government agency name in the same place you would place a more traditional author. If the source is commonly known by an acronym, give the **full name** the first time you reference it, followed by the acronym in parentheses.

2. There was "a 47 percent decrease since 2010" (<u>HUD</u>, 2016).

   > Subsequent references in the paper to the same organization or government agency use the <u>acronym</u> only.

H. Unknown Author

If you don't know the author of your source and it isn't an organization or government agency, do some detective work and try to find it out. It's not that hard, and librarians are great help with this, too. However, if the author is really unknown and the title is short, use the full title in the citation. If the title is not short, use a key work or two from the title in the citation.

1. The original source material deserves a close examination. Grendel is described as a "brutish demon who lived in darkness" (***Beowulf***, 2008, p. 4).

2. Grendel is described in ***Beowulf*** <u>(2008)</u> as a "brutish demon who lived in darkness" <u>(p. 4)</u>.

   > The author of the epic poem *Beowulf* is unknown, so use the **title** in the <u>parenthetical citation</u> where the author would typically go. When the **title** appears in the introduction, it doesn't go inside the <u>parenthetical citation</u>.

3. Ten years ago, the City of Portland set in motion an ambitious plan to end homelessness in this city, but today there are even more homeless men, women, and children living in Portland (**"Crisis,"** 2015).

4. As reported in **"**<u>Crisis in Portland's Homeless Populations</u>**"** (2015), there are more homeless men, women, and children living in Portland than there were ten years ago — in spite of the City of Portland's ten-year plan to end homelessness.

   > Many newspaper articles are published without a named author. In these cases, use a **key word** from the title in place of the full title in the parenthetical citation. In an introduction, however, it's easier to understand if you use the <u>full title</u> of the article. Because this is a shorter work within a larger publication, the title is enclosed by **quotation marks**.

APA

I. Sacred Text

Sacred texts are different because they often have an unclear author and multiple translations into English. You'll need to cite the book, chapter, verse, or other defining sections of the source. You also cite the translation you're using. However, you don't cite the source in your references list at the end of your paper.

1. **The instruction in 1 Thessalonians 5:16–17 of the Bible** (New International Version) to "Rejoice always, pray continually" is similar to instruction on meditation found in other sacred texts.

2. The instruction in the Bible to "Rejoice always, pray continually" is similar to instruction on meditation found in other sacred texts (1 Thessalonians 5:16–17, New International Version).

> Your citation can happen in the **signal phrase** or in the parenthetical citation. If you cite the same translation of a sacred text later, you do not need to indicate the version again. If you change versions, however, you have to cite the new version.

J. Indirect Citation

In her article, Dr. Shamah cites an idea from a book by William Damon. If you want to cite the same idea from Damon that Dr. Shamah cites in her article, what do you do? You go to the library, of course, and get Damon's book. That's what you should do. If it has one idea worth incorporating into your paper, it might have other and even better ideas to consider.

However, if you don't have time to get that book or your library can't access it, you can use an indirect citation. Give credit in the introduction to the person who came up with the idea, and use the parenthetical citation to show the reader exactly which of the sources on your list of references this idea appears within.

1. **Damon claimed that** "finding one's place in the world is a developmental process that spans the life course" (as cited in *Shamah,* 2011, p. 45).

> The indirectly cited author appears in the **introduction** while the *author whose work you actually read* appears within the parenthetical citation. Note that you must include the phrase "as cited in" before the author's name in that citation.

2. **One expert claimed that** "finding one's place in the world is a developmental process that spans the life course" (Damon, as cited in *Shamah*, 2011, p. 45).

> If neither of the authors is mentioned in the **introduction**, the indirectly cited author and the *author whose work you actually read* both go in the parenthetical citation.

K. Personal Communication

Personal communications like emails, letters, memos, phone calls, and personal interviews do not have recoverable data and will not appear in the Reference list. Cite them as personal communication within the body of your text instead.

1. The pecan pie was delicious (S. **Snoek-Brown**, personal communication, May 24, 2011).

> Include the *author's initials* as well as his or her **last name**.

L. Block Quote

Reserve block quotations for instances where you must quote more than forty words.

1. *Roy K. Humble (2010) argued for the use of note cards when organizing a college essay*:

> If you're using note cards, you simply unleash their awesome, low-tech power. You lay the note cards on the dinette table and move them around. I know that doesn't sound like much, but trust me — it's awesome and powerful. Note cards allow you to visually arrange the evidence into its natural patterns. (p. 97)

Despite the logic of the argument he presented, many students refuse to try the technique.

> Indent a block quote one half-inch from the left. Block quotations use formatting instead of quotation marks to show the material is a direct quotation. Typically, you should introduce a block quotation with a *complete sentence* that is followed by **colon**. The parenthetical citation sits just outside the **ending punctuation** of the quotation. If the paragraph continues after the block quote, do not indent the sentence that follows the block quote. That shows readers that this enormous quotation is supporting information within a longer paragraph.

2. *There are good reasons to use note cards while researching*:

> If you're using note cards, you simply unleash their awesome, low-tech power. You lay the note cards on the dinette table and move them around. I know that doesn't sound like much, but trust me — it's awesome and powerful. Note cards allow you to visually arrange the evidence into its natural patterns. (Humble, 2010, p. 97)

Despite the logic of this argument, however, many students refuse to try the technique.

> If you don't name the author and date in the *introduction*, then put that in the <u>parenthetical citation</u> and put the <u>parenthetical citation</u> just outisde the **ending punctuation**.

2. References

The APA list of references is a complete list of the works that are used in your paper. The complete publication information allows your readers to find any work that you used and study it themselves. APA divides that publication information into four elements, typically presented in this order:

A. Author

B. Publication date

C. Title

D. Publication information

A. Author

The author is the person or people or organization responsible for creating the source. This is the first piece of information you must find to build your citation.

With books, the author's name is usually on the spine. Magazines, newspapers, and journals typically put the author's name near the title of the article. However, the name may also appear at the end of short articles. If the source is a corporate or governmental publication and a specific author is not given, the organization itself is usually the author.

One Author

1. **Todd, D.** (2012). *Feeding back: Conversations with alternative guitarists from proto-punk to post-rock.* Chicago, IL: Chicago Review Press.

   List the author's last name first, followed by a **comma** and then the author's first initial. End the author section with a **period**.

2. **Georges, N. K.** (2013). *Calling Dr. Laura.* New York, NY: Houghton Mifflin Harcourt.

   Include the middle initial or initials if they are listed in the original text.

3. **Churchill, W.** (1953). *Triumph and tragedy.* Boston, MA: Houghton Mifflin.

   That's *Sir* Winston Churchill to you and me, but in a citation, don't include titles like "Sir," "PhD," "M.S.W.," "King," "Saint," or "Dr."

Two to Seven Authors

1. Ede, L., **& Lunsford,** <u>A.</u> <u>A.</u> (2012). *Writing together: Collaboration in theory and practice.* Boston, MA: Bedford/St. Martin's.

   > Use a **comma** and an **ampersand** between the name of the last author and the next-to-last author. Note that the second author's name is written with the **last name** followed by the <u>first initial</u> and, in this case, a <u>middle initial</u>. Always list the authors in the order they appear in the text, not alphabetically.

2. Murray, R. M., Jones, P. B., Susser, E., van Os, J., **&** Cannon, M. (2002). *The epidemiology of schizophrenia.* Cambridge, UK: Cambridge University Press.

   > The same pattern continues up to seven authors, with a **comma** separating each name until the last, which is marked with a **comma** and an **ampersand.**

Eight or More Authors

1. Raggi, A., Corso, B., Minicuci, N., Quintas, R., Sattin, D., De Torres, L., . . . Leonardi, M. (2016). Determinants of quality of life in aging populations: Results from a cross-sectional study in Finland, Poland and Spain. *PLoS ONE, 11*(7), e0159293. doi: 10.1371/journal.pone.0159293

   > With sources with eight or more authors, list the first six names, and then insert an **ellipsis**. End the list with the last author named in the original work. You'll notice that there's no ampersand in this list. Maybe you'll notice. You'll notice if you're paying attention.

Organizational or Governmental Author

Business and professional documents are often considered a work product and property of the company rather than that of the sad, nameless authors who work for that organization. In that case, list the organization as the author.

1. U.S. Census Bureau. (2010). *Strength in numbers: Your guide to 2010 census redistricting data from the U.S. Census Bureau.* Washington, DC: U.S. Dept. of Commerce, Economics and Statistics Administration.

   > For an organizational or government author, abbreviate commonly understood terms like "U.S." instead of writing out "United States." More complex or unfamiliar acronyms should be written out.

Screen Name

Many online authors write under a screen name. You don't have to go searching for the author's secret (true) identity. You can use the screen name.

1. **chewingofthecud.** (2014, March 13). What currents or movements are currently happening in literature? [Forum post]. Retrieved from https://www.reddit.com/r/literature/comments/20by05/what_currents_or_movements_are_currently/

   Simply list the screen name in the author's place in the citation. You can also see in this example the importance of choosing a good screen name.

No Author

If no author is listed for the text, skip the author's place and begin the citation with the title. Do not use the word "Anonymous" in place of the author.

1. **Facetious.** (2016). In *Vocabulary.com*. Retrieved from https://www.vocabulary.com/dictionary/facetious

   Don't use a date of publication for the first word of a citation. Move the title over to the author's place and then proceed as normal.

Nontraditional Authors

Occasionally, the person or organization most important to your discussion of a source contributed something other than the writing of the words. Some terms you are likely to use in your documentation are "performer," "director," "producer," and "reporter." However, abbreviate "editor(s)" to "Ed." or "Eds." and "translator(s)" to "Trans."

1. **Reiner, R. (Director).** (1987). *The princess bride* [**Motion picture**]. United States: Act III Communications.

   Capitalize the contributor's role, which appears inside **parentheses** and is followed by a **period**.

2. **Low, A. K. (Producer), & O'Brien, B. (Writer & Reporter).** (1985). *The Hoboken sound* [Documentary movie]. United States: Metromedia Telecenter. Retrieved from https://www.youtube.com/watch?v=clNuALHa_6E

   Place the role next to the contributor's name. If the contributor performed more than one key role, separate the roles as you would when listing multiple authors, using an **ampersand** in place of the "and."

3. **Boluk, S., & Lenz, W. (Eds.).** (2011). *Generation zombie: Essays on the living dead in modern culture.* Jefferson, NC: McFarland.

   When the principles responsible for a source are the editors, put the abbreviated role "Eds." within **parentheses**, followed by a **period**.

B. Publication Date

The publication date is the specific date the work was published. Because a book edition is published once, its publication date lists the year only. Because a periodical is published regularly throughout the year, its publication date identifies which part of the year it was published in. A monthly magazine notes the month and year. A daily newspaper lists the day, month, and year.

The location of the publication date varies from publication to publication. In a book, the date will be on the title page or copyright page. In articles that appear in periodicals, the date will often be next to the byline and title. This applies to online articles as well, but if a date is missing, you can also search the bottom of the web page for a publication year to stand in for something more precise.

1. McCloud, S. **(2015).** *The sculptor.* New York, NY: First Second Books.

   For books, movies, and other works published on a non-periodic basis, put the year inside a set of **parentheses** followed by a **period**.

2. Federoff, N., & Block, J. **(2016, April 6**). Mosquito vs. mosquito [Editorial]. *The New York Times,* p. A23.

   Daily publications will name the year followed by a **comma** and the month and day. Months are not abbreviated in APA.

3. Barone, R. **(2016, May/June**). The power of song: Recording Pete Seeger. *Tape Op,* 113, 36–44.

   Bimonthly publications will often use the year followed by a **comma** and a month range separated by a slash.

You may use the abbreviation "n.d." for no date, but do not use it lightly. It is rare that a publication date is truly not included in a print source. In web sources, the date can be difficult to find, but it almost always exists in the web page's HTML code. Most web browsers will allow you to search the HTML code, but that may take some work. Ask for help.

C. Title

The next key element in an APA citation is the title of the work. APA style requires you to format the title to distinguish between larger and smaller works. APA also requires you to capitalize the first word of the title, the first word of the subtitle, and all proper nouns while all other words are left in lowercase. However, this rule only applies to end-of-text references. When you write the title within the body of your paper, capitalize all the major words. In general, APA does not consider conjunctions, articles, and short prepositions to be major words, so you leave those lowercase. Whenever a word is more than three letters long, however, capitalize it.

Occasionally, you'll need to cite non-routine information in the title. In such case, put the information within brackets and a short description of the source. Common examples are as follows:

APA

APA
References: Title

> [Abstract]
> [Audio podcast]
> [Brochure]
> [Letter to the editor]
> [Motion picture]
> [MP3 file]

These are not to be confused with what APA considers "gray literature." Gray literature refers to sources like dissertations and technical reports that are not published formally but nevertheless contain valuable information for scholars. For these, follow the title with a description inside parentheses.

Look for the title of the source near the author's name, usually at the beginning of the work.

Larger Works

APA uses formatting to quickly indicate whether the title of the source is a larger, self-contained work or a smaller work within a larger one. In APA, you italicize titles of sources that are the name of the larger work itself. You'll see this often with books, anthologies and other collections, book-length poems, movie and album names, and the names of websites.

1. Georges, N. J. (2013). *Calling Dr. Laura.* New York, NY: Houghton Mifflin Harcourt.
   This is a full-length book, so the title is italicized. All the words are capitalized in this title because the words are either proper nouns or the first word of the title. Put a **period** at the end of this section.

2. Roemmele, J. A., & Batdorff, D. (2001). *Surviving the "flesh-eating bacteria": Understanding, preventing, treating, and living with the effects of necrotizing fasciitis.* New York, NY: Avery.

> Put a colon between the main title and a <u>subtitle</u>. With larger works, both remain italicized. If the title contains words within quotation marks, those words are also italicized. Also, notice that only the first word of the title and subtitle are capitalized because this time, the title includes no proper nouns.

3. Bishop, K. W. (2010). *American zombie gothic: The rise and fall (and rise) of* <u>The Walking Dead</u> *in popular culture.* Jefferson, NC: McFarland.

> In this unusual example, however, we have a <u>television series title</u> within the main book title that must be *de*-italicized to distinguish it from the rest of the book's title. If a part of the larger work's title would normally be italicized, then you must de-italicize it within the italics of the rest of the title.

4. Bartow, R. (1975). *After the fall III* [<u>Paint on clay</u>]. Portland, OR: Portland Art Museum.

> APA considers works of art to be larger works, even if they aren't physically very large, so those titles are also italicized. Non-routine sources will have a <u>short description</u> within brackets that describes the work. A **period** follows the description but not the title.

5. Kennison, K. R. (2011). *Smoke derived taint in grapes and wine* (<u>Doctoral dissertation</u>). Retrieved from http://espace.library.curtin.edu.au/R?func=dbin-jump-full&local_base=gen01-era02&object_id=185451.

> Non-routine works that have been published informally, such as a dissertation or thesis, come with a <u>short description</u> within brackets after the title. A **period** follows the description.

Smaller Works within a Larger Work

Smaller works are usually nested within a larger work. For these, APA leaves the title of the smaller work unitalicized and does not enclose it with quotation marks. The first word in a title or subtitle is capitalized but other than proper nouns, the other words are not capitalized. APA considers smaller works things like short stories and essays in an anthology, short poems within a collection, episodes within a television series, songs within an album, articles within a website, and so on.

1. Toobin, J. (2014, December 9). **Our broken Constitution**. *The New Yorker,* pp. 64–73.

> The article title is left unitalicized because it appears within a larger work, in this case a magazine. "Constitution" is capitalized because it is a proper noun.

2. Mahoney, P. (2011). **Gray is the new black: <u>Race, class, and zombies</u>.** In S. Boluk, & W. Lenz (Eds.), *Generation zombie: Essays on the living dead in modern culture* (pp. 55–72). Jefferson, NC: McFarland.

    This citation refers to an article within an edited book, so the title is not italicized. Notice how the first letter of the <u>subtitle</u> is capitalized.

3. Tuchman, B. (1962). **Ch. 19: Retreat.** *The guns of August.* (pp. 341–372). London, England: Macmillan.

    Chapters or other sections within a book are considered shorter works, even if they are quite long, so the title is not italicized.

4. Assistant Secretary for Public Affairs. (2016, March 24). **Opioids: The prescription drug & heroin overdose epidemic.** U.S. Department of Health & Human Services. Retrieved from https://www.hhs.gov/opioids

    Web pages are shorter works within websites, so the title is not italicized. No bracketed summary is needed to explain that this is a website because let's face it, information from websites is as routine as it gets.

5. ArtsAlive YamhillCo. (2015, March 25). **ArtsAlive: Stephanie Lenox <u>[Video file]</u>.** Retrieved from https://www.youtube.com/ watch?v=xOQIKeERJTE

    This is a smaller work within a website, so the title isn't italicized. While information from websites is routine, multimedia on the web is still considered non-routine. Therefore the title is followed by a <u>short description</u> within brackets that describes the work and a **period** that follows the description.

6. Grosvenor, E. (2010, August 7). **The Dude abides in Salem. <u>[Blog post]</u>.** Retrieved from https://desperatelyseekingsalem.wordpress.com/2010/08/08/the-dude-abides-in-salem/

    Yes, we know that blogs are routine, but APA has other ideas. Sometimes it seems to use these <u>short descriptions</u> in order to look down its collective nose at some sources. The title is not italicized.

7. Kenny, G. (2016, January 15). **A perfect day <u>[Review of the film *A perfect day*, by F. L. de Aranoa]</u>.** *Rogerebert.com.* Retrieved from http://www.rogerebert.com/ reviews/a-perfect-day-2016

    When the work is a review of another work, the title of the review is not italicized. Add a <u>short description</u> within brackets that includes "Review of," the type and title of the work, and the principle author responsible, followed by a **period**. A **comma** separates the *title of the reviewed work* from its author.

D. Publication Information

The fourth and most complex element of an APA citation is the one that captures publication information about the source. This section will include information about some or all of the following subcategories of information:

1. Other contributors

2. Title of publication

3. Version

4. Number

5. Publisher

6. Publisher location

Not every source will use each of the subcategories described in this section. For example, a periodical does not typically come in "versions," but in volumes and issues, two variations covered by "number." In cases when your source does not contain one of the subcategories, move on to the next one on the list.

1. Other Contributors

Other contributors are people who play integral roles in creating the publication but are secondary to the named author of the source. These contributors must be identified by their role in the publication with terms such as "Trans." (translator), "Ed.," (editor), and so on.

You'll find the names of other contributors on title pages or other places where credit is given to collaborators, like the credits of a film or the liner notes of an album. Only bring in the additional contributors whose work is directly applicable to the topic of your writing.

1. Bolano, R. (2008). *The savage detectives.* **(N. Wimmer, Trans.)**. New York, NY: Picador.

> When the main work has an additional contributor, the contributor name goes inside **parentheses**, followed by a **comma** and the role. Note that the first initial of the contributor comes before the last name.

2. Mahoney, P. (2011). Gray is the new black: Race, class, and zombies. **In S. Boluk, & W. Lenz (Eds.),** *Generation zombie: Essays on the living dead in modern culture* (pp. 55–72). Jefferson, NC: McFarland.

> When the work being cited is included within a larger work, start with the preposition "In" and then list the contributors' names. Use the first initial and then the last name. After that, put the role of the contributors within a set of **parentheses**, followed by a **comma**.

2. Title of Publication

The title of publication is used when a shorter work is published within a larger host publication, such as a news article inside a newspaper. The name of the shorter work goes in the regular title section of the citation (Part B). The name of the larger work goes after that as the title of publication.

1. Boluk, S., & Lenz, W. (Eds.). (2011). *Generation zombie: Essays on the living dead in modern culture.* Jefferson, NC: McFarland.

   > When the work cited is a larger work like this anthology, the title of the larger work goes into the main title section (Part B). There's nothing to put here for title of a host publication publication, like a magazine, because there is no host publication. That's okay. Move along.

2. Mahoney, P. (2011). Gray is the new black: Race, class, and zombies. In S. Boluk, & W. Lenz (Eds.), **Generation zombie: Essays on the living dead in modern culture** (pp. 55–72). Jefferson, NC: McFarland.

   > In this example, the citation is for on an article within the larger work. The name of the host anthology goes here as the title of publication.

3. Rockmore, E.B. (2015, October 15). How Texas teaches history. **The New York Times.** Retrieved from http://www.nytimes.com/2015/10/22/opinion/how-texas-teaches-history.html

   > With articles in periodicals, the title of the host publication is typically the name of the journal, magazine, or newspaper.

4. Assistant Secretary for Public Affairs. (2016, March 24). Opioids: The prescription drug & heroin overdose epidemic. **U.S. Department of Health & Human Services.** Retrieved from https://www.hhs.gov/opioids

   > When the focus of the source is on one page at a website, the title of the host publication is the name of the website.

5. Agrippina (Agrippina the younger). (1989). **In** *Encyclopedia of world crime* (Vol. 1, pp. 39–40). Wilmette, IL: CrimeBooks, Inc.

   > With an article in a reference work, the title of the publication is the title of the main reference work, preceded by the preposition "In."

6. Silence (2016). War drums. **On** *The deafening sound of absolutely nothing* [MP3 file]. Huntington, WV: Profane Existence.

   > When citing a song, the song title is in the main title section, and the name of the album is the title of publication, preceded by the preposition "On." A description of the non-routine source is in **brackets**.

3. Version

Works often have multiple versions or editions identified by numbers that tell you how many times the publication has been revised — 2nd edition, for example — or names that tell you the nature of the revision — like "unabridged" or "expanded."

When they exist, version numbers or names can usually be found next to the title of the publication.

1. Rottenberg, A. T., & Winchell, D. H. (Eds.). (2015). *The structure of argument* **(8th ed.)**. Boston, MA: Bedford/St. Martin's.

   Use numbers rather than spelling out editions distinguished by an ordinal number. Don't use superscript for the number either. Put the version within **parentheses** and follow that with a **period**.

4. Number

Books that are too long to be published in a single publication are often split into multiple publications, and each is given its own volume number. In addition, periodicals that are published on an ongoing basis — as is the case with most scholarly journals — are assigned volume, issue, or volume *and* issue numbers to distinguish one publication of the periodical from another.

The number is typically found near the title of the publication. However, it may be found within the publication on a page with more information about the publication, contributors, and so on.

1. Ruiz, G., & Sánchez, N. (2014). Wolfgang Köhler's *The Mentality of Apes* and the animal psychology of his time. *The Spanish Journal of Psychology, 17,* E69.

   When a journal is paginated by volume only, the italicized volume number will follow the publication title, followed by a **comma**.

2. Coates, T. The case for reparations. *The Atlantic, 313*(5), 54–71.

   If a journal has both volume number and issue number, mention the italicized volume number first, followed by the <u>issue number</u> within parentheses, leaving no space between the two.

3. Sheffield, R. (2015). Getting to know Colbert. *Rolling Stone,* **1295,** 30.

   If there is no volume number, mention the issue number only.

4. Agrippina (Agrippina the younger). (1989). In *Encyclopedia of world crime* (**Vol. 1,** pp. 39–40). Wilmette, IL: CrimeBooks, Inc.

   While you don't write "Vol." when referring to a periodical, you do use the abbreviation when citing one volume in a multivolume book.

5. Publisher

The publisher is the company or person who actually produced a book, government publication, film, or website. Film and television series generally involve multiple publishers. In such cases, cite the publisher primarily responsible for the work. Periodicals often do not have a publisher, in which case you can skip this section. In addition, APA does not record publishers of websites.

With a book, you can find the name of the publisher on the title page or on a page near the front of the book that provides more information about the publication and its copyright. On pamphlets, look on the back or the innermost leaf of the folded paper. On brochures, look at the front or back covers.

1. McCloud, S. (2015). *The sculptor.* **New York, NY: First Second Books.**

   For books printed in the United States, separate the city and state abbreviation with a **comma**. Then, add a **colon** and list the name of the publishing company.

2. Murray, R. M., Jones, P. B., Susser, E., van Os, J., & Cannon, M. (2002). *The epidemiology of schizophrenia.* **Cambridge, UK: Cambridge University Press.**

   With books published out of the country, separate the city and country with a **comma**, followed by a **colon** and the name of the publishing company.

3. Frank Lisciandro. [Television series episode]. (2016). In *The writing life.* **McMinn ville, OR: McMinnville Community Media, MCM-TV.**

   This reference begins with the title of the episode because no author is listed. With television broadcasts, films, and albums, the publisher is the company or organization that paid for the creation of the work.

4. Travel Guard. (2016). *Insure your next trip with Travel Guard* [Brochure]. Stevens Point, WI: **Author.**

   For self-published works, such as this brochure, write the word "Author" to show that the author and the publishing company are the same.

6. Location

The location varies by the type of work. For shorter works within anthologies or periodicals, the location is usually a page number or a range of pages. The location for a work of art is often the place where the piece is on exhibit. For online sources, the location is a URL or DOI. Because of the possibilities here, your main task is to be as precise as possible.

1. Behar, E., McGowan, S., McLaughlin, K., Borkovec, T., Goldwin, M., & Bjorkquist, O. (1998). Concreteness of positive, negative, and neutral repetitive thinking about the future. *Behavior Therapy, 43*(2), **300–312.**

   Use an **en dash** (–, usually option-hyphen or alt-hyphen) to separate a range of pages. Put a **period** after the last page.

2. OSU women try to keep a storied season going. (2016, April 2). *The Oregonian*, **p. A1**.

    Page numbers in a newspaper source are preceded by a "p." for information on one page or "pp." for information on multiple pages. The **page numbers** often include a letter that refers to one <u>section</u> of the newspaper.

3. Erlanger, S., Castle, S., & Gladstone, R. (2016, April 6). Airing of hidden wealth stirs inquiries and rage: Iceland premier steps down as release of files reverberates around world. *The New York Times*, **pp. A1, A6**.

    For a multipage work that appears on nonconsecutive pages, list each **page** separately, separated by a **comma**.

4. Grosvenor, E. (2010, August 7). The Dude abides in Salem [Blog post]. **Retrieved from** https://desperatelyseekingsalem.wordpress.com/2010/08/08/the-dude-abides-in-salem/

    For online works, write "Retrieved from" and the <u>URL</u>. Only use a URL if it will reliably and consistently allow a reader to navigate to the cited page and only give enough information to get to the desired source. Avoid using one-time URLs generated for a specific browsing session.

5. Aagaard, J. (2015, December.) Media multitasking, attention, and distraction: A critical discussion. *Phenomenology and the Cognitive Sciences, 14*(4), 885. **doi:10.1007/s11097-014- 9375-x**

    A digital object identifier (**DOI**) is more reliable than a URL, and if that's available, that's what you should use. You do not need to use "Retrieved from" when you use a DOI.

6. Racy, A. J. (2016, Spring/Summer). Domesticating otherness: The snake charmer in American popular culture. *Ethnomusicology, 60*(2), 197–232. **Retrieved from** www.jstor.org/stable/10.5406/ethnomusicology.60.2.0197

    In general, don't include database information unless the work can only be found in an electronic database. In such case, give the <u>URL</u> for the online archive and add "Retrieved from."

7. Bartow, R. (1975). *After the fall III* [Paint on clay]. **Portland, OR**: Portland Art Museum.

    For items that appear in physical locations, name the place the work is housed with sufficient distinguishing detail like <u>city</u>, <u>state</u>, or country.

E. Reference List Examples

As you see from the past section, APA style divides reference list information into four main sections:

A. Author

B. Publication date

C. Title

D. Publication information

In the examples that follow, we'll show you how to format citations for your references list and then the information that goes into each main section.

Even though these are common examples, you still have to adopt them to fit the information about the works you're using. You may have to tinker with the author section or the publication section to accurately capture the information about a given work.

But that's a good thing. It means that you can build each citation to match the works instead of having to somehow tailor the information about a work to fit a template that doesn't really fit.

Books

One Author (Print)

Georges, N. J. (2013). *Calling Dr. Laura*. New York, NY: Houghton Mifflin Harcourt.

> Author: Georges, N. J.
> Publication date: (2013).
> Title: *Calling Dr. Laura*.
> Publication information: New York, NY: Houghton Mifflin Harcourt.

Edition Other Than the First

Rottenberg, A. T., & Winchell, D. H. (Eds.). (2015). *The structure of argument* (8th ed.). Boston, MA: Bedford/St. Martin's.

> Author: Rottenberg, A. T., & Winchell, D. H. (Eds.).
> Publication date: (2015).
> Title: *The structure of argument* (8th ed.).
> Publication information: Boston, MA: Bedford/St. Martin's.

Boluk, S., & Lenz, W. (Eds.). (2011). *Generation zombie: Essays on the living dead in modern culture.* Jefferson, NC: McFarland.

> Author: Boluk, S., & Lenz, W. (Eds.).
> Publication date: (2011).
> Title: *Generation zombie: Essays on the living dead in modern culture.*
> Publication information: Jefferson, NC: McFarland.

Online Book

Twain, Mark. (1917). *Life on the Mississippi.* New York, NY: Harper & Brothers Publishers. Retrieved from books.google.com

> Author: Twain, M.
> Publication date: (1917).
> Title: *Life on the Mississippi.*
> Publication information: New York, NY: Harper & Brothers Publishers. Retrieved from books.google.com

Sacred Text

APA directs you to cite sacred texts within your text, so there's no need for a reference entry. See the section in this chapter on sacred text and in-text citations for more about this.

Parts of Books

Chapter of a Book

Tuchman, B. (1962). Ch. 19: Retreat. *The guns of August.* (pp. 341–372). London, England: Macmillan.

> Author: Tuchman, B.
> Publication date: (1962).
> Title: Ch. 19: Retreat.
> Publication information: *The guns of August.* (pp. 341–372). London, England: Macmillan.

Work in an Anthology

Mahoney, P. (2011). Gray is the new black: Race, class, and zombies. In S. Boluk, & W. Lenz (Eds.), *Generation zombie: Essays on the living dead in modern culture* (pp. 55–72). Jefferson, NC: McFarland.

> Author: Mahoney, P.
> Publication date: (2011).
> Title: Gray is the new black: Race, class, and zombies.
> Publication information: In S. Boluk, & W. Lenz (Eds.), *Generation zombie: Essays on the living dead in modern culture* (pp. 55–72). Jefferson, NC: McFarland.

Agrippina (Agrippina the younger). (1989). In *Encyclopedia of world crime* (Vol. 1, pp. 39–40). Wilmette, IL: CrimeBooks, Inc.

> Author: —
> Publication date: (1989).
> Title: Agrippina (Agrippina the younger).
> Publication information: In *Encyclopedia of world crime* (Vol. 1, pp. 39–40). Wilmette, IL: CrimeBooks, Inc.

Articles

Journal Article (Print)

APA

Racy, A. J. (2016, Spring/Summer). Domesticating otherness: The snake charmer in American popular culture. *Ethnomusicology, 60*(2), 197–232.

> Author: Racy, A. J.
> Publication date: (2016, Spring/Summer).
> Title: Domesticating otherness: The snake charmer in American popular culture.
> Publication information: *Ethnomusicology, 60*(2), 197–232.

Journal Article (Library Database)

Racy, A. J. (2016, Spring/Summer). Domesticating otherness: The snake charmer in American popular culture. *Ethnomusicology, 60*(2), 197–232. Retrieved from www.jstor.org/stable/10.5406/ethnomusicology.60.2.0197

> Author: Racy, A. J.
> Publication date: (2016, Spring/Summer).
> Title: Domesticating otherness: The snake charmer in American popular culture.
> Publication information: *Ethnomusicology, 60*(2), 197–232. Retrieved from www. jstor.org/stable/10.5406/ethnomusicology.60.2.0197

Magazine Article (Print)

Barone, R. (2016, May/June). The power of song: Recording Pete Seeger. *Tape Op*, 113, 36–44.

> Author: Barone, R.
> Publication date: (2016, May/June).
> Title: The power of song: Recording Pete Seeger.
> Publication information: *Tape Op*, 113, 36–44.

Magazine Article (Website)

Engber, D. (2016, January 26). The neurologist who hacked his brain— and almost lost his mind. *Wired*. Retrieved from http://www.wired.com/ phil-kennedy-mind-control-computer/

> Author: Engber, D.
> Publication date: (2016, January 26).
> Title: The neurologist who hacked his brain—and almost lost his mind.
> Publication information: Retrieved from http://www.wired.com/phil-kennedy-mind-control-computer/

Newspaper Article (Print)

Erlanger, S., Castle, S., & Gladstone, R. (2016, April 6). Airing of hidden wealth stirs inquiries and rage: Iceland premier steps down as release of files reverberates around world. *The New York Times*, pp. A1, A6.

> Author: Erlanger, S., Castle, S., & Gladstone, R.
> Publication date: (2016, April 6).
> Title: Airing of hidden wealth stirs inquiries and rage: Iceland premier steps down as release of files reverberates around world.
> Publication information: *The New York Times*, pp. A1, A6.

Newspaper Article (Website)

Rockmore, E.B. (2015, October 15). How Texas teaches history. *The New York Times*. Retrieved from http://www.nytimes.com/2015/10/22/opinion/how-text-teaches-history.html

> Author: Rockmore, E.B.
> Publication date: (2015, October 15).
> Title: How Texas teaches history.
> Publication information: *The New York Times*. Retrieved from http://www.nytimes.com

Reference Article (Print)

Agrippina (Agrippina the younger). (1989). In *Encyclopedia of world crime* (Vol. 1, pp. 39–40). Wilmette, IL: CrimeBooks, Inc.

> Author: —
> Publication date: (1989).
> Title: Agrippina (Agrippina the younger).
> Publication information: In *Encyclopedia of World Crime* (Vol. 1, pp. 39–40). Wilmette, IL: CrimeBooks, Inc.

Reference Article (Website)

Facetious. (2016). In *Vocabulary.com*. Retrieved from https://www.vocabulary.com/dictionary/facetious

> Author: —
> Publication date: (2016).
> Title: Facetious.
> Publication information: In *Vocabulary.com*. Retrieved from https://www.vocabulary.com/dictionary/facetious

Iūlia Agrippīna (Agrippina the younger). (2007). In Roberts, J. (Ed.), *Oxford dictionary of the classical world*, Oxford, England: Oxford University Press. Retrieved from http://www.oxfordreference.com/view/10.1093/acref/9780192801463.001.0001/acref-9780192801463-e-1165

> Author: —
> Publication date: (2007).
> Title: Iūlia Agrippīna (Agrippina the younger).
> Publication information: In Roberts, J. (Ed.), *Oxford dictionary of the classical world*, Oxford, England: Oxford University Press. Retrieved from http://www.oxfordreference.com/view/10.1093/acref/9780192801463.001.0001/acref-9780192801463-e-1165

Online Publications

Entire Website

APA rules state that you should *not* include an entire website in the list of references. Instead, the URL should be included in the text of the paper in parentheses.

Web Page

Assistant Secretary for Public Affairs. (2016, March 24). Opioids: The prescription drug & heroin overdose epidemic. *U.S. Department of Health & Human Services.* Retrieved from https://www.hhs.gov/opioids

> Author: Assistant Secretary for Public Affairs.
> Publication date: (2016, March 24).
> Title: Opioids: The prescription drug & heroin overdose epidemic. *U.S. Department of Health & Human Services.*
> Publication information: Retrieved from https://www.hhs.gov/opioids

Social Media

LibrariansTNT. (2016, January 6). Cassandrasaurs for sure roamed this earth. Retrieved from https://twitter.com/LibrariansTNT/status/684778779034517504

> Author: LibrariansTNT.
> Publication date: (2016, January 6).
> Title: Cassandrasaurs for sure roamed this earth.
> Publication information: Retrieved from https://twitter.com/LibrariansTNT/status/684778779034517504

APA

APA
References: Examples

Blog

Grosvenor, E. (2010, August 7). The Dude abides in Salem [Blog post].
Retrieved from https://desperatelyseekingsalem.wordpress.com/2010/08/07/
the-dude-abides-in-salem/

> Author: Grosvenor, E.
> Publication date: (2010, August 7).
> Title: The Dude abides in Salem [Blog post].
> Publication information: Retrieved from https://desperatelyseekingsalem.word-
> press.com/2010/08/07/the-dude-abides-in-salem/

Online Video

ArtsAlive YamhillCo. (2015, March 25). ArtsAlive: Stephanie Lenox [Video file].
Retrieved from https://www.youtube.com/watch?v=xOQIKeERJTE

> Author: ArtsAlive YamhillCo.
> Publication date: (2015, March 25).
> Title: ArtsAlive: Stephanie Lenox [Video file].
> Publication information: Retrieved from https://www.youtube.com/
> watch?v=xOQIKeERJTE

Media and Performance

Film

Reiner, R. (Director). (1987). *The princess bride* [Motion picture]. United States:
Act III Communications.

> Author: Reiner, R. (Director).
> Publication date: (2015).
> Title: *The princess bride* [Motion picture].
> Publication information: United States: Act III Communications.

Television Show (Broadcast)

Frank Lisciandro [Television series episode]. (2016). In *The writing life*.
McMinnville, OR: McMinnville Community Media, MCM-TV.

> Author: —
> Publication date: (2016).
> Title: Frank Lisciandro [Television series episode].
> Publication information: In *The writing life*. McMinnville, OR: McMinnville
> Community Media, MCM-TV.

Television Show (Digital)

Cox, C., & D'Onofrio, V. (Performers). (2015). World on fire [Television series episode]. In F. Blackburn (Director), *Daredevil*. Burbank, CA: ABC Studios.

> Author: Cox, C., & D'Onofrio, V. (Performers).
> Publication date: (2015).
> Title: World on fire [Television series episode].
> Publication information: In F. Blackburn (Director), *Daredevil*. Burbank, CA: ABC Studios.

Audio (Album)

Mould, B. (1989). *Workbook*. Beverly Hills, CA: Virgin Records America.

> Author: Mould, B.
> Publication date: (1989).
> Title: *Workbook*.
> Publication information: Beverly Hills, CA: Virgin Records America.

Audio (Digital)

Adams, S. (2016, December 29). Be cool to the pizza dude. *This I believe* [Audio podcast]. Retrieved from http://cdn.audiometric.io/9487820912.mp3

> Author: Adams, S.
> Publication date: (2016, December 29).
> Title: Be cool to the pizza dude.
> Publication information: *This I believe* [Audio podcast]. Retrieved from http://cdn. audiometric.io/9487820912.mp3

Advertisement

BF Goodrich Co. (2016, July). Put the magazine down and go [Advertisement]. *Automobile Magazine, 31*(4). (p. 5). Ann Arbor, MI: The Enthusiast Network.

> Author: BF Goodrich Co.
> Publication date: (2016, July).
> Title: Put the magazine down and go [Advertisement].
> Publication information: *Automobile Magazine, 31*(4). (p. 5). Ann Arbor, MI: The Enthusiast Network.

Fine Art

Bartow, R. (1975). *After the fall III* [Paint on clay]. Portland, OR: Portland Art Museum.

> Author: Bartow, R.
> Publication date: (1975).
> Title: *After the fall III* [Paint on clay].
> Publication information: Portland, OR: Portland Art Museum.

Sikking, D. (Director). (2015, March 5–14). *Pride and prejudice*, by J. Austen [Theater performance]. ACMA Theater Company, Arts & Communications Magnet Academy Theater, Beaverton, OR.

> Author: Sikking, D. (Director).
> Publication date: (2015, March 5–14).
> Title: *Pride and prejudice*, by J. Austen [Theater performance].
> Publication information: ACMA Theater Company, Arts & Communications Magnet Academy Theater, Beaverton, OR.

Other

Pamphlet, Brochure, or Press Release

Travel Guard. (2016). *Insure your next trip with Travel Guard*. Stevens Point, WI: Author.

> Author: Travel Guard.
> Publication date: (2016).
> Title: *Insure your next trip with Travel Guard*.
> Publication information: Stevens Point, WI: Author

Government Report

U.S. Census Bureau. (2010). *Strength in numbers: Your guide to 2010 census redistricting data from the U.S. Census Bureau*. Washington, DC: U.S. Dept. of Commerce, Economics and Statistics Administration.

> Author: U.S. Census Bureau.
> Publication date: (2010).
> Title: *Strength in numbers: Your guide to 2010 census redistricting data from the U.S. Census Bureau*.
> Publication information: Washington, DC: U.S. Dept. of Commerce, Economics and Statistics Administration.

Dissertation

Kennison, K. R. (2011). *Smoke derived taint in grapes and wine* (Doctoral dissertation). Retrieved from http://espace.library.curtin.edu.au/R?func=dbin-jump-full&local_base=gen01-era02&object_id=185451

> Author: Kennison, K. R.
> Publication date: (2011).
> Title: *Smoke derived taint in grapes and wine* (Doctoral dissertation).
> Publication information: Retrieved from http://espace.library.curtin.edu.au/R?-func=dbin-jump-full& local_base=gen01-era02&object_id=18545

Personal Interview

APA does not require a citation in your references. Simply indicate the personal interview within the text of your essay. See the section in this chapter on personal communications and in-text citations for more about this.

Email

APA directs you to cite emails within your text, so there's no need for a reference entry. See the section in this chapter on personal communications and in-text citations for more about this.

3. Paper Format

APA style also offers guidance about how to format your paper so that it looks like all the other APA papers. This helps ensure that readers will stay focused on your ideas. Here are the general guidelines to keep in mind:

1. Type your paper on a computer and print it out on standard, white 8.5 x 11 inch paper. Set the margins of your document to one inch on all four sides.

2. Use a businesslike font that doesn't draw attention to itself and is easy to read. Times New Roman is a popular choice, and a 12-point size in this font is readable.

3. Double-space everything—no more, no less.

4. Leave two spaces after periods.

5. Indent the first line of paragraphs one half-inch from the left margin. Use the tab key to do that. Pushing the space bar five times to create a half-inch indentation worked on a typewriter, but it doesn't work with computers. These are different times.

6. Create a header in the upper right-hand corner of each page that is one half-inch from the top of the page and even with the right margin. This should include the page number. Use automatic page numbering for that. Trying to do that manually will cause needless suffering.

7. Never use boldface. Only use italics as required for the titles of larger works and some publications and, with grave restraint, for emphasis.

In addition to these general guidelines, APA style also provides guidelines for how to format different pages within a paper. In the following pages, we'll show you how that works with formatted examples.

A. Title Page

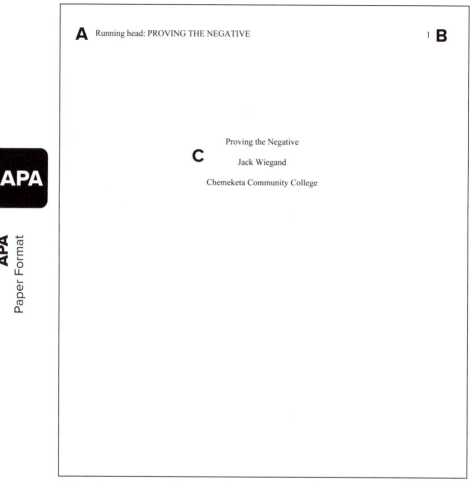

APA style requires a title page, so here are points to keep in mind for that page:

A. In the upper left corner, one half-inch from the top, put "Running head," followed by a colon and then the title of your paper in all capital letters. Do not include a subtitle here.

B. In the upper right corner, one half-inch from the top, put the page number without any other words. This runs throughout the entire paper, so use automatic numbering in the header section of your document for that.

C. In the upper half of the title page, put the title of your paper, and beneath that your name, and beneath that the name of the school you attend. If your paper contains a subtitle, put a colon after the title and put the subtitle on its own line beneath that. Center all of these lines on the page.

B. Abstract

E Abstract

F Folk logic holds that you can't prove a negative. The purpose of this paper is to explain why this sentiment is universally rejected among logicians. The author explains that negative categorical propositions come in two forms and describes methods by which each can be proven true. Type O propositions take the form $(\exists x)(Sx \cdot \sim Px)$, or "Some S are not P." A Type O statement such as "not all dogs have four legs" can be proven by observing a dog with any number of legs besides four. Type E propositions take the form $(x)(Sx \Rightarrow \sim Px)$, or "No S is P." The majority of these statements can only be proven by way of inference, as observation of every x is not possible. However, exceptions exist. For example, a statement such as "no bachelors are married" can be proven by illustrating that the phrase "married bachelor" is internally inconsistent. This paper also points out that the statement "You can't prove a negative" is, itself, a Type E proposition, and that if you could prove it, it wouldn't be true. This paper further argues that the lack of absolute proof does not preclude reasonable certainty and that sufficient absence of evidence should be regarded as evidence of absence.

APA

APA
Paper Format

The second page contains an abstract, which is a short summary of your paper's contents. The abstract should be 250 words or fewer.

D. The title of your paper in all caps appears in the upper left hand corner but without the "Running head" from the title page.

E. The title is "Abstract." Center the title.

F. Note that you do not indent the abstract paragraph.

C. First Page

H Proving the Negative

With the arrival of social media, society has seen a marked increase in armchair academia. Like the dilettantes of the Victorian era, today's hobbyist intellectuals spend their free time engaging in the gentleman's sport of debate, study, and showing off their brains, rather than their muscles. Also like the dilettantes of old, they treat it as strictly leisure, while eschewing rigorous academic commitment. While they might be able to regale their friends for hours about the brilliance of Voltaire, they've likely read his Wikipedia page, rather than *Candide,* or *Plato's Dream.* While they may be able to offer a criticism of a documentary about humanism, they would likely struggle to offer a worthwhile analysis of Thomas More's *Utopia.* Not that there's anything wrong with dilettantism. If anything, it does for society much more than reality television or competitive Frisbee.

I It can, however, create a few issues. In every scholarly field, information tends to change slightly as it moves from the academic sphere to the public sphere. When simplifying ideas to make them accessible to the public, the foundational information — that can, in many cases, take years of study to understand — is necessarily lost. To borrow from *The Science of Discworld,* we tend to "bend the truths just sufficiently to make the basic principles of the operation clear to a layman while not actually being entirely wrong" (Pratchett, Stewart, and Cohen, 2003, p. 14). What the authors repeatedly described as "lies to children" may seem wholly benign (p. 15), but they often lead to small misunderstandings, which can accumulate to form vast misunderstandings.

In philosophy, we might call these bits of misinformation folk logic. These are most easily described as bad ideas that agree with common sense. While most people tend to hold common sense in high regard, it is a very inefficient means of understanding the universe, as it

Now it's time for the actual paper. On the first page, follow these rules:

G. Put the title of your paper in all caps in the upper left corner and the page number in the right corner. The running header continues through the rest of the paper, so we'll shut up about it.

H. Center the title on the next double-spaced line. Don't add extra spaces.

I. Indent the first sentence of each paragraph exactly one half-inch. Use tabs to do that. Spaces are not precise enough.

D. Middle Pages

moon, as it moved through its annual cycle, indicated that the moon was a sphere (StarChild Team, 2013).

Many people have used this example as an argument against scientific understanding, **J** claiming that if we were wrong about something like that, we could be wrong about anything. In rebuttal, rationalists are fond of saying that while we may not be absolutely right about certain things, we are continuously becoming less wrong. As Richard Feynman (1999) put it in a lecture given at the 1964 Galileo Symposium:

> **K** A scientist is never certain. We all know that. We know that all our statements are approximate statements with different degrees of certainty; that when a statement is made, the question is not whether it is true or false but rather how likely it is to be true or false. . . . We must discuss each question within the uncertainties that are allowed. . . . We absolutely must leave room for doubt or there is no progress and there is no learning. (pp. 111–112)

People tend to think of correctness as a binary; one is simply correct or incorrect. To wit, we now know that the Earth is not round, or at least not perfectly so. Isaac Newton observed, correctly, that the Earth is an oblate spheroid rather than a perfect sphere (Choi, 2007). While both previously held positions are incorrect, surely it is *less* incorrect to describe the Earth as round rather than flat.

Just as positive evidence can be used to make more reasonable positive statements, so too can negative evidence — or, the *absence* of evidence — be used to make more reasonable negative statements. Unfortunately, this is another case of widespread misunderstanding. The popular belief, known as Rees' Maxim, is that absence of evidence is not evidence of absence. This misunderstanding is not only prevalent in the public sphere, but has also found a foothold

APA

APA
Paper Format

In the middle pages of the paper, there are few more things to remember:

J. Continue to double-space every line, no more and no less. Check your word processing software's paragraph formatting to make sure it doesn't add extra spacing at the end of each paragraph.

K. For block quotations, it's best to use your word-processor's ruler tool to indent the entire paragraph one half-inch from the left margin. Leave the right margin alone. Don't try to do this with tabs or spaces. To do so will only cause painful and permanent regret.

E. References

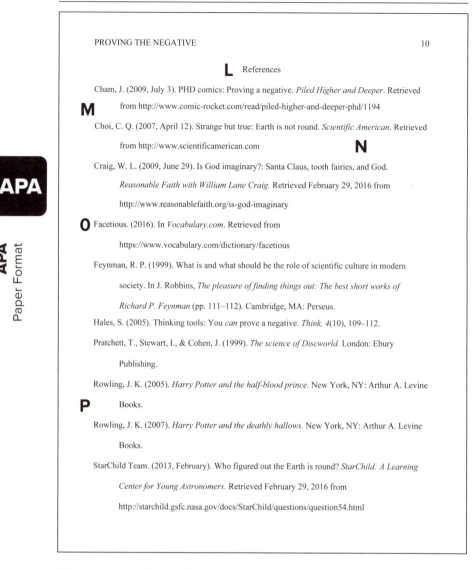

L References

Cham, J. (2009, July 3). PHD comics: Proving a negative. *Piled Higher and Deeper*. Retrieved

M from http://www.comic-rocket.com/read/piled-higher-and-deeper-phd/1194

Choi, C. Q. (2007, April 12). Strange but true: Earth is not round. *Scientific American*. Retrieved

from http://www.scientificamerican.com **N**

Craig, W. L. (2009, June 29). Is God imaginary?: Santa Claus, tooth fairies, and God.

Reasonable Faith with William Lane Craig. Retrieved February 29, 2016 from

http://www.reasonablefaith.org/is-god-imaginary

O Facetious. (2016). In *Vocabulary.com*. Retrieved from

https://www.vocabulary.com/dictionary/facetious

Feynman, R. P. (1999). What is and what should be the role of scientific culture in modern

society. In J. Robbins, *The pleasure of finding things out: The best short works of*

Richard P. Feynman (pp. 111–112). Cambridge, MA: Perseus.

Hales, S. (2005). Thinking tools: You *can* prove a negative. *Think, 4*(10), 109–112.

Pratchett, T., Stewart, I., & Cohen, J. (1999). *The science of Discworld*. London: Ebury

Publishing.

Rowling, J. K. (2005). *Harry Potter and the half-blood prince*. New York, NY: Arthur A. Levine

P Books.

Rowling, J. K. (2007). *Harry Potter and the deathly hallows*. New York, NY: Arthur A. Levine

Books.

StarChild Team. (2013, February). Who figured out the Earth is round? *StarChild: A Learning*

Center for Young Astronomers. Retrieved February 29, 2016 from

http://starchild.gsfc.nasa.gov/docs/StarChild/questions/question54.html

When you get to the end of your paper, insert a manual page break so that the references list will start at the top of its own page. The list includes all the works that you actually use in your paper. Here is what to keep in mind:

L. The title is "Reference" if you just cite one work or "References" if you cite more than one work. Capitalize and center the title.

M. The first line of each citation begins at the left margin. Subsequent lines are indented a half-inch. This is called a hanging indent. The most sensible way to do this is with the ruler tool that comes with your writing software. Even that isn't easy to figure out on your own, so search for video tutorials online. Once you get the hang of it, though, it's no big deal.

N. Double-space everything here just like you did on all the other pages. Be steadfast. Do *not* add a little extra space after each entry.

O. Alphabetize your sources by the first word or words in each citation. If the author isn't known, then you use the title for that work.

P. If you cite more than one source by the same author, you alphabetize by the next part of the citation. If the next part of the citation is a second author, use the second author. If the next part of the citation is the year, use the year. The earliest goes first.

APA

Chicago Style

The Chicago style of citation emerged out of the needs of the University of Chicago Press, beginning in 1891. To aid in the printing of professors' academic work, the editorial staff at the Press developed a style sheet. That sheet developed into a published book, and the *Chicago Manual of Style* has gone through seventeen editions in the years since. Today, the Chicago style is used by many disciplines in the humanities, including history, as a set of agreed-upon guidelines for scholars in these disciplines to follow when writing for classes or for publication. When we follow these guidelines, our readers can quickly understand and evaluate our sources while remaining focused on the ideas in the writing.

Chicago style is particularly well suited for historical research because the citations for historical writing are often quite long. Historical citations need to identify individual primary documents as well as the name of the collection in which they are located and the name and location of the historical archive. It's common in historical research to have multiple sources written by the same author, too, such as letters or diaries in a large collection. We can cite these using the longer citation format for footnotes, allowing future researchers to more readily retrace the author's steps through historical archives to locate the source.

Chicago style consists of three main categories—footnotes, bibliography, and paper formatting. In the body of the paper, you cite outside sources with Chicago-style footnotes. At the end of the paper, you will add a Chicago-style bibliography. The paper as a whole uses Chicago-style formatting to set margins, line spacing, page-numbering, and so on.

Think of Chicago style as a filter. When your ideas pass through this filter, your paper will conform to Chicago guidelines and emerge looking like every other Chicago manuscript. The two things different about your paper will be the two most important ingredients—the idea you present and how you explain it to your readers.

1. Footnotes

Chicago style allows authors to document citations within the text through one of two methods—footnotes or endnotes. Both systems have advantages and disadvantages, but this chapter focuses on footnotes due to their usefulness to the college writer. Footnotes allow readers to see the complete citation quickly with a downward glance of the eyes that doesn't interrupt the visual flow of the words in the text itself. Footnotes also allow readers to quickly understand whether you're using primary or secondary sources, whether you're using popular or academic sources, and whether your sources are up-to-date and relevant. This allows the reader to assess the quality of your research based on the choice of sources you make.

A footnote comes in two parts. In the body of the paper, you identify outside materials with a superscript number. Put the number at the end of the sentence or the clause that refers to a source. The number goes after any punctuation mark except for the dash, which it precedes. A corresponding, numbered note appears at the bottom—or foot—of the page where the idea appears. Start your footnotes with the number one, and then continue from there. If your paper only uses a few footnotes, you can use symbols instead. The order for the symbols you use should be *, †, ‡, and §. Any more than that, and you should really just use numbers.

1. Shamah argues that it's not just one specific or even one type of out-of-school activity that matters: "Out-of-school activities of all kinds appear to support the development of a sense of purpose."[1]

   The **footnote number** appears in superscript after the final punctuation—in this case, a closing quotation mark.

2. At least one expert claims that there's a clear relationship between out-of-school activities and a student's sense of purpose[4] — an idea that's been the subject of an increasing amount of attention by scholars.

   The idea being referenced appears before the dash, so the **footnote number** appears before the dash as well.

3. There's been an increasing amount of attention by scholars (at least one expert claims that there's a clear relationship between out-of-school activities and a student's sense of purpose[8]), but more still needs to be learned.

> A **footnote number** can appear inside of the closing parenthesis when the footnote refers to material inside the parentheses rather than to the sentence the parentheses appears within.

At the bottom of the page containing the footnote, include reference material about the work you just noted. How you document that source material will vary depending upon how many times you've cited the work, what you cited directly before this citation, and sometimes where you found the source material.

A. Initial Footnote

The first time you cite a source with a footnote, include the full citation information. Footnotes will include the author's name, the title of the work, and the publication information. The entire note will be single spaced, and the first line will be indented half an inch.

1. **Example:**

   1. **Scott** McCloud**,** *The Sculptor.* (New York: First Second Books, 2015), 28.

   > With books and works appearing in books, list the **first name**, followed by the last name, followed by a **comma**. Next, list the *title* of the book. The publication information goes inside a set of parentheses. Follow the closing parenthesis with a comma and the page number where the material referenced by your footnote appears. Close the note with a period.

2. **Example:**

   2. Nicole **J.** Georges, *Calling Dr. Laura* (New York: Houghton Mifflin Harcourt, 2013), 5–6.

   > If the author lists a **middle name** or **middle initial**, include it in the initial note. If the material you reference appears within a page range, separate the pages in that range with an en dash (–, usually option-hyphen or alt-hyphen).

3. **Example:**

   3. Devora Shamah, "Supporting a Strong Sense of Purpose: Lessons from a Rural Community," *New Direction for Youth Development* 132 (2011): 56.

   > When the title of the work is different from the *publication*, separate the two with a **comma**, not parentheses.

4. **Example:**

4. Lisa Ede, and Andrea A. Lunsford, *Writing Together: Collaboration in Theory and Practice* (Boston: Bedford/St. Martin's, 2012), 46.

> When citing two or three authors, separate each entry with a **comma**. Use the conjunction "and" before the last author named.

5. **Example:**

5. Robin M. Murray et al., *The Epidemiology of Schizophrenia* (Cambridge: Cambridge University Press, 2002), 14.

> When more than three authors share the authorship of a text, list the first author listed in the source. Follow the name with "et al.," a Latin phrase that means "and others." Place a **comma** after the period in "al." but not between "et al." and the author's name.

6. **Example:**

6. Julian Symons, preface to *Nineteen Eighty-Four*, by George Orwell (London: David Campbell Publishers, 1992), xix; Robert McCrum, "The Masterpiece that Killed George Orwell," *Guardian*, May 9, 2009, accessed February 29, 2016, https://www.theguardian.com/books/2009/may/10/1984-george-orwell.

> When the same idea is conveyed by two different works, separate the two notes with a **semicolon**. Use only one footnote number to mark the idea in the text. The lower case Roman numeral refers to an introductory page in the book. No page numbers are listed for the McCrum source because it's online.

B. Subsequent Footnotes

After providing the full reference material in the initial note, use a shortened version for any later notes that refer to the same source. Just like the initial note, the subsequent notes are single-spaced and indented one half-inch.

1. **Example:**

7. **Shamah,** "Supporting," 57.

> Only **last names** are needed in subsequent notes. Shorten the title to a key word or words unless it's already four words or fewer. Separate the author, title, and page number with **commas**. End the note with a **period**.

2. **Example:**

> 8. **D**. Shamah, "Supporting," 57.

> 8. **Devora** Shamah, "Supporting," 57.

> If **an initial** or **full name** is required to prevent confusion with another author already cited, add it to the note.

3. **Example:**

> 9. **Ede** and **Lunsford**, *Writing Together*, 46.

> When citing a work with two or three authors, give the **last names of each**. Be sure to maintain the order the names appear in the publication. That's how we know which one is the primary author.

4. **Example:**

> 10. **Murray** <u>et al.</u>, *The Epidemiology of Schizophrenia*, 14.

> If citing a work with more than three authors, list the **first author** followed by <u>et al.</u> and a **comma.**

C. Citing the Same Source Consecutively

In previous editions, Chicago style advised writers to use "ibid.," a Latin abbreviation that means "in the same place," to site the same source consecutively. It worked like this:

> 1. Shamah, "Supporting," 56.

> 2. Ibid., 57.

Chicago style now discourages the use of this term because it saves so little space over the shorted citations presented in Part B, "Subsequent Footnotes." The use of "ibid." can be confusing in electronic formats, too, which is another reason Chicago style now recommends that you abandon it just like you abandoned Facebook after your parents started posting pictures of you as a five-year-old.

D. Indirect Citation

Within her article, Dr. Shamah cites an idea from a book by William Damon. If you want to cite the same idea from Damon that Dr. Shamah cites in her article, what do you do? You go to the library, of course, and get Damon's book. That's what you do. If it has *one* idea worth incorporating into your paper, it might have more and better ideas for you to consider.

However, if you don't have time to get that book or your library can't access it, you can use an indirect citation. Within the footnote, cite the work where the information first appeared. Then cite the information for the work where you found the material. At the end of the paper, your Bibliography will also contain a single entry with information about both works.

1. **Initial Example:**

    1. William Damon, *The Path to Purpose: Helping Our Children Find Their Calling in Life*. (New York: Free Press), 17**,** quoted in **Devora Shamah, "Supporting a Strong Sense of Purpose: Lessons from a Rural Community,"** *New Direction for Youth Development* **132 (2011): 56**.

    > Cite the work where the material was first published followed by a **comma** and the phrase "quoted in." Then, provide information for **the work you actually found and read**.

2. **Subsequent Example:**

    2. William Damon, *The Path to Purpose: Helping Our Children Find Their Calling in Life* (New York: Free Press), 17, quoted in **Shamah, "Supporting," 56**.

    > This cites the same indirect source, but it only provides information required for subsequent citations for **the work you actually found** because this isn't the first time you've cited it. You've cited it a lot, actually.

E. Sacred Text

Sacred texts are different because they often have an unclear author and are available in many multiple translations with updated language. For these texts, cite the book, chapter, and verse—or other defining section—of the source, along with the translation you're using. In the footnote, abbreviate the book name, but spell out the translation title the first time you cite it. You do not cite these sources in the Bibliography at the end of your paper.

1. **Initial Examples:**

    1. **1 Thess.** 5:16–17 (New International Version).

    2. Qur'an 19:17–21 (Sahih International).

    > In the initial footnote, abbreviate **longer book names**, but spell out the translation title. Notice that chapter and verse are divided by a **colon**.

2. **Subsequent Examples:**

    8. 1 Thess. 5:18.

    9. Qur'an 19:21.

    > Subsequent footnotes are about the same. The only difference is that you no longer include the translation — unless you change to a different translation.

F. Block Quotations

Use block quotations for those rare occasions when you must quote five or more lines, two or more paragraphs of prose, or two or more lines of poetry.

Roy K. Humble argues for the use of note cards:

> If you're using note cards, you simply unleash their awesome, low-tech power. You lay the note cards on the dinette table and move them around. I know that doesn't sound like much, but trust me — it's awesome and powerful. Note cards allow you to visually arrange the evidence into its natural patterns. Those patterns might be steps in a process, competing answers, or different subtopics within the topic. It's different with every question and every set of evidence, but note cards are great for allowing you to look for patterns in the evidence you've collected. [17]

Despite the logic of the argument he presents, many students refuse to try the technique.

> Block quotations use formatting instead of quotation marks to show that this is a direct quotation. Typically, you should introduce a block quotation with a statement and a **colon**. Indent a block quotation one half-inch from the left margin, and double-space it like the rest of the paper. The <u>footnote number</u> sits just outside the ending punctuation of the quotation. If the paragraph continues after the block quotation, do not indent the sentence that follows the block quotation. That shows readers that this enormous quotation of yours is supporting information within a longer paragraph.

2. Bibliography

A Chicago-style Bibliography includes every source examined in the course of research, regardless of whether or not every source is mentioned in the essay text itself. In this way, it is distinct from the MLA-style work(s) cited page or the APA-style reference(s) page.

The complete publication information allows your readers to find any work that you consulted and study it themselves. Chicago divides that publication information into three elements, typically presented in this order:

    A. Author

    B. Title

    C. Publication information

A. Author

The author is the person or people or organization responsible for creating the source. This is the first piece of information you must find to build your citation.

With books, the author's name is usually on the spine. Magazines, newspapers, and journals typically put the author's name near the title of the article. However, the name may also appear at the end of short articles. If the source is a corporate or governmental publication and a specific author is not given, the organization itself is usually the author.

One Author

In Chicago style bibliography, the author's last name comes first, similar to what you'll see if you use MLA or APA.

1. **McCloud, Scott.** *The Sculptor*. New York: First Second Books, 2015.

   List the author's **last name** first, followed by a **comma** and then the author's first name. End the author section with a **period**.

2. **Williams, John Sibley.** *Controlled Hallucinations*. Hayesville, NC: FutureCycle Press, 2013. Kindle edition.

   Include the middle name or middle initial if it's listed in the original text. Don't provide the full name if the author (C. S. Lewis or J. D. Salinger, for example) prefers initials.

3. **Churchill, Winston.** *Triumph and Tragedy*. Boston: Houghton Mifflin, 1953.

   That's *Sir* Winston Churchill to you and me, but in a citation, don't include titles like "Sir," "PhD," "M.S.W.," "King," "Saint," or "Dr."

Two to Ten Authors

Chicago likes to make sure its authors get full credit. If your source has between two and ten authors, list all the authors' names.

1. **Ede, Lisa, and <u>Andrea A. Lunsford</u>.** *Writing Together: Collaboration in Theory and Practice.* Boston: Bedford/St. Martin's, 2012.

   Use a **comma** and the conjunction "and" between the authors' names. Note that the <u>second author's name</u> is written with the first name followed by the last name. Always list the authors in the order they appear in the text, not alphabetically.

2. **Murray, Robin M., Peter B. Jones, Ezra Susser, Jim van Os, and Mary Cannon.** *The Epidemiology of Schizophrenia.* Cambridge, UK: Cambridge University Press, 2012.

   The same pattern continues up to ten authors, with a **comma** separating each name until the last, which is marked with a **comma** and the conjunction "and." List them all.

Eleven or More Authors

If your source has eleven or more authors, the first names are compressed into initials, and only the top seven authors are even listed.

1. **Anastassopoulos, V., M. Arik, S. Aune, K. Barth, A. Belov, H. Bräuninger, G. Cantatore, et al.** "Search for Chameleons with CAST." *Physics Letters B* 749, no. 7 (October 2015): 72–180. doi:10.1016/j.physletb.2015.07.049.

   Eleven or more authors? If you can believe that such a thing exists, list the first seven names, separating each with a **comma**. After the seventh, put "et al." for "and others" and a **period**. You can be sure the seventh author is breathing a sigh of relief to not be stuck in "et al." with all the losers.

Authors of Scientific Sources

With scientific sources, Chicago style also compresses first names to initials.

1. **Roy, N., and N. Banerjee.** "Dynamical Systems Study of Chameleon Scalar Field." *Annals of Physics* 356 (2015): 452–466. doi:10.1016/j.aop.2015.03.013.

   With scientific sources, Chicago style abbreviates author first names just like APA style does. With Chicago, however, the first author is named with the last name followed by initials but all other authors are listed with the initials before the last name. **Commas** also separate the names of all the authors from one another.

Organizational or Governmental Author

Business and professional documents are often considered a work product and property of the company rather than that of the nameless, faceless authors who work for that organization. In that case, list the organization as the author.

> 1. <u>U.S.</u> **Census Bureau.** *Strength in Numbers: Your Guide to 2010 Census Redistricting Data from the U.S. Census Bureau.* Washington, DC: U.S. Dept. of Commerce, Economics and Statistics Administration, U.S. Census Bureau, 2010.
>
> > Abbreviate <u>commonly understood terms</u> like "U.S." instead of writing out "United States." More complex or particular acronyms should be written out.

Screen Name

Many online authors write under a screen name. You don't have to go searching for the author's secret (true) identity. You can use the screen name.

> 1. **chewingofthecud.** "What Currents or Movements are Currently Happening in Literature?" Reddit. March 13, 2014. Accessed February 29, 2016. https://www.reddit.com/r/literature/comments/20by05/what_currents_or_movements_are_currently/.
>
> > Simply list the screen name in the author's place.
>
> 2. **[Fittz, Christopher].** "The Unbridled Joy of Adrian Beltre." *Lone Star Ball* (blog), April 16, 2016. Accessed April 17, 2016. http://www.lonestarball.com/2016/4/16/11443156/the-unbridled-joy-of-adrian-beltre.
>
> > If the author's real name is known but not named as the author of the work, you can include that real name in the author's place in the citation but you must use **brackets** around the name. In this case, Christopher Fittz is the known author of a blog article posted under the screen name ghostofErikThompson.

No Author

If no author is listed for the text, skip the author's place and begin the citation with the information for the next element—the title of the work. Avoid the word "Anonymous" in place of the author unless grouping several anonymous works together in a bibliography.

> 1. *Go Ask Alice.* New York: Simon and Schuster, 1971.
>
> > If there is no author listed for the text, skip the author's place and begin the citation with the information for the next element—the *title*.

Other Contributors

Occasionally the person or organization most important to your discussion of a source contributed something other than the writing of the words. When you list the person or organization's role as a noun, it is abbreviated in the bibliography. For example, "editors" becomes "eds.," and "translator" becomes "trans." When you use the term as a verb, as in "edited by" or "translated by," the role is not abbreviated.

1. **Bevington, David, and David Scott Kastan, eds.** *Macbeth.* By William Shakespeare. New York: Bantam, 2005.

> If a paper about Shakespeare's play *Macbeth* emphasizes the edited collection in which the play appears rather than the play itself, list the editors in the author's place. Follow the contributors' names with a **comma** and their <u>role</u>.

B. Title

The second key element in a Chicago citation is the title. Chicago style requires you to capitalize the first word and all nouns, pronouns, verbs, adjectives, adverbs, and some conjunctions — *not* including the FANBOYS coordinating conjuctions ("for," "and," "nor," "but," "or," "yet," "so"). Don't capitalize any prepositions, no matter how long and substantial they appear. Chicago also requires you to format the title to distinguish between larger or smaller works.

Look for the title of the source near the author's name, usually at the beginning of the work.

Larger Works

Chicago uses formatting to quickly indicate whether the title of the work is a larger, self-contained work or a smaller work within a larger one. Larger works include books, anthologies, magazines, newspapers, websites, book-length poems, movies, and so on. Italicize the titles of these larger works.

1. Georges, Nicole J. ***Calling Dr. Laura.*** New York: Houghton Mifflin Harcourt, 2013.

> *Calling Dr. Laura* is the title of an entire book and should be italicized. Put a **period** at the end of this section.

2. Roemmele, Jacqueline A., and Donna Batdorff. ***Surviving the "Flesh-Eating Bacteria": Understanding, Preventing, Treating, and Living with the Effects of Necrotizing Fasciitis.*** New York: Avery, 2001.

> Put a **colon** between the <u>main title</u> and a subtitle. With larger works, both remain italicized. If the title contains words within quotation marks, those words are also italicized.

3. Rayburn, Kevin. *The 1920s.* October 12, 2008. Accessed February 29, 2016. http://www.louisville.edu/~kprayb01/1920s.html.

> Chicago only italicizes website titles when the websites function like printed books or magazines. If the site provides a comprehensive or steady stream of content, it's safe to italicize the website name.

4. Bartow, Rick. *After the Fall III.* <u>1975</u>, Portland Art Museum, Portland, OR.

> Chicago style considers most works of art to be larger works, even if they aren't physically large, so those titles are also italicized. Put a period after the title and then the <u>year it was produced</u>.

5. Bishop, Kyle W. *American Zombie Gothic: The Rise and Fall (and Rise) of* <u>The Walking Dead</u> *in Popular Culture.* Jefferson, NC: McFarland, 2010.

> If a part of the larger work's title would normally be italicized, as with the <u>title of a television show</u>, de-italicize it within the italics of the rest of the title.

Smaller Works within a Larger Work

When the work is nested within a larger work—such as articles within newspapers, journals, or reference books—it's considered a shorter work, and the article titles go inside quotation marks. You'll also use quotation marks for short stories and essays in an anthology, short poems within a collection, episodes within a television series, songs within an album, articles within a website, and so on.

1. Toobin, Jeffrey. "**Our Broken Constitution.**" *New Yorker*, December 9, 2013, 64–73.

> A magazine article is a shorter work that's nested inside a larger publication, so it's marked by **quotation marks** rather than italics. Notice that the **period** after this part of the citation slips inside those **quotation marks**.

2. Mahoney, Phillip. "**Gray Is the New Black: Race, Class, and Zombies.**" In *Generation Zombie: Essays on the Living Dead in Modern Culture*, edited by Stephanie Boluk and Wylie Lenz, 55–72. Jefferson, NC: McFarland, 2011.

> The Mahoney article appears within a larger collection of essays, so its title also appears within **quotation marks.**

3. Tuchman, Barbara. "**Retreat.**" Chap. 19 in *The Guns of August*. New York: Macmillan, 1962.

> Chapters or other sections within a book are considered shorter works, even if they're quite long.

4. Assistant Secretary for Public Affairs. "**Opioids: The Prescription Drug & Heroin Overdose Epidemic.**" U.S. Department of Health & Human Services. March 24, 2016. Accessed February 28, 2017. https://www.hhs.gov/opioids.

> Web pages are shorter works within websites.

5. Miller, Elise. "The ' Maw of Western Culture': James Baldwin and the Anxieties of Influence." *African American Review* 38, no. 4 (Winter 2004): 625–636.

> When quotation marks appear within the title of a shorter work, the inner quotation marks become **single quotation marks**. With shorter works, you also put a **colon** between the main title and a subtitle.

6. Kenny, Glenn. "A Perfect Day." Review of *A Perfect Day*, directed by Fernando Leon de Aranoa. *Rogerebert.com*. January 15, 2016. Accessed February 29, 2016. http://www.rogerebert.com/reviews/a-perfect-day-2016.

> The title of an individual article reviewing another work should be in **double quotation marks** even if the title of the work being reviewed is italicized. In this case, the review is a small work appearing on a website, and the film of the same title is the larger work.

C. Publication Information

The third and most complex section of a Chicago citation is the one that captures publication information about the source. This section will include information about some or all of the following subcategories of information:

1. Title of publication

2. Other contributors

3. Version

4. Number

5. Publisher

6. Publication date

7. Publisher location

Not every source will use each of the subcategories described in this section. For example, a book by a single author may not have "other contributors" to recognize. A periodical does not typically come in "versions," but in volumes and issues, two variations covered by "number." When your source does not contain one of the subcategories, move on to the next one on the list. Once you are done, place a period at the end of this section to show readers that your publication information is complete.

1. Title of Publication

For a larger work, the title of the work and the title of the publication are the same thing, so that title goes after the author in the title section (as seen in "Larger Works" three pages ago).

> **1.** Boluk, Stephanie, and Wylie Lenz, eds. *Generation Zombie: Essays on the Living Dead in Modern Culture*. Jefferson, NC: McFarland, 2011.
>
> > Because the citation focuses on the larger book as a whole, there's nothing to list as the title of the host publication. That's okay. Move along. Remember, don't italicize websites unless they produce regular content like a magazine or newspaper.

> **2.** Mahoney, Phillip. "Gray is the New Black: Race, Class, and Zombies." **In *Generation Zombie: Essays on the Living Dead in Modern Culture*,** edited by Stephanie Boluk and Wylie Lenz, 55–72. Jefferson, NC: McFarland, 2011.
>
> > However, this citation focuses on the shorter Mahoney article within the larger collection from Example 1. The title of the zombie anthology therefore appears in the title-of-publication section of this citation.

> **3.** Rockmore, Ellen Bresler. "How Texas Teaches History." ***New York Times,*** October 12, 2015. Accessed February 29, 2016. http://www.nytimes.com/2015/10/22/opinion/how-texas-teaches-history.html.
>
> > With articles in periodicals, the title of the publication is typically the name of the journal, magazine, or newspaper. Chicago style removes "The" from the start of the titles, which is fine.

> **4.** Assistant Secretary for Public Affairs. "Opioids: The Prescription Drug & Heroin Overdose Epidemic." **U.S. Department of Health & Human Services.** March 24, 2016. Accessed February 28, 2017. https://www.hhs.gov/opioids.
>
> > When the focus of the source is on one page at a website, the name of the website goes into the title-of-publication slot. Remember, don't italicize websites unless they produce regular content like a magazine or newspaper.

> **5.** Silence. "War Drums." *The Deafening Sound of Absolutely Nothing*. Profane Existence EXIST 161, 2016, vinyl LP.
>
> > When citing a song, the title of the song goes in the title section as a shorter work, and the name of the album or collection goes in this slot.

2. Other Contributors

Other contributors are people who play integral roles in creating the publication but are secondary to the named author of the work. Contributors can be identified by their role in the work, such as "performer," "director," "editor(s)," "translator," "writer," and "producer." Use phrases like "edited by," "translated by," or "directed by" with these contributors.

You'll find the names of other contributors on title pages or other places where credit is given to collaborators, like the credits of a film or the liner notes of an album.

1. Shakespeare, William. *Macbeth*. **Edited by <u>David Bevington</u> and <u>David Scott Kastan</u>**. New York: Bantam, 2005.

   | Name the role first. Then, list the <u>contributors</u> by first and then last name.

2. Bolano, Roberto. *The Savage Detectives*. **Translated by Natasha Wimmer.** New York: Picador, 2008.

   | The same goes for any **role.**

3. Mahoney, Phillip. "Gray is the New Black: Race, Class, and Zombies." In *Generation Zombie: Essays on the Living Dead in Modern Culture***, edited by Stephanie Boluk and Wylie Lenz**, 55–72. Jefferson, NC: McFarland, 2011.

   | When the work cited is within a larger work, a **comma** separates the title of the publication and the other contributors, so the <u>role</u> is written lowercase.

3. Version

Works often have multiple versions or editions identified by numbers that tell you how many times the publication has been revised—2nd edition, for example—or names that tell you the nature of the revision—like "unabridged" or "expanded."

When they exist, version numbers or names can usually be found next to the title of the publication within the original source.

1. Rottenberg, Annette T., and Donna Haisty Winchell. *The Structure of Argument*, **8th ed.** Boston: Bedford/St. Martin's, 2015.

   | Use numbers rather than spelling out editions distinguished by an ordinal number.

4. Number

Books that are too long to be published in a single publication are often split into multiple publications, and each is given its own volume number. In addition, periodicals that are published on an ongoing basis—as is the case with most scholarly journals—are assigned volume, issue, or volume *and* issue numbers to distinguish one publication of the periodical from another.

Like versions, the number is typically found near the title of the publication. However, it may be found within the publication on a page with more information about the publication, contributors, and so on.

1. Conan Doyle, Arthur. *Sherlock Holmes: The Complete Novels and Stories*, **vol. <u>1</u>.** New York: Bantam Classics, 1986.

   | "Vol." is an abbreviation for "volume" and should precede the volume number in large works. Use a <u>number</u> rather than spelling out the word.

2. Racy, A. J. "Domesticating Otherness: The Snake Charmer in American Popular Culture." *Ethnomusicology* **60, no. 2** (2016): 197–232.

> For academic journals and other small works, there is no "vol." before the volume number, but there is an abbreviated "no." for "number" before the issue number. You'll notice, hopefully, that there is no punctuation before the volume or after the issue.

3. Sheffield, Rob. "Getting to Know Colbert." *Rolling Stone*, October 8, 2015, 30.

> For magazines, Chicago style doesn't list issue or volume numbers, even if the original sources have them.

5. Publisher

The publisher is the company or person who actually produced a book, government publication, film, or website. Film and television series generally involve multiple publishers. In such cases, cite the publisher primarily responsible for the work. Periodicals often do not have a publisher, in which case you can skip this section.

With a book, you can find the name of the publisher on the title page or on a page near the front of the book that provides more information about the publication and its copyright. On pamphlets, look on the back or the innermost leaf of the folded paper. On brochures, look at the front or back covers. A website will usually list the publisher at the bottom of the page in the footer or on its version of the "About" page.

1. McCloud, Scott. *The Sculptor*. New York**:** **First Second Books**, 2015.

> Name the city where the publisher is located, then place a **colon** and then the **name** of the publishing company.

2. Bishop, Kyle W. *American Zombie Gothic: The Rise and Fall (and Rise) of* The Walking Dead *in Popular Culture*. **Jefferson,** NC: **McFarland**, 2010.

> When the city of publication is not immediately recognizable, add a **comma** and the state, using the two-character postal code.

3. Murray, Robin, Peter Jones, Ezra Susser, Jim van Os, and Mary Cannon. *The Epidemiology of Schizophrenia*. **Cambridge: Cambridge University Press**, 2002.

> When you have two cities known for publishing, the less well-known city is distinguished with a state abbreviation. That means you, Cambridge, MA.

4. Mayo Clinic Staff. "Gallstones-Definition." Mayo Clinic. **Mayo Foundation for Medical Education and Research.** July 25, 2013. Accessed February 29, 2016. http://www.mayoclinic.org/diseases-conditions/gallstones/basics/definition/con-20020461.

> Websites are often published by a sponsoring organization. List them if they are not the same as the name of the website and if the website is not considered analogous to a larger work like a periodical or a book.

5. Engber, Daniel. "The Neurologist Who Hacked His Brain—And Almost Lost His Mind." *Wired*, February 8, 2016. Accessed February 29, 2016. http://www.wired.com/2016/01/phil-kennedy-mind-control-computer/.

> *Wired* is published by Condé Nast, but because Chicago considers it an online magazine, don't list the publisher. In general, if you italicize the website, you don't need to list a publisher. If you don't italicize the website name, then you do list the publisher. Unless it's the same name as the site. Got that?

6. Lisciandro, Frank. Interview by Steve Long. *The Writing Life*. **McMinnville Community Media**, March 21, 2016.

> For broadcast works, name the network.

7. Silence. "War Drums." *The Deafening Sound of Absolutely Nothing*. **Profane Existence EXIST 161**, 2016, vinyl LP.

> For albums, name the publishing company and the <u>catalog number</u> with no intervening punctuation.

6. Publication Date

The publication date is the specific date the work was published. A book is published once and therefore only features the year. A periodical is published regularly throughout the year, so its publication date identifies which part of the year it was published in. A monthly magazine notes the month and year. A daily newspaper lists the day, month, and year.

The location of the publication date varies from publication to publication. In a book, the date will be on the title page or copyright page. Articles that appear in periodicals will often appear next to the byline and title of the source. This applies to online articles as well, but if a date is missing, you can also search the bottom of the web page for a publication year to stand in for something more precise.

1. Humble, Roy K. *The Humble Argument*. Dallas, OR: Problem Child Press**, 2010**.

> With books, movies, and other works published on a non-periodic basis, put a **comma** after the name of the publisher and then the year.

2. Federoff, Nina, and John Block. "Mosquito vs. Mosquito." *New York Times*, **April 6, <u>2016</u>**, p. A23.

> With works like magazines, journals, and newspapers that are published periodically, the most common format is month and day followed by a **comma** and the <u>year</u> since so many works come out on a specific day. Months are not abbreviated in Chicago style.

3. Barone, Richard. "The Power of Song: Recording Pete Seeger." *Tape Op.* **May–June 2016**, 36–44.

| Bimonthly publications will often use a month range followed by a year.

You may use the abbreviation "n.d." for no date, but do not use it lightly. It is rare that a publication date is truly not included in a print source. In web sources, the date can be difficult to find, but it almost always exists in the web page's HTML code. Most web browsers will allow you to search the HTML code, but that may take some work. Ask for help.

7. Location

The location varies by the type of publication. For stand-alone books, the location is usually the city where the publisher is located. For shorter works within anthologies or periodicals, the location is usually a page number or a range of pages. In online sources, the location is a URL or DOI. Film and music locations might be physical discs or their digital equivalent. The location for a work of art is often the place where the piece is on exhibit or housed in a collection. With the abundance of variety among mediums, the general rule is that you should document the location as accurately and precisely as possible.

1. Behar, Evelyn, Sarah McGowan, Katie McLaughlin, T. D. Borkovec, Michelle Goldwin, and Olivia Bjorkquist. "Concreteness of Positive, Negative, and Neutral Repetitive Thinking About the Future." *Behavior Therapy* 43, no. 2 (1998): **pp. 300–312**.

   | For more than one continuous page, put "pp." before the page range if you think it will cause confusion about what the number refers to. Chicago does not strictly require "p." or "pp." before a page number. Use an en dash (–, usually option-hyphen or alt-hyphen) to separate a range of pages.

2. "OSU Women Try to Keep a Storied Season Going." *Oregonian*, April 2, 2016, A1.

   | Some page numbers (especially print newspapers) include letters that identify the section of the newspaper in which those pages are located.

3. Erlanger, Steven, Stephen Castle, and Rick Gladstone. "Airing of Hidden Wealth Stirs Inquiries and Rage: Iceland Premier Steps Down as Release of Files Reverberates Around World." *New York Times*, April 6, 2016, **early edition, sec. A**.

   | That being said, Chicago style does not consider the page number an essential element for newspaper articles, so it can be omitted if you feel like it. When you know the edition of the newspaper, you can include that information here with the abbreviated section, separated by a **comma**.

4. Grosvenor, Emily. "The Dude Abides in Salem." *Desperately Seeking Salem* (blog). August 8, 2010. **Accessed <u>February 29, 2016</u>.** https://desperatelyseekingsalem.wordpress.com/2010/08/08/the-dude-abides-in-salem/**.**

> For online works, include a URL if it will reliably and consistently allow a reader to navigate to the cited page. Avoid using one-time URLs generated during a specific browsing session. Note that Chicago style requires a **period** at the end of the URL, unlike APA. Also note that you must include "Accessed" and the <u>date</u> you reviewed the site before the URL. Follow the accessed date with a **period**.

5. Aagaard, Jesper. "Media Multitasking, Attention, and Distraction: A Critical Discussion." *Phenomenology and the Cognitive Sciences* 14, no. 4 (December 2015): <u>885</u>**.** **Accessed February 29, 2016. doi:10.1007/s11097-014- 9375-x.**

> **DOIs** (digital object identifiers) are more stable online locations than URLs, so use them when they are available. Add when you accessed the work, too. The DOI location is in addition to the page location conveyed by the <u>page number</u>.

6. Kerr, William R., Ramana Nanda, and Matthew Rhodes-Kropf. "Entrepreneurship as Experimentation." *The Journal of Economic Perspectives* 28, no. 3 (2014): <u>25–48</u>**.** **www.jstor.org/stable/23800574.**

> For sources found through a database, add a stable URL or DOI if the database provides one. You don't need a date of access unless the original source doesn't have a publication date. If there are <u>page numbers</u>, include those first as part of the location.

7. Koster, John. "Hating the 'Hun' at Home: When America Went to War against the Kaiser, German-Americans Caught Hell." *American History* 51, no. 3 (2016): **58.** **Accessed February 29, 2016. <u>General OneFile</u> (A453285833).**

> When the database doesn't provide a stable URL or DOI, list the <u>name</u> of the database and, in parentheses, any identification number included with the source. And, as you might expect, add any page numbers first. Add the accessed date, too.

8. Mould, Bob. *Workbook.* Virgin Records America OVED 340, 1989, **vinyl LP**.

> For physical objects, describe the type of work that it is.

D. Bibliography Examples

As you see from the past section, Chicago style divides bibliographic information into three main sections:

A. Author

B. Title

C. Publication information

In the examples that follow, we'll break down citations into these three categories of information and then show you how to format both the initial footnote and the bibliography citation.

Even though these are common examples, you still have to adapt them to fit the information about the works you're using. You may have to tinker with the author section or the publication information section to accurately capture the information about a given work. But that's a good thing. It means that you can build each citation to match the works instead of having to somehow tailor the information about a work to fit a template that doesn't really fit.

Books

One Author (Print)

Todd, David. *Feeding Back: Conversations with Alternative Guitarists from Proto-Punk to Post-Rock.* Chicago: Chicago Review Press, 2012.

> Author: Todd, David.
> Title: *Feeding Back: Conversations with Alternative Guitarists from Proto-Punk to Post-Rock.*
> Publication information: Chicago: Chicago Review Press, 2012.
>
> **Initial Footnote**
> 1. David Todd, *Feeding Back: Conversations with Alternative Guitarists from Proto-Punk to Post-Rock* (Chicago: Chicago Review Press, 2012), 14.

Edited Collection

Boluk, Stephanie, and Wylie Lenz, eds. *Generation Zombie: Essays on the Living Dead in Modern Culture.* Jefferson, NC: McFarland, 2011.

> Author: Boluk, Stephanie, and Wylie Lenz, eds.
> Title: *Generation Zombie: Essays on the Living Dead in Modern Culture.*
> Publication information: Jefferson, NC: McFarland, 2011.
>
> **Initial Footnote**
> 1. Stephanie Boluk and Wylie Lenz, eds., *Generation Zombie: Essays on the Living Dead in Modern Culture* (Jefferson, NC: McFarland, 2011), 19.

Williams, John Sibley. *Controlled Hallucinations*. Hayesville, NC: FutureCycle
Press, 2013. Kindle edition.

> Author: Williams, John Sibley.
> Title: *Controlled Hallucinations*.
> Publication information: Hayesville, NC: FutureCycle Press, 2013. Kindle edition.
>
> **Initial Footnote**
> 1. John Sibley Williams, *Controlled Hallucinations* (Hayesville, NC:
> FutureCycle Press, 2013), Kindle edition, pt. 3.

Online Book

Twain, Mark. *Life on the Mississippi*. New York: Harper, 1917. Google Books,
books.google.com/books?id=h99O07cNtEMC.

> Author: Twain, Mark.
> Title: *Life on the Mississippi*.
> Publication information: New York: Harper, 1917. Google Books, books.google.
> com/books? id=h99O07cNtEMC.
>
> **Initial Footnote**
> 1. Twain, Mark, *Life on the Mississippi* (New York: Harper, 1917), Google
> Books, books.google.com/books?id=h99O07cNtEMC, 153.

Sacred Text

For sacred texts, only use footnotes. Do not cite them in the bibliography. Sacred
texts are different from other works, so read more about them in the footnote
part of this chapter.

> **Initial Footnote**
> 1. 1 Thess. 5:16–17 (New International Version).
>
> 1. Qur'an 19:17–21 (Sahih International).

Parts of Books

Chapter of a Book

Tuchman, Barbara. "Retreat." Chap. 19 in *The Guns of August*. New York:
Macmillan, 1962.

> Author: Tuchman, Barbara.
> Title: "Retreat."
> Publication information: Chap. 19 in *The Guns of August*. New York: Macmillan,
> 1962.
>
> **Initial Footnote**
> 4. Barbara Tuchman, "Retreat," chap. 19 in *The Guns of August* (New York:
> Macmillan, 1962), 341–72.

Mahoney, Phillip. "Gray is the New Black: Race, Class, and Zombies." In *Generation Zombie: Essays on the Living Dead in Modern Culture*, edited by Stephanie Boluk and Wylie Lenz, 55–72. Jefferson, NC: McFarland, 2011.

> Author: Mahoney, Phillip.
> Title: "Gray is the New Black: Race, Class, and Zombies."
> Publication information: In *Generation Zombie: Essays on the Living Dead in Modern Culture*, edited by Stephanie Boluk and Wylie Lenz, 55–72. Jefferson, NC: McFarland, 2011.

> **Initial Footnote**
> 1. Phillip Mahoney, "Gray is the New Black: Race, Class, and Zombies," in *Generation Zombie: Essays on the Living Dead in Modern Culture*, eds. Stephanie Boluk and Wylie Lenz (Jefferson, NC: McFarland, 2011), 55–72.

Articles

Journal Article (Print)

Racy, A. J. "Domesticating Otherness: The Snake Charmer in American Popular Culture." *Ethnomusicology* 60, no. 2 (2016): 197–232.

> Author: Racy, A. J.
> Title: "Domesticating Otherness: The Snake Charmer in American Popular Culture."
> Publication information: *Ethnomusicology* 60, no. 2 (2016): 197–232.

> **Initial Footnote**
> 1. A. J. Racy, "Domesticating Otherness: The Snake Charmer in American Popular Culture," *Ethnomusicology* 60, no. 2 (2016): 232.

Journal Article (With DOI)

Aagaard, Jesper. "Media Multitasking, Attention, and Distraction: A Critical Discussion." *Phenomenology and the Cognitive Sciences* 14, no. 4 (December 2015): 885. Accessed February 29, 2016. doi:10.1007/s11097-014- 9375-x.

> Author: Aagaard, Jesper.
> Title: "Media Multitasking, Attention, and Distraction: A Critical Discussion."
> Publication information: *Phenomenology and the Cognitive Sciences* 14, no. 4 (December 2015): 885. Accessed February 29, 2016. doi:10.1007/s11097-014- 9375-x.

> **Initial Footnote**
> 1. Jesper Aagaard, "Media Multitasking, Attention, and Distraction: A Critical Discussion," *Phenomenology and the Cognitive Sciences* 14, no. 4 , December 2015: 885, accessed February 29, 2016, doi:10.1007/ s11097-014- 9375-x.

Kerr, William R., Ramana Nanda, and Matthew Rhodes-Kropf.
"Entrepreneurship as Experimentation." *The Journal of Economic Perspectives*
28, no. 3 (2014): 25–48. http://www.jstor.org/stable/23800574.

> Author: Kerr, William R., Ramana Nanda, and Matthew Rhodes-Kropf.
> Title: "Entrepreneurship as Experimentation."
> Publication information: *The Journal of Economic Perspectives* 28, no. 3 (2014):
> 25–48. www.jstor.org/stable/23800574.
>
> **Initial Footnote**
> 1. William R. Kerr, Ramana Nanda, and Matthew Rhodes-Kropf,
> "Entrepreneurship as Experimentation," *The Journal of Economic Perspectives* 28,
> no. 3, 2014: 40, http://www.jstor.org/stable/23800574.

Koster, John. "Hating the 'Hun' at Home: When America Went to War against
the Kaiser, German-Americans Caught Hell." *American History* 51, no. 3
(2016): 58. Accessed February 29, 2016. General OneFile (A453285833).

> Author: Koster, John.
> Title: "Hating the 'Hun' at Home: When America Went to War against the Kaiser,
> German-Americans Caught Hell."
> Publication information: *American History* 51, no. 3 (2016): 58. Accessed February
> 29, 2016. General OneFile (A453285833).
>
> **Initial Footnote**
> John, Koster, "Hating the 'Hun' at Home: When America Went to War
> against the Kaiser, German-Americans Caught Hell," *American History* 51, no.
> 3, 2016: 58, accessed February 29, 2016, General OneFile (A453285833).

CHI

Behar, Evelyn, Sarah McGowan, Katie McLaughlin, T. D. Borkovec, Michelle Goldwin, and Olivia Bjorkquist. "Concreteness of Positive, Negative, and Neutral Repetitive Thinking About the Future." *Behavior Therapy* 43, no. 2 (1998): 300–312. Accessed February 29, 2016. www.sciencedirect.com/science/article/pii/S0005789411001109.

> Author: Behar, Evelyn, Sarah McGowan, Katie McLaughlin, T. D. Borkovec, Michelle Goldwin, and Olivia Bjorkquist.
> Title: "Concreteness of Positive, Negative, and Neutral Repetitive Thinking About the Future."
> Publication information: *Behavior Therapy* 43, no. 2 (1998): 300–312. Accessed February 29, 2016. www.sciencedirect.com/science/article/pii/S0005789411001109.
>
> **Initial Footnote**
> 1. Evelyn Behar, Sarah McGowan, Katie McLaughlin, T. D. Borkovec, Michelle Goldwin, and Olivia Bjorkquist, "Concreteness of Positive, Negative, and Neutral Repetitive Thinking About the Future," *Behavior Therapy* 43, no. 2 (1998): 312, accessed February 29, 2016, http://www.sciencedirect.com/science/article/pii/S0005789411001109.

Barone, Richard. "The Power of Song: Recording Pete Seeger." *Tape Op*, May–June 2016, 36–44.

> Author: Barone, Richard.
> Title: "The Power of Song: Recording Pete Seeger."
> Publication information: *Tape Op*. May–June 2016, 36–44.
>
> **Initial Footnote**
> 1. Richard Barone, "The Power of Song: Recording Pete Seeger," *Tape Op*, May–June 2016, 42.

Engber, Daniel. "The Neurologist Who Hacked His Brain—And Almost Lost His Mind." *Wired*, February 8, 2016. Accessed February 29, 2016. http://www.wired.com/2016/01/phil-kennedy-mind-control-computer/.

> Author: Engber, Daniel.
> Title: "The Neurologist Who Hacked His Brain—And Almost Lost His Mind."
> Publication information: *Wired*, February 8, 2016. Accessed February 29, 2016. http://www.wired.com/2016/01/phil-kennedy-mind-control-computer/.
>
> **Initial Footnote**
> 1. Daniel Engber, "The Neurologist Who Hacked His Brain—And Almost Lost His Mind," *Wired*, February 8, 2016, accessed February 29, 2016, http://www.wired.com/2016/01/phil-kennedy-mind-control-computer/.

Erlanger, Steven, Stephen Castle, and Rick Gladstone. "Airing of Hidden Wealth Stirs Inquiries and Rage: Iceland Premier Steps Down as Release of Files Reverberates Around World." *New York Times*, April 6, 2016, early edition, sec. A.

> Author: Erlanger, Steven, Stephen Castle, and Rick Gladstone.
> Title: "Airing of Hidden Wealth Stirs Inquiries and Rage: Iceland Premier Steps Down as Release of Files Reverberates Around World."
> Publication information: *New York Times*, April 6, 2016, early edition, sec. A.
>
> **Initial Footnote**
> 1. Steven Erlanger, Stephen Castle, and Rick Gladstone, "Airing of Hidden Wealth Stirs Inquiries and Rage: Iceland Premier Steps Down as Release of Files Reverberates Around World," *New York Times*, April 6, 2016, early edition, sec. A.

Newspaper Article (Online)

Rockmore, Ellen Bresler. "How Texas Teaches History." *New York Times*, October 12, 2015. Accessed February 29, 2016. http://www.nytimes.com/2015/10/22/opinion/how-texas-teaches-history.html.

> Author: Rockmore, Ellen Bresler.
> Title: "How Texas Teaches History."
> Publication information: *New York Times*, October 12, 2015. Accessed February 29, 2016. http://www.nytimes.com/2015/10/22/opinion/how-texas-teaches-history.html.
>
> **Initial Footnote**
> 1. Ellen Bresler Rockmore, "How Texas Teaches History," *New York Times*, October 12, 2015, accessed February 29, 2016, http://www.nytimes.com/2015/10/22/opinion/how-texas-teaches-history.html.

Reference Article

Only use footnotes. Do not cite in bibliography.

> **Initial Footnote (Print)**
> 1. *The Encyclopedia of World Crime*, 1st ed., s.v. "Agrippina (Agrippina the Younger)."
>
> **Initial Footnote (Digital)**
> 2. *Vocabulary.com*, s.v. "facetious," accessed February 10, 2016, https://www.vocabulary.com/dictionary/facetious.

> The term "s.v." is a Latin abbreviation that means "under the word." Its use here means that you find the reference article by looking up the title within the reference book.

CHI

CHI
Bibliography: Examples

Website Publications

Entire Website

Chicago style recommends citing specific pages or articles on a website rather than the site as a whole.

Page from a Website

Assistant Secretary for Public Affairs. "Opioids: The Prescription Drug & Heroin Overdose Epidemic." U.S. Department of Health & Human Services. March 24, 2016. Accessed February 28, 2017. https://www.hhs.gov/opioids.

> Author: Assistant Secretary for Public Affairs.
> Title: "Opioids: The Prescription Drug & Heroin Overdose Epidemic."
> Publication information: U.S. Department of Health & Human Services. March 24, 2016. Accessed February 28, 2017. https://www.hhs.gov/opioids.
>
> **Initial footnote**
>
> 1. Assistant Secretary for Public Affairs, "Opioids: The Prescription Drug & Heroin Overdose Epidemic," U.S. Department of Health & Human Services, March 24, 2016, accessed February 28, 2017, https://www.hhs.gov/opioids.

Social Media

The Librarians. "Cassandrasaurs for Sure Roamed this Earth." Twitter. January 6, 2016. Accessed February 29, 2016. https://twitter.com/LibrariansTNT/status/684778779034517504.

> Author: The Librarians.
> Title: "Cassandrasaurs for Sure Roamed this Earth."
> Publication information: Twitter. January 6, 2016. Accessed February 29, 2016. https://twitter.com/LibrariansTNT/status/684778779034517504.
>
> **Initial Footnote (Digital)**
>
> 1. The Librarians, "Cassandrasaurs for Sure Roamed this Earth," Twitter, January 6, 2016, accessed February 29, 2016, https://twitter.com/LibrariansTNT/status/684778779034517504.

Blog

Grosvenor, Emily. "The Dude Abides in Salem." *Desperately Seeking Salem* (blog). August 8, 2010. Accessed February 29, 2016. https://desperatelyseekingsalem.wordpress.com/2010/08/08/the-dude-abides-in-salem/.

> Author: Grosvenor, Emily.
> Title: "The Dude Abides in Salem."
> Publication information: *Desperately Seeking Salem* (blog). August 8, 2010. Accessed February 29, 2016. https://desperatelyseekingsalem.wordpress.com/2010/08/08/the-dude-abides-in-salem/.

Initial Footnote

    1. Emily Grosvenor, "The Dude Abides in Salem," *Desperately Seeking Salem* (blog), August 8, 2010, accessed February 29, 2016, https://desperatelyseeking-salem.wordpress.com/2010/08/08/the-dude-abides-in-salem/.

Media and Performance

Film

Kasdan, Lawrence, J. J. Abrams, and Michael Arndt. *Star Wars: The Force Awakens*. Directed by J. J. Abrams. 2015. San Francisco: Lucasfilm, 2016. DVD.

    Author: Kasdan, Lawrence, J. J. Abrams, and Michael Arndt.
    Title: *Star Wars: The Force Awakens*.
    Publication information: Directed by J. J. Abrams. 2015. San Francisco: Lucasfilm, 2016. DVD.

Initial Footnote

    1. Lawrence Kasdan, J. J. Abrams, and Michael Arndt, *Star Wars: The Force Awakens*, directed by J. J. Abrams, 2015 (San Francisco: Lucasfilm, 2016.) DVD.

Television Show (Broadcast)

Lisciandro, Frank. Interview by Steve Long. *The Writing Life*. McMinnville Community Media, March 21, 2016.

    Author: Lisciandro, Frank. Interview by Steve Long.
    Title: *The Writing Life*.
    Publication information: McMinnville Community Media, March 21, 2016.

Initial Footnote

    1. Frank Lisciandro, interview by Steve Long, *The Writing Life*, McMinnville Community Media, March 21, 2016.

Television Show (Digital)

Luke Kalteux. *Daredevil*. Season 1, episode 5, "World on Fire." Aired April 10, 2015, on ABC. https://www.netflix.com/watch/80018195.

    Author: Kalteux, Luke.
    Title: *Daredevil*.
    Publication information: Season 1, episode 5, "World on Fire." Aired April 10, 2015, on ABC. https://www.netflix.com/watch/80018195.

Initial Footnote

    1. *Daredevil*. Season 1, episode 5, "World on Fire," directed by Farren Blackburn, written by Luke Kalteux, featuring Charlie Cox and Vincent D'Onofrio, aired April 10, 2015, on ABC. https://www.netflix.com/watch/80018195.

"ArtsAlive Stephanie Lenox." YouTube video, 14:49. Posted by
    ArtsAlive YamhillCo. March 25, 2015. https://www.youtube.com/
    watch?v=xOQIKeERJTE.

> Author: —
> Title: "ArtsAlive Stephanie Lenox."
> Publication information: YouTube video, 14:49. Posted by ArtsAlive YamhillCo.
>   March 25, 2015. https://www.youtube.com/watch?v=xOQIKeERJTE.

> **Initial Footnote**
>   1. "ArtsAlive Stephanie Lenox," YouTube video, 14:49, posted by
> ArtsAlive YamhillCo, March 25, 2015, https://www.youtube.com/
> watch?v=xOQIKeERJTE.

Audio (Album)

Mould, Bob. *Workbook*. Virgin Records America OVED 340, 1989, vinyl LP.

> Author: Mould, Bob.
> Title: *Workbook*.
> Publication information: Virgin Records America OVED 340, 1989, vinyl LP.

> **Initial Footnote**
>   1. Bob Mould, *Workbook*, Virgin Records America OVED 340, 1989,
> vinyl LP.

Audio (Digital)

Adams, Sarah. "Be Cool to the Pizza Dude." *This I Believe*. NPR. Podcast audio.
    December 29, 2015. Accessed February 29, 2016. http://cdn.audiometric.
    io/9487820912.mp3.

> Author: Adams, Sarah.
> Title: "Be Cool to the Pizza Dude."
> Publication information: *This I Believe*. NPR. Podcast audio. December 29, 2015.
>   Accessed February 29, 2016. http://cdn.audiometric.io/9487820912.mp3.

> **Initial Footnote**
>   1. Sarah Adams, "Be Cool to the Pizza Dude," *This I Believe*, NPR, podcast
> audio, December 29, 2015, accessed February 29, 2016, http://cdn.audiometric.
> io/9487820912.mp3.

CHI

Bibliography: Examples

BF Goodrich Co. "Put the Magazine Down and Go." Advertisement. *Automobile
    Magazine,* July 2016, 5.

> Author: BF Goodrich Co.
> Title: "Put the Magazine Down and Go." Advertisement.
> Publication information: *Automobile Magazine,* July 2016, 5.
>
> **Initial Footnote**
> 1. BF Goodrich Co., "Put the Magazine Down and Go," advertisement,
> *Automobile Magazine,* July 2016, 5.

Performance

Pride and Prejudice. Readers can't access and consider live performances like they
can recordings. For that reason, you should mention details about the performance in the text itself or a footnote rather than in bibliography.

> **Initial Footnote**
> 1. *Pride and Prejudice*, by Jane Austen, directed by David Sikking, ACMA
> Theater Company, Arts & Communications Magnet Academy Theater,
> Beaverton, OR, March 5–14, 2015.

Other

Pamphlet, Brochure, or Press Release

Travel Guard. *Insure Your Next Trip with Travel Guard*. Stevens Point, WI:
    Travel Guard, 2016.

> Author: Travel Guard.
> Title: *Insure Your Next Trip with Travel Guard.*
> Publication information: Stevens Point, WI: Travel Guard, 2016.
>
> **Initial Footnote**
> 1. Travel Guard, *Insure Your Next Trip with Travel Guard* (Stevens Point,
> WI: Travel Guard, 2016), 1.

CHI

CHI
Bibliography: Examples

U.S. Census Bureau. *Strength in Numbers: Your Guide to 2010 Census Redistricting Data from the U.S. Census Bureau.* Washington, D.C.: U.S. Dept. of Commerce, Economics and Statistics Administration, U.S. Census Bureau, 2010.

> Author: U.S. Census Bureau.
> Title: *Strength in Numbers: Your Guide to 2010 Census Redistricting Data from the U.S. Census Bureau.*
> Publication information: Washington, D.C.: U.S. Dept. of Commerce, Economics and Statistics Administration, U.S. Census Bureau, 2010.
>
> **Initial Footnote**
> 1. U.S. Census Bureau, *Strength in Numbers: Your Guide to 2010 Census Redistricting Data from the U.S. Census Bureau*, (Washington, DC: U.S. Dept. of Commerce, Economics and Statistics Administration, U.S. Census Bureau, 2010), 2.

Unpublished Dissertation

Kennison, Kristen Renee. "Smoke Derived Taint in Grapes and Wine." PhD diss., Curtin University, Bentley, Australia, 2011. eSpace (185451).

> Author: Kennison, Kristen Renee.
> Title: *Smoke Derived Taint in Grapes and Wine.*
> Publication information: PhD diss., Curtin University, Bentley, Australia, 2011. eSpace (185451).
>
> **Initial Footnote**
> 1. Kristen Renee Kennison, "Smoke Derived Taint in Grapes and Wine" (PhD diss, Curtin University, Bentley, Australia, 2011), eSpace (185451), 3.

Personal Interview, Letter, Or Email

Only use footnotes. Do not cite personal sources like this in the Bibliography.

> **Initial Footnote (Personal Interview)**
> 1. Tom Franklin, interview by Sam Snoek-Brown, March 21, 2000.
>
> **Initial Footnote (Unpublished Letter)**
> 2. Walter Biggins, letter to Daniel Couch, March 23, 2015.
>
> **Initial Footnote (Email)**
> 3. Tom Franklin, e-mail message to Gertrude Mornenweg, April 3, 2003.

3. Paper Format

Chicago style also offers guidance about how to format your paper so that it looks like all the other Chicago papers. This helps ensure that readers will stay focused on your ideas. Here are the general guidelines to keep in mind:

1. Type your paper on a computer and print it out on standard, white 8.5 x 11 inch paper. Set the margins of your document to 1 inch on all four sides.

2. Use a businesslike font that doesn't draw attention to itself and is easy to read. Times New Roman is a popular choice, and a 12-point size in this font is pleasant and readable.

3. Double-space the text of your paper.

4. Leave only one space after periods or other punctuation marks—unless you're told otherwise by an elderly person who has fond memories of the days when typewriters ruled the land.

5. Indent the first line of paragraphs one half-inch from the left margin. Use the tab key to do that, too. Pushing the space bar five times to create a half-inch indentation doesn't work with computers.

6. Create a header in the upper right-hand corner of each page that is one half-inch from the top of the page and even with the right margin for the page number. Use automatic page numbering for that. Trying to do that manually will cause you anguish.

7. Never use boldface. Only use italics as required for the titles of larger works and some publications and, with grave restraint, for emphasis within the paper.

We'll show you how this works in the following pages by looking at some examples of actual pages. As we do, we'll add a few more guidelines that apply only in specific situations.

A. Title Page

A Proving the Negative

B & C Jack Wiegand
Writing 122
Prof. Roy K. Humble
February 29, 2016

Chicago style requires a title page, so keep these points in mind:

A. Place your title one-third of the way down the page. If your paper contains a subtitle, put it on a separate line directly after the title.

B. Place your name, the course, your instructor's name, and the date about two-thirds of the way down the page.

C. Center and single-space all the lines on this page.

B. First Page

E   With the arrival of social media, society has seen a marked increase in armchair academia. Like the dilettantes of the Victorian era, today's hobbyist intellectuals spend their free time engaging in the gentleman's sport of debate, study, and showing off their brains, rather than their muscles. Also like the dilettantes of old, they treat it as strictly leisure, while eschewing **F** rigorous academic commitment. While they might be able to regale their friends for hours about the brilliance of Voltaire, they've likely read his Wikipedia page, rather than *Candide,* or *Plato's Dream.* While they may be able to offer a criticism of a documentary about humanism, they would likely struggle to offer a worthwhile analysis of Thomas More's *Utopia.* Not that there's anything wrong with dilettantism. If anything, it does for society much more than reality television or competitive Frisbee.

E   It can, however, create a few issues. In every scholarly field, information tends to change slightly as it moves from the academic sphere to the public sphere. When simplifying ideas to make them accessible to the public, the foundational information — that can, in many cases, take years of study to understand — is necessarily lost. To borrow from *The Science of Discworld,* we tend to "bend the truths just sufficiently to make the basic principles of the operation clear to a layman while not actually being entirely wrong."[1] What the authors go on to describe as "lies to children"[2] may seem wholly benign, but they often lead to small misunderstandings, which can accumulate to form vast misunderstandings.

E   In philosophy, we might call these bits of misinformation folk logic. These are most easily described as bad ideas that agree with common sense. While most people tend to hold common sense in high regard, it is a very inefficient means of understanding the universe, as it requires that any new information conform to old information.

G   1. Terry Pratchett, Ian Stewart, and Jack Cohen, "Science and Magic," in *The Science of Discworld* (London: Ebury Publishing, 1999), 14–15.
   2. Pratchett, Stewart, and Cohen, "Science," 15.

On the first page, you don't put a title, but there are other things to do:

D. Place the page number in the upper- or lower-right-hand corner of the page. The first page of text should be page two.

E. Indent the first sentence of each paragraph one half-inch.

F. Double-space every line of text.

G. Footnotes should appear on the same page as their corresponding number within the paper. Unlike the rest of your text, they are single-spaced.

C. Middle Pages

things, we are continuously becoming less wrong. As Richard Feynman put it, in a lecture given at the 1964 Galileo Symposium:

> A scientist is never certain. We all know that. We know that all our statements are
> approximate statements with different degrees of certainty; that when a statement is made,
> the question is not whether it is true or false but rather how likely it is to be true or
> false. . . . We must discuss each question within the uncertainties that are allowed. . . .
> We absolutely must leave room for doubt or there is no progress and there is no learning.[10]

People tend to think of correctness as a binary; one is simply correct or incorrect. To wit, we now know that the Earth is not round, or at least not perfectly so. Isaac Newton observed, correctly, that the Earth is an oblate spheroid, rather than a perfect sphere.[11] While both previously-held positions are incorrect, surely it is *less* incorrect to describe the Earth as round rather than flat.

Just as positive evidence can be used to make more reasonable positive statements, so too can negative evidence — or, the *absence* of evidence — be used to make more reasonable negative statements. Unfortunately, this is another case of widespread misunderstanding. The popular belief, known as Rees' Maxim, is that absence of evidence is not evidence of absence. This misunderstanding is not only prevalent in the public sphere, but has also found a foothold among academics, including science educator and cosmologist Carl Sagan, and Christian apologist William Lane Craig.[12]

---

10. Feynman, "Role of Scientific Culture," 111–112.
11. Choi, "Strange but True: Earth Is Not Round."
12. Carl Sagan, *The Demon-Haunted World: Science as a Candle in the Dark* (New York: Ballantine, 1997); William Lane Craig, "#115 Is God Imaginary?: Santa Claus, Tooth Fairies, and God," Reasonable Faith with William Lane Craig, June 29, 2009, accessed January 10, 2016, http://www.reasonablefaith.org/is-god-imaginary.

The middle pages continue on with double spacing for the text and single spacing for the footnotes.

H. For block quotations, use your word processor's ruler tool to indent the entire paragraph one half-inch from the left margin.

I. Footnotes 10 and 11 are shortened because the author referred to the sources earlier in the paper. Footnote 12 cites the same idea found in two sources.

D. Bibliography Page

K 9

J Bibliography

Cham, Jorge. "PHD Comics: Proving a Negative." *Comic Rocket*. July 3, 2009. Accessed
L January 10, 2016. http://www.comic-rocket.com/read/piled-higher-and-deeper-phd/1194.

Choi, Charles Q. "Strange but True: Earth Is Not Round." *Scientific American*, April 12, 2007. **M**
Accessed January 10, 2016. http://www.scientificamerican.com/article/earth-is-not-round/.

Craig, William Lane. "#115 Is God Imaginary?: Santa Claus, Tooth Fairies, and God"
Reasonable Faith with William Lane Craig. June 29, 2009. Accessed January 10, 2016.
http://www.reasonablefaith.org/is-god-imaginary.

Feynman, Richard P. "What Is and What Should Be the Role of Scientific Culture in Modern
Society," In *The Pleasure of Finding Things Out: The Best Short Works of Richard P.*
O *Feynman*, 111–112. New York: Perseus, 1999. **N**

Hales, Steven. "Thinking Tools: You *Can* Prove a Negative." *Think* 4, no. 10, 2005: 109–112.

Jillette, Penn. "There is no God." *This I Believe*. National Public Radio. November 21, 2005.
Accessed January 10, 2016. http://www.npr.org/2005/11/21/5015557/there-is-no-god.

Pratchett, Terry, Ian Stewart, and Jack Cohen. "Science and Magic." In *The Science of*
Discworld, 14-15. London: Ebury Publishing, 1999.

Rowling, J. K. *Harry Potter and the Deathly Hallows*. New York: Arthur A. Levine Books, 2007.

P ———. *Harry Potter and the Half-Blood Prince*. New York: Arthur A. Levine Books, 2005.

Sagan, Carl. *The Demon-Haunted World: Science as a Candle in the Dark*. New York:
Ballantine, 1997.

StarChild Team. "Who Figured out the Earth Is Round?" *StarChild: A Learning Center for*
Young Astronomers. NASA. February 2013. Accessed January 10, 2016.
http://starchild.gsfc.nasa.gov/docs/StarChild/questions/question54.html.

CHI

CHI
Paper Format

When you get to the end of your paper, insert a manual page break so that the bibliography will start at the top of its own page. The list includes all the works that you examined in the writing of your paper. If you read and thought about a work but didn't end up using it, put it on this list.

Here's what you keep in mind while formatting this page:

J. The title is "Bibliography," regardless of how many sources appear on the list. Center the title.

K. The page numbering continues on this page, too.

L. The first line of each citation should begin at the far left margin. Any subsequent lines are indented a half-inch. This is called a hanging indent. The most sensible way to do this is with the ruler tool that comes with your writing software. It's not hard once you get the hang of it.

M. Single-space each reference.

N. Add an extra line of space *after* each reference to create space that makes the references more distinct visually.

O. Alphabetize your sources by the first word or words in each citation. If the author isn't known, then you use the title for that work.

P. If you cite more than one source by the same author, alphabetize by the next word in the citation — from the first word of title that isn't an article like "a" or "the," in other words — and with those other works by the same author, you replace the author's name with three em dashes.

This is another place where taking good notes during the research process will save you time and heartache. You need to include all the information that the Chicago style demands. So if you don't already have that information at your fingertips, you need to go back to the work and gather it after the fact, which you may or may not have time to do.

Glossary / Index

A

Abbreviation: A shortened version of a word.
105, 110–111
> *In MLA citations: 195, 197*
> *In APA citations: 228–229*
> *In Chicago citations: 259, 263–264*

Acronym: Initials that stand for a group of words.
101, 105, 110–111
> *In MLA citations: 143*
> *In APA citations: 222–223*
> *In Chicago citations: 264*

Active voice: A sentence where the subject of the sentence performs the action of the sentence.
74–77

Adjective: A word that describes a noun.
44
> *Types of: 44–48*

Adverb: A word that describes a verb, adjective, or adverb.
60

Anecdote: A short story used to illustrate a point.
12, 14

Antecedent: The word to which a pronoun refers.
134

Apostrophe: (') A punctuation mark that 1) replaces missing letters in contractions, 2) indicates possession, or 3) makes a single-letter word plural.
98–101, 117

Appositive: A noun that renames the noun beside it in the sentence.
36

Article (part of speech): A type of adjective that precedes a noun to qualify it as specific or general.
46

Attribution: Credit given to a source for an idea, a fact, or other information.
92, 158

B

Bias: A preconceived attitude toward a person, group of people, or idea that obscures objectivity.
132, 156

Block quotation: The correct formatting for long quotations (length determined by the style manual you are using), indented one half-inch from the left margin.
187
> *In MLA citations: 214*
> *In APA citations: 225, 251*
> *In Chicago citations: 261, 288*

C

Citation: An attribution or credit to the original author of material used by another author.
> *End-of-paper: 163*
> *In-text: 157–163*

Clause: A group of words containing a subject and a verb that express an idea.
25–28, 89
> *Dependent: 26, 65–68*
> *Independent: 25, 65–69, 89, 95*
> *Subordinate: 26–27*

Cliché: An overused phrase or metaphor.
21, 139–141

Colon: (:) A punctuation mark that either introduces an elaboration or clarifies meaning in a technical way.
97–98

Comma: (,) A punctuation mark that is used to divide ideas from one another. This happens with lists of items, multiple clauses, introductory ideas, interruptions to main ideas, introductions to quotations and attributions, multi-part numbers and nouns, and sometimes just to avoid confusion. *87–96*

> *In lists: 87*
> *In compound sentences: 89*
> *In introductory phrases: 90*
> *In interruptions: 91*
> *In direct quotations and attributions: 92*
> *In multi-part numbers and nouns: 93–94*
> *To avoid confusion: 95*

Comma splice: A writing error caused by two independent clauses joined with a comma. This creates a run-on sentence. *69–72*

Complement: A noun phrase that completes the meaning of a subject or object of a sentence by describing it with necessary information. *36*

Complex sentence: A sentence in which at least one independent clause is coupled with one or more dependent clauses. *72, 90–92*

Compound sentence: A sentence in which at least two independent clauses are joined with the appropriate punctuation. *71, 89–90*

Conclusion: An ending paragraph in a paper that 1) shows how the body paragraphs have explained and defended the thesis of the paper and 2) looks to the future implications of that thesis being true. *13–14, 157*

Conjunction: A word that joins parts of a sentence. *62–64, 89*

> *Coordinating: 62*
> *Subordinating: 64*

Connotation: The psychological or ideological values that color a word through cultural, historical, or personal associations. *127*

Contraction: Two words combined into one with an apostrophe standing in for the missing letter(s). *98–99, 129*

Coordinating conjunction: One of seven specific conjunctions—and, but, or, yet, for, nor, so—that join parts of a sentence.
62

D

Dash: (—) A punctuation mark that separates, introduces, interrupts, or omits information within a sentence. Other punctuation marks do these things more precisely, so avoid the dash in most cases.
105–106

Dependent clause: A group of words that depend on a main clause to express their full meaning. Dependent clauses, which cannot stand alone as a sentence, often begin with a subordinating conjunction like after, although, or as if.
26, 65–68

Demonstrative pronoun: A pronoun that can refer back to or identify a noun. A demonstrative pronoun may also be used as a determiner to modify a noun.
51, 68

Determiner: A word that precedes and modifies a noun. Articles, possessive pronouns, and demonstrative pronouns are all types of determiners.
46

Direct quotation: A verbatim inclusion of another author's writing in your own.
159–161

DOI (digital object identifier): An alphanumeric designation used in source citation of electronic publications, often assigned to online or digital documents as a permanent, stable identifier.
In MLA citations: 198
In APA citations: 237–238
In Chicago citations: 272–273, 277

E

Ellipses: (. . .) A punctuation mark, made of three successive periods, that indicates that the author has removed words from a direct quotation.
106, 119

End-of-paper citation: The listing of a source or sources used in a paper that contains the information necessary for the reader to locate the origin of the source(s).
163
In MLA citations: 188–211
In APA citations: 227–246
In Chicago citations: 262–284

F

Fragment: An incomplete sentence. See also: Clause, dependent.
65–68

G

Gerund: A noun derived from a verb by adding –ing to the end.
29, 65, 78

Gray literature: A broad category of literature that is not produced to be published and may have only limited distribution within an academic, professional, or governmental field.
231

H

Hanging indent: The indentation of the second and all subsequent lines of text while the first line remains in line with the margin.
In MLA citations: 216
In APA citations: 252
In Chicago citations: 290

Helping verb: Also known as auxiliary verbs, these are words used in combination with the main verb to show time, duration, or mood.
58–59

Hyphen: (-) A punctuation mark that connects two or more words, creating a compound word that combines the meanings of both into a single unit.
114–115

I

Idiom: A common figurative expression.
129

Independent clause: A group of words that express a complete thought. Independent clauses contain a subject and a verb that can stand alone as a sentence.
25, 65–69, 89, 95

Infinitive: A noun or adverb phrase formed by "to" plus the root form of a verb and indicating no specific tense.
30–31

In-text citation: A method of attributing quoted, paraphrased, and summarized ideas to their sources within a paragraph.
157–163, 173
> *In MLA citations: 180–187*
> *In APA citations: 218–226*
> *In Chicago citations: 256–261*

Introduction: An opening paragraph that introduces three pieces of information that will appear in your paper: 1) the topic of your paper, 2) the focus of your paper on a part of that topic, and 3) the main idea (thesis) that your paper will explain.
10–12

Irregular verb: Verbs that do not follow a standard pattern of conjugation.
55–56

J

Jargon: Wording that is usually familiar only to a specific group of people such as within a profession, field, or hobby.
143–144

L

Linking verb: A verb that connects a subject and a complement. Usually a form of "to be" but can include any of the five sense verbs or verbs that show a particular state of being.
38–39

M

Metaphor: A non-literal comparison that suggests by association some quality of a person, thing or action.
139

N

Nonrestrictive clause: A dependent clause that is not essential to the main idea of the sentence and is often set off from the rest of the sentence with commas.
27

Noun: A word that represents people, places, things, or ideas.
28, 29–37, 42–43, 99–100
> *Proper nouns: 107*
> *Pronouns: 49–53, 109, 141*

Noun phrase: A word or group of words that includes a noun and together serve the same purpose as a noun in a sentence; also called a nominal phrase. *29–39*

> *Subjects: 23, 25*
> *Objects: 34–35*
> *Complements: 36*
> *Gerunds: 29, 65, 78*
> *Infinitives: 30–31*
> *Appositives: 36*

O

Object: The part of a sentence that receives or explains the action of the verb. *34–35*

P

Paragraph: A grouping of sentences that together express a single, focused idea. *3*

> *Topic sentences: 4–5, 15–16*
> *Supporting sentences: 5–6*
> *Opening paragraphs: 10–12*
> *Body paragraphs: 4–9*
> *Closing paragraphs: 13–14*

Parallelism: A grammatical pattern in sentences and paragraphs that demonstrates that things, actions, or ideas are similar in nature and importance. *78–79*

> *In lists: 87–88*

Paraphrase: A sentence or paragraph of synthesis and simplification of another author's writing, with the goal of making complex ideas easier to understand. *162*

Parentheses: [( )] A pair of punctuation marks that enclose information that is important but is not part of the main idea in a sentence. *104*

Parenthetical citation: The portion of an in-text citation that appears within parentheses at the end of a word or phrase.

> *See In-text citation*

Parts of speech: The categories of words in a language.
42–64
> *Nouns: 28, 29–37, 42–43, 99–100*
> *Adjectives: 48*
> *Pronouns: 49–53, 109, 141*
> *Verbs: 23, 31–32, 37, 54–59*
> *Adverbs: 60*
> *Prepositions: 40–41, 61*
> *Conjunctions: 62–64, 89*

Passive voice: A sentence where the object of the sentence is placed in the subject's place and appears to perform the action of the sentence.
74–77

Patchwriting: The swapping out of words in a sentence while maintaining the general structure and meaning from the original source.
171

Period: A punctuation mark that is used to end a sentence that is an idea or information.
86

Phrase: A group of words that act as a unit in a sentence for a common purpose.
29–41
> *Noun phrases: 29–36*
> *Verb phrases: 37–39*
> *Prepositional phrases: 40–41*

Plural: A noun or verb that that is more than one. The grammatical structure of other words in a sentence is affected by whether a noun or verb is plural.
> *Nouns: 43*
> *Verbs: 55*
> *Agreement: 81–83*

Possessive: An adjective form that indicates that one noun belongs to another noun.
50, 99–100

Possesive adjective: An adjective that shows ownership.
99

Predicate: The verb or verb phrase that expresses the action of the sentence.
23

Preposition: Words used with an object in a phrase to express some quality of time, space, or reason.
40–41, 61

Prepositional phrase: A preposition followed by a determiner and any adjectives coupled with a noun or pronoun.
40–41

Pronoun: A word that stands in for or refers to a previously expressed noun.
49–53, 109, 141
> *Personal: 49*
> *Possessive: 50*
> *Reflexive: 50*
> *Other types of: 51–52*

Proper noun: A capitalized word that is the name of a specific person, place, or thing.
107

Q

Quotation: The inclusion of the words or phrases of another author in your own writing. You must always give credit to the author of a quotation.
157–163
> *Direct: 159–161*
> *Block: 187*

Quotation marks: (" ") A pair of punctuation marks that enclose words or phrases, indicating that 1) the enclosed phrases are quotations of another author's writing, 2) the enclosed word is being written about as a word, or 3) the enclosed word or words are the title of a shorter work.
102–103
> *To indicate direct quotations : 102*
> *To indicate a word as a word: 103*
> *To indicate titles of short works: 103*
> *To indicate irony: 104*

R

Relative clause: A dependent clause that starts with a relative pronoun. A relative clause can be either restrictive or nonrestrictive and refers to something that precedes it in the sentence.
27, 29
> *Nonrestrictive: 27*
> *Restrictive: 27–28*

Relative pronoun: A pronoun such as this, that, these, or those that relates groups of words to nouns or pronouns. A relative pronoun often introduces relative clauses.
27–28, 68

Restrictive clause: A dependent clause that is essential to the main idea of the sentence and unlike nonrestrictive clauses is not usually set off with commas.
27, 28

Run-on sentence: Two or more independent clauses joined in a single sentence without the punctuation necessary to separate them.
69–71

S

Semicolon: (;) A punctuation mark that 1) joins related, independent clauses or 2) separates items in a complex list.
95–96

Sentence: A group of words that state an idea, made up of a noun and a verb.
23–25
> *Simple: 23*
> *Complex: 72, 90–92*
> *Compound: 71, 89–90*
> *Run-ons: 69–73*
> *Fragments: 65–69*

Signal phrase: A phrase that introduces evidence or other information by attributing it to the source in the body of the sentence.
159

Slanted language: Words that skew the reader toward a particular point of view.
132–133, 156

Subject: The part of a sentence that joins with a verb to form a clause. The subject performs the action of the verb.
23, 25

Subject-verb agreement: A grammatical structure where the singular and plural forms of the subject and verb in a sentence align with one another correctly. An error results in subject-verb disagreement.
81–83

Subordinate clause: A dependent clause that explains a main clause and is joined to it by a subordinating conjunction.
26, 27

Summary: A sentence or paragraph that compresses detailed information into a shorter statement that describes what the information means or adds up to.
161–162

Superscript: Typographical category for a number or other symbol that is small in size and placed slightly higher on the line than other type in a document. Superscript is often used to indicate a footnote or endnote.
256

T

Thesis: A reasonable idea you have about a topic that serves as the central argument of a piece of writing.
10–12

Topic sentence: The main idea of a paragraph expressed in a sentence within that paragraph.
7–8, 20

Transition: Words or phrases that help readers understand how different supporting sentences are organized or how different ideas relate to one another.
7, 8, 19, 20, 21, 128

U

URL (uniform resource locator): The web address used to locate web resources and other online material.
In MLA citations: 198
In APA citations: 237–238
In Chicago citations: 272–273

V

Verb: A word that expresses action or state of being.
23, 31–32, 37, 54–59

Verb phrase: A group of words that describe an action or — when the verb is a linking verb — the subject of a sentence.
37–39
With action verbs: 37
With linking verbs: 38–39

Expanded Table of Contents

A Note to Students

A. How the Handbook Works v
B. How to Find What You Need vii
C. How to Use What You Find ix

A Note to Faculty

A. What We've Done xi
B. What You Can Do. xii

Chapter 1: Paragraphs

1. Body Paragraphs   4

A. Topic Sentences 4
B. Supporting Sentences 5
C. Transitional Words and Phrases 7
D. Paragraph Groups. 9

2. Opening and Closing Paragraphs   10

A. Opening Paragraphs 10
   Moving from General to Specific. 10
   An Attention Grabber 11
   An Engaging Anecdote 12
B. Closing Paragraphs 13
   Doing Something about It. 13
   The Danger of Doing Nothing 13
   Return to the Opening 14

3. Common Problems   15

A. Unfocused Paragraphs. 15
B. Disorganized Paragraphs. 19
C. Clichéd Opening Paragraphs 21

Chapter 2: Sentences

1. Clauses   25

A. The Main Clause 25

B. Dependent Clauses 26

C. Types of Dependent Clauses. 26

    Subordinate Clauses 26

    Relative Clauses. 27

    Noun Clauses 28

2. Phrases   29

A. Noun Phrases 29

    Gerund Phrases. 29

    Infinitive Phrases. 30

B. Noun Phrases in Sentences 32

    Subjects. 32

    Objects 34

    Complements 36

    Appositives 36

C. Verb Phrases 37

    With Action Verbs. 37

    With Linking Verbs. 38

D. Prepositional Phrases 40

    As Adjectives. 40

    As Adverbs 40

    As Introductions and Transitions. 41

3. Parts of Speech   42

A. Nouns. 42

B. Adjectives 44

    Descriptive Adjectives 44

    Quantity Adjectives. 45

    Determiners 46

    Adjective Order. 48

C. Pronouns 49

    Personal Pronouns. 49

    Possessive Pronouns. 50

    Reflexive Pronouns 50

    Demonstrative Pronouns. 51

    Indefinite Pronouns. 52

    Interrogative Pronouns 52

D. Verbs. 54

    Verb Forms 54

    Helping Verbs 58

E. Adverbs 60

F. Prepositions 61

G. Conjunctions 62

    Coordinating Conjunctions. 62

    Correlating Conjunctions 63

    Subordinating Conjunctions 64

4. Common Problems   65

A. Sentence Fragments 65

B. Run-On Sentences 69

C. Passive Voice. 74

D. Faulty Parallelism. 78

E. Subject-Verb Disagreement 81

Chapter 3: Punctuation and Mechanics

1. Ending Punctuation (. ? !)   86

2. Commas (,)   87

A. Items in a List. 87

B. Clauses in Compound Sentences 89

C. Introductory Words or Phrases. 90

D. Interruptions to the Main Clause. 91

E. Direct Quotations and Attributions 92

F. Multipart Numbers and Nouns 93

    Numbers. 93

    Cities. 93

    Addresses. 94

    People 94

    Dates. 94

G. To Avoid Confusion 95

3. Semicolons (;)   95

A. Join Independent Clauses. 95

B. Separate Multi-Part Items in a List. 96

4. Colons (:)   97

A. Introduce Elaborations 97

B. Technical Clarity. 98

5. Apostrophes (')   98

A. Missing Words or Numbers 98

B. Possessive Adjectives 99

    Singular Noun Phrases 99

    Plural Noun Phrases 100

C. Plural Letters 101

6. Quotation Marks (" ")   102

A. Direct Quotations. 102

B. Words as Words. 103

C. Titles of Shorter Works. 103

D. Ironic Meaning. 104

7. Other Punctuation Marks   104

A. Parentheses ( ) 104

B. Dash (—). 105

    Dramatic Introduction 105

    Dramatic Interruption. 105

C. Ellipses (. . .). 106

8. Capitalization   107

A. The First Word of a Sentence 107

B. Proper Nouns 107

C. Major Words in Titles of Created Works 108

D. Days, Months, and Holidays 108

E. The Pronoun "I". 109

9. Abbreviations   110

A. Abbreviations with Names 110

B. Acronyms 110

C. Technical and Scientific Terms. 111

10. Italics   112

A. Emphasis. 112

B. Titles of Larger Created Works. 112

C. Names of Vehicles 113

D. Non-English Words and Sounds. 113

11. Hyphens (-)   114

A. Compound Adjectives. 114

B. Compound Nouns and Numbers 114

C. Line Breaks. 115

12. Common Problems — 115

A. Excessive Ending Punctuation 115

B. Apostrophe Abuse. 117

C. Punctuation for Sound Effects 119

D. Errors with Titles. 120

Chapter 4: Word Choice

1. Appropriate Words — 124

A. Correct Words. 124

B. Objective Attitude. 127

C. Formal Writing Style. 128

2. Precise Words — 130

3. Common Problems — 132

A. Slanted Language 132

B. Exclusionary Language 134

C. Wordy Sentences. 138

D. Clichés 139

E. Unnecessary Self-Reference 141

F. Jargon 143

4. Commonly Confused Words — 145

Chapter 5: Research

1. The Research Process — 152

A. Ask a Good Question 152

B. Gather and Assess Information. 153

    Identify Key Terms 153

    Find Your Information through the Library. 154

    Types of Publications. 154

    Evaluate the Quality of Your Sources. 155

    Take Notes 156

C. Form a Conclusion 157

2. Documentation 157

A. In-Text Documentation 158

Source Framing... 159

Direct Quotation 159

Summary.. 161

Paraphrase 162

Common Knowledge 163

B. End-of-Paper Documentation............................. 163

3. Common Problems 164

A. Poor Note-Taking 164

B. Missing Citations 166

C. Relying on Citation Generators 167

D. Unquoted Quotations 169

E. Patchwriting 171

F. Quote Bombs.. 172

G. Incorrectly Using and Citing Images 173

Chapter 6: MLA Style

1. In-Text Citations 180

A. Author in the Introduction............................. 180

B. Author Absent from the Introduction.................... 181

C. More than One Work by an Author 182

D. Authors with the Same Last Name....................... 183

E. Two or More Authors 183

F. Organization or Agency as Author...................... 184

G. Unknown Author 185

H. Indirect Citation..................................... 186

I. Block Quotations...................................... 187

2. List of Works Cited 188

A. Author.. 188

One Author 189

Two Authors 189

Three or More Authors 189

Organizational or Governmental Author.................... 189

Screen Name... 190

No Author... 190

Other Contributors.. 190

B. Title 191

Larger Works.. 191

Smaller Works (within a Larger Work) 192

C. Container (Publication) 193

   1. Title of Publication 193

   2. Other Contributors. 194

   3. Version 195

   4. Number 195

   5. Publisher. 196

   6. Publication Date 197

   7. Location 198

D. Other Information 199

   Second Container (Publication) 199

   Date of Access 200

   City of Publication 200

E. Putting It All Together 201

F. Works Cited Examples. 202

   Books 202

   Parts of a Book 204

   Articles 205

   Online Publications. 207

   Media and Performance. 208

   Other Works 210

3. Paper Format   **212**

A. First Page 213

B. Middle Pages. 214

C. Works Cited Page 215

Chapter 7: APA Style

1. In-Text Citations   **218**

A. Author in the Introduction 218

B. Author Absent from the Introduction. 219

C. More Than One Work by an Author. 220

D. Authors with the Same Last Name. 220

E. Two Authors 221

F. Three or More Authors 222

G. Organization or Agency as Author 222

H. Unknown Author. 223

I. Sacred Text. 224

J. Indirect Citation 224

K. Personal Communication. 225

L. Block Quote 225

2. References   227

A. Author 227
One Author 227
Two to Seven Authors 228
Eight or More Authors 228
Organizational or Governmental Author 228
Screen Name 229
No Author 229
Nontraditional Authors 229

B. Publication Date 230

C. Title 231
Larger Works 231
Smaller Works within a Larger Work 232

D. Publication Information 234
1. Other Contributors 234
2. Title of Publication 235
3. Version 236
4. Number 236
5. Publisher 237
6. Location 237

E. Reference List Examples 239
Books 239
Parts of Books 240
Articles 241
Online Publications 243
Media and Performance 244
Other 246

3. Paper Format   247

A. Title Page 248

B. Abstract 249

C. First Page 250

D. Middle Pages 251

E. References 252

Chapter 8: Chicago Style

1. Footnotes   **256**

  A. Initial Footnote 257

  B. Subsequent Footnotes 258

  C. Citing the Same Source Consecutively 259

  D. Indirect Citation 259

  E. Sacred Text 260

  F. Block Quotations 261

2. Bibliography   **262**

  A. Author 262

    One Author 262

    Two to Ten Authors 263

    Eleven or More Authors 263

    Authors of Scientific Sources 263

    Organizational or Governmental Author 264

    Screen Name 264

    No Author 264

    Other Contributors 265

  B. Title 265

    Larger Works 265

    Smaller Works within a Larger Work 266

  C. Publication Information 267

    1. Title of Publication 268

    2. Other Contributors 268

    3. Version 269

    4. Number 269

    5. Publisher 270

    6. Publication Date 271

    7. Location 272

  D. Bibliography Examples 274

    Books 274

    Parts of Books 275

    Articles 276

    Website Publications 280

    Media and Performance 281

    Other 283

3. Paper Format   **285**

  A. Title Page 286

  B. First Page 287

  C. Middle Pages 288

  D. Bibliography Page 289

Notes for Multilingual Writers

Chapter 2: Sentences

Gerunds and Infinitives 31
It Is / There Is 33
Linking Verbs 39
Adjectives 45
Articles 46
Pronouns 53
Verb Forms 55
Verb Tense 57
Negation 60
Prepositions 61

Chapter 3: Punctuation and Mechanics

Apostrophe 101
Capitalization 109

Chapter 4: Word Choice

Correct Word Form 126
False Friends 148

Chapter 5: Research

Plagiarism 158